DATE DUE

DE2 0'00			
MR 1 9'01			

DEMCO 38-296

Designing Campus Networks

Terri Quinn-Andry
Kitty Haller

CISCO SYSTEMS
CISCO PRESS

M T P
MACMILLAN
TECHNICAL
PUBLISHING
U·S·A

Macmillan Technical Publishing
201 West 103rd Street
Indianapolis, IN 46290 USA

Designing Campus Networks

Terri Quinn-Andry
Kitty Haller

Copyright © 1998 Macmillan Technical Publishing

Cisco Press logo is a trademark of Cisco Systems, Inc.

Published by:
Macmillan Technical Publishing
201 West 103rd Street
Indianapolis, IN 46290 USA

Printed in the United States of America   4 5 6 7 8 9 0

Library of Congress Cataloging-in-Publication Number 97-81037

ISBN: 1-57870-030-2

Warning and Disclaimer

This book is designed to provide information about **Designing Campus Networks**. Every effort has been made to make this book as complete and as accurate as possible, but no warranty or fitness is implied.

The information is provided on an "as is" basis. The authors, Macmillan Technical Publishing, and Cisco Systems, Inc. shall have neither liability nor responsibility to any person or entity with respect to any loss or damages arising from the information contained in this book or from the use of the discs or programs that may accompany it.

The opinions expressed in this book belong to the authors and are not necessarily those of Cisco Systems, Inc.

Associate Publisher	Jim LeValley
Executive Editor	Julie Fairweather
Cisco Systems Program Manager	H. Kim Lew
Managing Editor	Caroline Roop
Acquisitions Editor	Tracy Hughes
Development Editor	Laurie McGuire
Project Editor	Sherri Fugit
Copy Editors	Leah Williams Nancy Sixsmith
Book Designer	Louisa Klucznik
Cover Designer	Jean Bisesi
Cover Production	Casey Price
Production Team Supervisor	Vic Peterson
Graphics Image Specialists	Laura Robbins Marvin Van Tiem
Production Analysts	Dan Harris Erich J. Richter
Production Team	Mary Hunt Nicole Ritch
Indexers	Kevin Fulcher Tim Wright

Trademark
Acknowledgments

About the Authors

Terri Quinn-Andry has been in the networking industry for seven years. She has been a systems engineer, FDDI technical support specialist, systems test engineer, product manager, and trade show technical consultant. Currently, she works as a technical marketing engineer with emphasis on network designs at Cisco Systems. Terri holds a B.S. degree from the University of New Hampshire, where she focused on both electrical engineering and business administration.

Kitty Haller is a professional writer and editor with over 17 years of experience. She has produced numerous technical documents, user guides, and manuals covering such topics as semiconductor automation, networking protocols, voice messaging systems, LAN management software, and electronic mail programs. Kitty owns and operates Haller Publication Services and has worked for both start-up and established companies, including 3Com, Hughes Electronics, Novell, Oracle, Rolm, and Sun Microsystems. She holds a B.A. in Journalism from the University of Montana.

Contents at a Glance

	Introduction to the Campus Network
Part I	Traffic Patterns
Chapter 1	Understanding Traffic Patterns
Chapter 2	Server Placement
Chapter 3	The Effects of Broadcast Traffic
Chapter 4	Factoring in Multimedia Traffic
Chapter 5	Looking at Local versus Cross-Campus Traffic
Part II	Essential Elements of Design
Chapter 6	Network Reliability and Resiliency
Chapter 7	Setting Traffic Priorities
Chapter 8	Addressing Security Issues

Chapter 9   Designing for Change and Growth

Part III   Campus Design and Implementation

Chapter 10   Understanding the Structural Foundation of Network Design

Chapter 11   Design One—A Barebone Network

Chapter 12   Design Two—A Scalable Network

Chapter 13   Design Three—A Complex Network

Chapter 14   Preparing for the Future

Appendix A Technical References

Glossary

Index

Table of Contents

Introduction 1
Objectives 1
Audience 2
Organization 2
Approach 3

PART I   TRAFFIC PATTERNS 4

Chapter 1   Understanding Traffic Patterns 7
Summary 10

Chapter 2   Server Placement 13
Enterprise Servers 13
Distributed Servers 15
Migration Patterns 16
New Server Trends 17
Summary 23

Chapter 3   **The Effects of Broadcast Traffic 27**

How Broadcasts are Sent and Received 28

How Switches Handle Broadcast Traffic 34

How Routers Handle Broadcast Traffic 36

How Broadcast Traffic Affects Endstations 41

Controlling Broadcast Traffic 45

Summary 47

Chapter 4   **Factoring in Multimedia Traffic 51**

Multimedia Application Types 52

Multimedia Traffic Characteristics 53

IP Multicast Operation 57

Multicast Network Requirements 59

Routing Methods for Multimedia 68

How the Switch Handles Multimedia 81

Summary 85

Chapter 5   **Looking at Local versus Cross-Campus Traffic 89**

Local Traffic 89

Cross-Campus Traffic 93

Effects of Internet Traffic on the Campus 101

Broadcast and Multimedia Through the
   Campus 108

Determining How Much Traffic is Local versus
   Cross-Campus 115

Summary 116

PART II   **ESSENTIAL ELEMENTS OF DESIGN 118**

Chapter 6   **Network Reliability and Resiliency 121**

The Meaning and Importance of Redundancy 121

Redundancy Methods 126

Summary 145

Chapter 7   Setting Traffic Priorities 149
What Needs to be Prioritized 150
Using a Software Approach 151
Using a Hardware Approach 162
How ATM Networks Prioritize Traffic 164
Summary 167

Chapter 8   Addressing Security Issues 171
How Much Security? 172
User Identity 172
Security Within the Network 180
Data Security and Integrity 184
Summary 199

Chapter 9   Designing for Change and Growth 203
Addressing Network Rate of Growth 204
Looking at User Mobility 206
Scaling with Virtual LANs 220
Summary 243

PART III   CAMPUS DESIGN AND IMPLEMENTATION 246

Chapter 10   Understanding the Structural Foundation of Network Design 249
The Building Block 249
The Core Block 251
The Server Block 253
Scale of the Campus Designs 256
Summary 260

Chapter 11   Design One—A Barebone Network 263
Design Requirements and Characteristics 263
Barebone Blueprint 264
Traffic Patterns 266
Designing Redundancy 269

Designing Mobility 273
Designing Security 275
Other Network Services 276
Small Barebone Network Design 276
Summary 277

Chapter 12   Design Two—A Scalable Network 281
Design Requirements and Characteristics 281
Scalable Blueprint 282
Traffic Patterns 285
Designing Redundancy 293
Addressing Multimedia 313
Designing Security 322
Designing Mobility 324
Building VLANs 326
Setting Traffic Priorities 339
Summary 341

Chapter 13   Design Three—A Complex Network 345
A Complex Network Blueprint 346
Traffic Patterns 349
Broadcast Domains in the Server Block 350
Designing Redundancy 355
Addressing Multimedia 376
Designing Security 383
Implementing VLANs 391
Setting Traffic Priorities 418
Summary 420

Chapter 14   Preparing for the Future 425
Voice-over-Data 425
Internet-Influenced Changes 426
Technology and Device Evolution 426
Network Management 427
Summary 428

Appendix A   Technical References 430
Where to Get Information 430
RFC Reports 431
Internet-Drafts 432
ATM Forum Standards 433
IEEE Specifications 434
Additional Reading 435

Glossary   436

Index   475

Introduction

A number of good books have been written on the various technical aspects of networking, including devices, networking protocols, routing protocols, and technologies. Network administrators and designers wishing to learn and apply the technical nuts and bolts of networking have no shortage of references to consult.

More difficult to find have been system-wide perspectives; resources for ways to put all the nuts and bolts together to form an elegant, well-designed network. We wrote this book to address that shortage of information for one category of networks—campus LANs—by examining them from a practical design perspective. The scope extends from individual design characteristics to the ways that multiple design goals must be integrated and built into the campus LAN.

OBJECTIVES

Too often, network designers get caught up in the technology du jour, or get sold on the fastest product on the market, without looking at what their networks truly need to run efficiently. The goal of *Designing Campus Networks* is to help network designers and administrators understand the issues and problems they face within campus networks today, and then design their networks for optimal performance and future scalability.

1

AUDIENCE

Network administrators and designers, who are either developing new campus networks or managing the evolution of existing ones, are the intended audience for *Designing Campus Networks*. The concepts in this book are generally straightforward and intuitive, so the prerequisite knowledge is simply a basic understanding of what a network is, what it does, and why it exists. However, to apply this book's concepts you will need a deeper understanding—from experience or other resources—of network devices, technologies, network protocols, and routing protocols.

ORGANIZATION

This book is organized into three parts, reflecting the increasing complexity of design characteristics, and concludes with sample blueprints of campus LANs.

Part One, "Traffic Patterns," focuses on traffic, the most fundamental, pervasive element that must be analyzed and managed in order to design an efficient network. Critical patterns and types of traffic are examined in distinct chapters.

Part Two, "Essential Elements of Design," turns to the more complex, often intertwined design characteristics that designers and administrators must build into the network, including redundancy, security, and mobility.

Part Three, "Campus Design and Implementation," brings together the concepts and network characteristics from Parts One and Two into sample designs for, respectively, simple, scalable, and complex networks.

The text explains technical terms and references as they arise in chapters. For reference purposes, a glossary of terms and an appendix of technical references, including RFCs and Internet-drafts, are presented at the end of the book.

APPROACH

This book takes a system-wide design approach to campus LANs. As such, we do not delve into details of implementation and configuration; presumably, readers are already familiar with such details for the applications and devices on their particular networks. For the same reason, we also do not go into detail about the individual technologies, devices, and protocols that exist in campus networks. The concern here is developing the overall campus network to meet critical design goals: efficient traffic flow, resiliency, security, mobility, and scalability.

In particular, the design goal of scalability emerges as a theme throughout campus LAN design. Scalability is a ubiquitous, but sometimes neglected, goal. The designer's perspective almost never can be just on the present uses and circumstances of the network. Questions about future growth and change must be considered, even if they need not be addressed immediately. Individual chapters and topics throughout *Designing Campus Networks* address ways to design scalability into the network.

We provide network blueprints as a basis for network design. The blueprints are detailed enough to enable understanding and implementation, but generic enough so that each network designer can use a blueprint as a foundation on which to build the desired unique network design.

Part I

Traffic Patterns

- **Chapter 1**—Understanding Traffic Patterns

- **Chapter 2**—Server Placement

- **Chapter 3**—The Effects of Broadcast Traffic

- **Chapter 4**—Factoring in Multimedia Traffic

- **Chapter 5**—Looking at Local versus Cross-Campus Traffic

The first goal of successful network design is to understand which applications and traffic the network needs to support. The characteristics of the applications play an important role in designing the right network. These characteristics include such things as: client-to-server communication, the amount of bandwidth that the application uses, delay and response time requirements, and where the application travels on the network. The network needs to support traffic from the applications as well as traffic in the form of routing updates, service advertisements, queries/responses, handshakes, and so forth. Each chapter in Part 1 of this book focuses on a different type of traffic found in today's networks.

CHAPTER 1

Understanding Traffic Patterns

All network designers and administrators want their campus LAN to run efficiently. The goal is to have a smart, tight network that will operate when it's supposed to, provide the services that users and businesses need, and leave nothing for the network administrator to do except plan for and implement new services as the need arises.

In the real world, however, networks don't operate this way. Servers get overloaded with traffic and stall out or quit altogether; network bottlenecks slow the traffic and adversely impact user productivity; network devices fail, causing connection loss; and so on. The network support group ends up spending all of its time troubleshooting problems.

As one approach to solving these problems, network administrators have added more power and bandwidth to the network—faster and bigger servers, more high-speed connections to the endstations, increased bandwidth on the backbone—whatever is necessary to relieve congestion or bandwidth problems.

Adding power and bandwidth to the campus LAN to solve network problems is relatively easy and inexpensive. The solution seems to work for the short term, so the network designer is shocked when congestion problems crop up again. Simply throwing bandwidth and power at a problem that hasn't been carefully scrutinized probably won't solve it in the long run.

The good news is that many network problems can be solved—even prevented—when the network designer understands the traffic patterns on the network. Where the network traffic comes from, goes to, and circulates within the campus (in other words, the traffic patterns) dictates how efficient the current network design is.

Think of the campus as an airline hub. The flights coming into and going out of the hub impact the performance of the hub. Air traffic control must know and control the traffic patterns and schedules of the arriving and departing planes to prevent chaos and accidents.

In the same manner, data traffic going into, out of, and through the campus impacts the performance of the campus network. In this case, network designers can be viewed as air traffic control. They must know the traffic patterns of the network to create smooth travel through the campus and to schedule upgrades and routine maintenance for times that will cause the least network interruption.

Data traffic is generated by the devices and associated software applications that are running on the network. Most likely, your network has at least the typical applications—word processing, file transfer, and electronic mail. These applications generally do not require a lot of bandwidth, and their traffic patterns are pretty intuitive. However, most modern campus LANs have and need much more than these basic applications. Multifaceted applications, like desktop publishing, video conferencing, and WebTV broadcast programs, are all gaining in popularity. The characteristics of these applications are not always as easy to predict.

One of the keys to operating networks successfully is to understand the nature of the traffic generated by the applications on it. You can avoid many network problems by understanding and controlling the traffic patterns that are generated by the applications and devices on the network.

One crucial element to understanding traffic patterns is to baseline the traffic patterns on the campus. By *baseline*, we mean gathering data on the traffic flow through the network during normal operation.

Once you baseline the traffic multiple times during the day, you can then understand what the network's basic performance level is. This includes response times through the network during peak traffic times and low traffic periods of the day, types of traffic traveling through the campus, network utilization of different parts of the network, and so forth. With this information, you can:

- Understand where the bottlenecks could be

- Know quickly when a significant change occurs on the network

- Know when peak and low usage times occur

- Make troubleshooting easier because you know the norm

- Plan for improvement and future expansion

- Schedule upgrades and routine maintenance during low network-utilization periods

SUMMARY

One of the most fundamental, pervasive tasks in a campus LAN design is to understand the traffic patterns. Other design criteria—scalability, security, resilience—and their implementations all depend on this understanding. In Chapters 2–5, we discuss some common applications and traffic types that impact the performance of campus networks.

This chapter covers the following topics:

- Enterprise servers

- Distributed servers

- Migration patterns

- New server trends

CHAPTER 2

Server Placement

Servers play a defining role in campus LAN design. After all, they're the devices that provide services to all or part of the network and control access to its resources (such as disk drives and printers).

Servers are identified by the function they perform in the network and the users they support. Two of the most common types are *enterprise servers* and *distributed servers*. Recently, new types have emerged, including the super server, the networked computer server, and the Web-based application server.

Where and how you set up these servers for the campus network can have a direct effect on network performance. This chapter defines the various server types and how they can be put to optimum use. This chapter also discusses the advantages and drawbacks of the emerging server trends.

ENTERPRISE SERVERS

Enterprise servers (also known as *centralized servers*) support either all or a majority of network users. An e-mail server would fall into this category because its users can access the server to read and send their e-mail, no matter where on the campus they're located.

The physical placement of enterprise servers is one of the least-flexible areas in network design. Because enterprise servers handle traffic from all users and are considered critical for network operation, many network managers prefer to place them in the data center, where they are in a single, secure location.

The location of the enterprise servers on the network has a significant impact on the traffic patterns within that network. By placing enterprise servers close to the network backbone, each group of users' traffic generally travels through the same number of networking devices in order to reach the servers, as shown in Figure 2–1.

Figure 2–1

Enterprise server connections on the network.

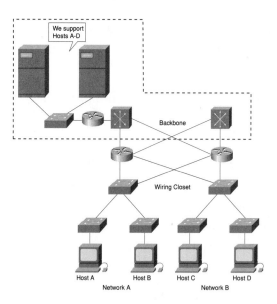

Let's say, for example, that your campus has Building 1, Building 2, and Building 3, and your e-mail server is located in Building 2. Even though users in Building 2 are physically closer to the e-mail server, their requests for e-mail service must still go through a router, just like the users in Buildings 1 and 3. This is important from a traffic standpoint, because it results in more consistent performance for all users instead of unbalanced network behavior throughout the campus.

DISTRIBUTED SERVERS

Distributed servers (also known as *local* or *workgroup servers*) support a specific group of users. For example, the distributed server containing payroll information typically supports only the Accounting or Human Resources group. When an engineering server is set up to only support the engineering group, it is considered a distributed server as well. But if that engineering server supports many end users—the engineers, customer support personnel, and so on—it is then an enterprise server, not a distributed server.

A distributed server is usually placed on the same network subnet as the users it supports. Therefore, it may not be located at the data center, but instead may reside at the wiring or distribution closets of the network, as shown in Figure 2–2.

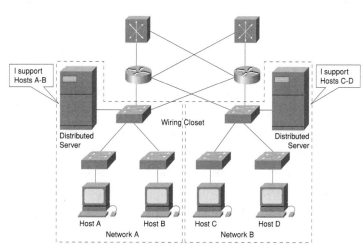

Figure 2–2

Typical distributed server connection to the network.

Distributed servers can effectively reduce the amount of traffic traveling across the network core. Since a distributed server is typically connected to the same switch as the users it supports, the traffic never needs to be routed to another location. This lowers the amount of traffic on the backbone, thereby increasing network performance and response times. Refer to Figure 2–2 to see how distributed servers are connected to users.

In addition, distributed servers let you localize where the traffic is going on your network, which means that you can keep a better monitoring system of the traffic patterns and traffic characteristics.

Enterprise servers and distributed servers both have their advantages. The best situation is to have a mix of both. That is, use distributed servers where you can localize the application; use enterprise servers where you have the common applications that everyone needs to access, such as e-mail or public Web pages.

MIGRATION PATTERNS

Choosing how to set up each server—as an enterprise server or a distributed server—has been and continues to be a major challenge for the network designer. In the early 1990s, it was common to have nothing but enterprise servers, meaning that all data went through the core of the network to the servers. This made good design sense because the applications running on the servers were relatively few and small in size, which kept network performance issues to a minimum. A typical design ratio placed 80 percent of the traffic on enterprise servers and a mere 20 percent on the distributed servers (if there were any on the network).

As applications increased in bandwidth and performance requirements, a change in philosophy occurred. Network managers began to place popular programs on distributed servers to get them closer to the users and alleviate traffic on the network core. In the mid-1990s, the ideal design ratio shifted to placing 80 percent of the traffic through the local distributed servers and 20 percent of the traffic through the central enterprise servers.

In the late 1990s, the design philosophy is shifting again, this time reverting back to a focus on central enterprise servers. This is due in large part to emerging new software applications such as multimedia. For example, many multimedia applications (which we discuss in Chapter 4, "Factoring in Multimedia Traffic" in detail) use a centralized video server. As the popularity and usefulness of multimedia increases, more network traffic will be coming from these centralized servers.

Additional new technologies and power-hungry applications have forced network designers to continually rethink how servers are used in their networks. Fortunately, server hardware has been able to keep pace with the new demands—servers are bigger, faster, and more powerful than they were just two years ago. This has allowed designers to use servers in some new and creative ways, which we describe in the sections that follow.

NEW SERVER TRENDS

For some networks, the capabilities of the enterprise server and the distributed server cannot satisfy all of the network's needs. As a result, other ways of using servers have evolved. These include:

- Network super servers

- Network computer servers

- Web-based application servers

Network Super Server

Many enterprise servers are just too slow to handle the magnitude of traffic they receive. To keep pace with new demands, the idea of a *super server* has emerged. This server is comprised of several enterprise servers that have been consolidated into a single, more powerful machine (hence the name *super server*). These servers have much more processing power and speed, multiple network interface cards for handling more data, and a lot more memory for data storage. Super servers were "in" when large mainframes were common, and the need for their power is making them popular again.

Although the super server may seem like a good idea, there can be a down side to consolidating several servers into one, depending on the consolidated servers' original functions. For example, if all e-mail servers are replaced by one super e-mail server, then there exists one important single point of failure on the network. Or, if a bandwidth-intensive application server is combined with two other bandwidth-intensive application servers, there may not be enough processing power and bandwidth connections at the super server to effectively handle the traffic that those applications generate.

Another possible problem may be that the network cannot handle the increased traffic that travels through it to reach the super servers. For example, if the network was originally designed to handle mostly local traffic to the distributed servers, implementing super servers and changing the traffic patterns may require a substantial amount of upgrading within the network infrastructure to handle the increased traffic load. As another example, replacing regular enterprise servers with super servers presupposes more network traffic, as more users and higher bandwidth applications place higher demands on the network.

Figure 2–3 shows how enterprise servers are set up today for a hypothetical, growing network, and Figure 2–4 shows the network scheme that will likely be required to implement these super servers within a year. Note that Figure 2–3 has 150 enterprise servers, and Figure 2–4 has 50 super servers, resulting in a server consolidation ratio of 3:1. More traffic will be going to each super server (Figure 2–4) than to each enterprise server (Figure 2–3), even though the total amount of traffic remains the same.

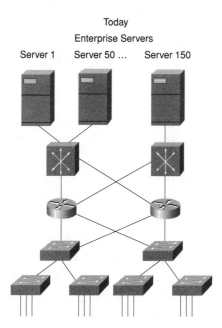

Today

Enterprise Servers

Server 1   Server 50 ...   Server 150

Figure 2–3

Enterprise server connections today.

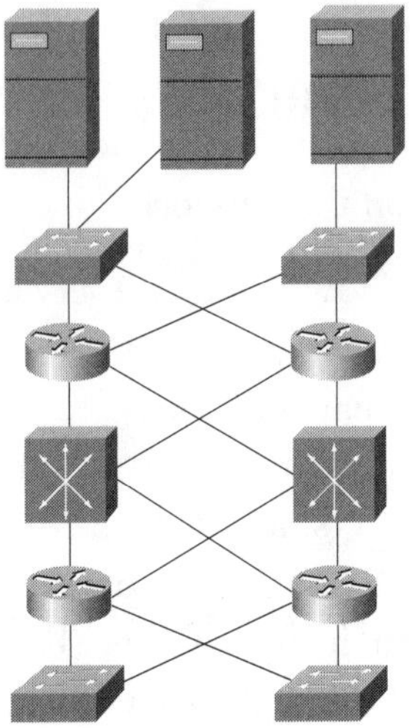

Figure 2–4

Super server connections within a year.

Next Year

Enterprise Servers

Super Server 1   Super Server 2 ...   Super Server 50

Network Computer Server

Another trend that is affecting network traffic is the migration toward the *network computer server*. This type of server is reminiscent of the beginning days of computing, when workers had a keyboard connected to a "dumb" terminal that was hard-wired to the central computer server. The only thing users had to do was power up—they had immediate server access. The network computer server is set up in a similar fashion. Users simply use the network to work with all of their applications—there is no need for hard drives because the network server holds and supplies all of the information. This creates a very cost-effective machine for the network computer client. Users can place their machines anywhere they want or take them wherever they go, and as long as they can connect to the network, they have all of their work located in one place—the network server.

Using these machines, of course, can cause an increase in traffic across the network. Just as with enterprise and distributed servers, the amount of traffic affecting the backbone of the network is determined by the network computer server location.

If, for example, each network computer server is responsible for only a certain group of users, then the network computer server can become a distributed server. The traffic can stay local between the stations and the server—it doesn't need to travel through much of the network. This makes the assumption, though, that the users work exclusively from the office and do not move around or telecommute. Figure 2–5 shows this scenario.

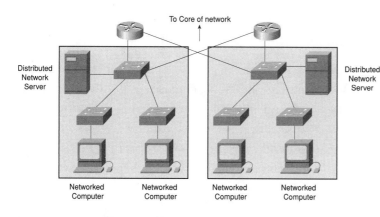

Figure 2–5
A network computer server as a distributed server.

If, however, the network computer server services a large group of users throughout the network, or if many of the users telecommute from multiple places, the data traffic will necessarily travel across a larger part of the network. The network computer server then becomes more like an enterprise server because it supports many users on the network, and the traffic travels throughout several areas of the network, as shown in Figure 2–6.

Figure 2–6

A network computer server as an enterprise server.

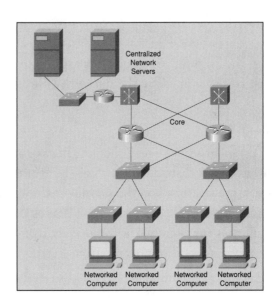

Web-based Application Server

The *Web-based application server* is another type of server. With Web-based applications, clients tap into the Web server to access and run the application from the server. The Web-based application server is usually at the enterprise level, because a wide variety of users typically need access to it. Figure 2–7 shows a typical network scheme for Web-based application servers.

It has also become very easy for users to set up their own Web servers right on their machines. Now clients can become servers as well. The trend toward "client Web servers" is so new that it has not created a large impact on the traffic characteristics of most networks yet; it is too early to know whether the new traffic produced will be primarily local or enterprise traffic.

Web Application Servers

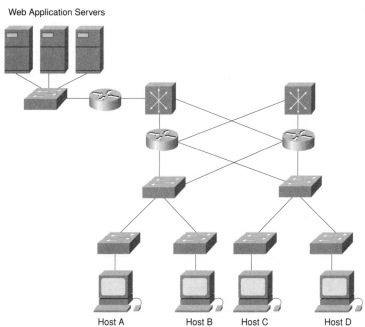

Figure 2–7
Networking scheme for
Web-based application
servers.

Host A   Host B   Host C   Host D

Summary

The location of servers and their functions can have quite an impact on traffic patterns. Conversely, traffic patterns can have a substantial impact on the servers, especially in terms of network performance and response times for users. Understanding where network traffic is coming from and going to, as well as the type of traffic being generated, is a key factor in determining the optimal location for your servers. It is also important to plan ahead for the migrations that will occur in the future for server roles and responsibilities. In the next chapter, we cover the effects of broadcast traffic, a traffic type that is common to all networks.

Keep in mind the following design considerations in placing servers:

- Enterprise servers support most or all users on the network.

- Distributed servers support a specific group of users on the network.

- Consider whether the server is performing a distributed- or enterprise-level task to determine where to place it physically.

- Emerging software applications such as multimedia are driving a shift toward enterprise servers and away from distributed servers.

- Adding enterprise-level servers changes the overall network traffic patterns, possibly requiring network infrastructure changes.

This chapter covers the following topics:

- How broadcasts are sent and received

- How switches handle broadcast traffic

- How routers handle broadcast traffic

- How broadcast traffic affects endstations

- Controlling broadcast traffic

CHAPTER 3

The Effects of Broadcast Traffic

Broadcast traffic, just as in radio or television, is a transmission sent to more than one recipient. It is a point-to-multipoint transmission. On data networks, broadcasts are formed as broadcast frames and distributed to all stations.

Understanding how broadcast traffic works is an important element in effective network design. By their very nature, broadcasts have the capability to empower a network by sending important messages to everyone or to cripple a network by blanketing it with too much traffic.

Keep in mind that broadcasts are necessary and provide useful information. For example, broadcasts include routing updates so that the routers know how to direct traffic. Some network servers, such as IPX servers, announce the services they support via broadcasts. The simple act of requesting your address to get onto the network or asking for the address of the station you want to send data to can also generate broadcast frames.

Table 3–1 lists the key broadcast frame types that we discuss in this chapter. All of these broadcast frames, as well as many others, are necessary to make a network run successfully. But you can't let broadcast traffic overwhelm the other traffic on the network. This chapter explains how broadcasts operate and offers suggestions on ways to control their effect.

Table 3–1   *Broadcast Frame Types*

Broadcast Frame	Abbreviation	Definition
IP Address Resolution Protocol request	IP ARP	Broadcast to learn the MAC address that corresponds to a known IP address
Dynamic Host Configuration Protocol request	DHCP Request	Broadcast to obtain an IP address for an endstation
IPX Service Advertisement Packet	IPX SAP	Broadcast that advertises the services that an IPX server supports
Routing update	n/a	Broadcast sent by routers with routing table updates to other routers

HOW BROADCASTS ARE SENT AND RECEIVED

All data sent through the network must have a source address and a destination address to get from the sending station to the receiving station. A broadcast frame automatically contains the sending station's unique address as the source address. The destination address for a broadcast frame is formed in the frame's two destination address fields.

The two destination address fields in a frame correspond to Layers 2 and 3 of the OSI reference model. Figure 3–1 shows the OSI reference model and the layers that compose it.

The destination address fields start at Layer 2, the Media Access Control (MAC) layer. For some broadcast frames, this field consists of all fs (hexadecimal notation), which means "send me to everyone." Figure 3–2 shows a Layer 2 broadcast frame.

A MAC address is 48 bits in length. This is normally represented as 12 sequential hexidecmial values. For example, a router's MAC address might be 0000.0ce5.b7cl. A MAC broadcast address would be depicted as ffff.ffff.ffff. For the purposes of this book, the authors have truncated the depiction of MAC addresses to simplify discussions. All MAC addresses presented here will be six-digit values (e.g., e5b7cl), appearing without the high order portion of the address (which encodes the manufacturer's designation). The MAC broadcast addresses will be depicted as ffffff.

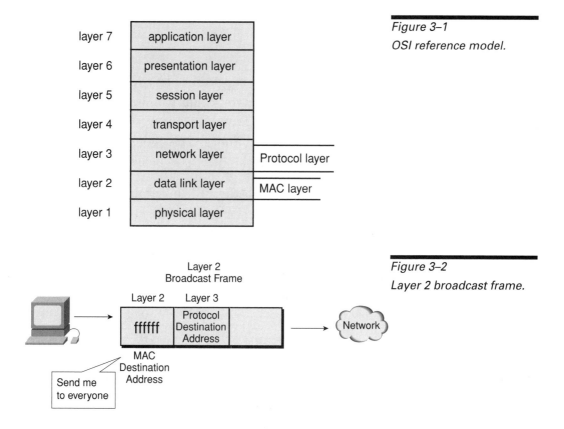

Figure 3–1
OSI reference model.

Figure 3–2
Layer 2 broadcast frame.

The second destination address field for the frame includes Layer 3, the Network layer, commonly known as the protocol layer. This address provides protocol-specific information. A typical broadcast destination address for the IP protocol that says "send me to everyone" (such as a DHCP request) is 255.255.255.255. Figure 3–3 shows a broadcast frame with the MAC and protocol destination addresses designated.

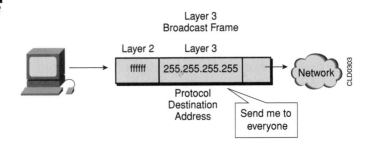

Figure 3–3
Layer 3 broadcast frame.

To put this example in perspective, let's relate it to the telephone system. Suppose you could pick up the phone, press ** on your dialing pad, and thus have your call placed to everyone in the United States. This would be similar to a "send me to everyone" broadcast, as depicted in Figure 3–3.

A broadcast can also be limited to certain segments of the network. The IP protocol uses subnetting for fine-tuning specific device locations. Figure 3–4 provides the broadcast destination address for the different IP classes of addresses with no subnetting. Figure 3–5 shows the broadcast destination address with an 8-bit subnet mask.

Figure 3–4
IP class network broadcasts.

	IP Class Network	Network Portion	Host Portion
Class A	1.255.255.255	1.	255.255.255
Class B	130.130.255.255	130.130.	255.255.
Class C	200.200.200.255	200.200.200.	255

send me to everyone broadcast

255.255.255.255	all networks	all hosts

	IP Class Network	With 8 bit subnet mask		
		Network Portion	Subnet Portion	Host Portion
Class A	1.100.255.255	1.	100.	255.255
Class B	150.150.100.255	150.150.	100.	255
Class C	200.200.200.255	200.200.200.	N/A	255

Figure 3–5

IP class subnetwork broadcasts.

For example, let's suppose that the network has a class B IP network address of 150.150.0.0 with an 8-bit subnet mask, and the broadcast specifies 150.150.100.255 as the protocol destination address. This address translates to "send me to everyone on the 150.150.100 subnet of the 150.150.0.0 network." The network is 150.150, the subnet is 100, and the host portion is 255—which specifies everyone. Figure 3–6 shows this scenario.

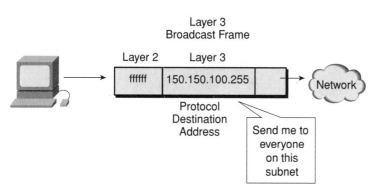

Figure 3–6

Layer 3 subnet broadcast frame.

To use the telephone analogy again, let's say you could dial *555, and the phone call would reach everyone in the 555 area code. This would be the same as having a broadcast in the MAC destination address and a subnet-specific broadcast in the protocol destination address. A routing update broadcast frame has a format similar to this.

Broadcast frames do not need to have a broadcast in the MAC destination address field and the protocol destination field to send data through the network. An example of this is when a station uses the IP Address Resolution Protocol (ARP). When Station A wants to send data to Station B, it first must learn Station B's MAC Layer address. To get it, Station A sends out an IP ARP request frame, which contains Station B's Protocol destination address (IP address and a broadcast in the layer 2 (MAC) destination address.

In the context of the telephone example, suppose you dial 1411 for directory assistance and ask for the phone number of John Doe. This is similar to an IP ARP request because you know the IP destination address (John Doe), but you use a general Layer 2 broadcast destination address (1411) to learn the specific MAC address (the specific number for John Doe).

Figure 3–7 shows the IP ARP request address scheme. When Station B responds to Station A, it sends a unicast frame, not a broadcast frame, back to Station A. It places Station A's MAC and IP addresses into the corresponding destination address fields, and puts its own MAC and IP addresses into the source MAC address and source protocol address fields.

Figure 3–8 shows the IP ARP response back to Station A. Station A learns Station B's MAC address from the response. Station A can now send data to Station B because it knows Station B's MAC and IP addresses.

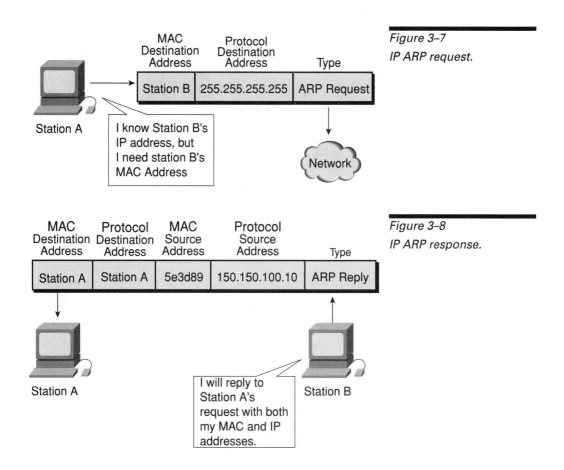

Figure 3–7
IP ARP request.

Figure 3–8
IP ARP response.

Figure 3–9 shows four broadcast examples and where they use a broadcast destination address. The IP ARP request uses a broadcast in the Layer 2 (MAC) destination address. The DHCP request uses a broadcast in both the MAC and protocol destination addresses. The IPX SAP uses a broadcast in both the MAC destination address and in the host portion of the protocol destination address. The network portion is not a broadcast. Routing updates use broadcasts in a fashion similar to the IPX SAP.

Figure 3–9

Broadcast frame examples.

Broadcast frame	MAC Destination Address	Protocol Destination Address
IP ARP Request	ffffff	Known IP address
DHCP Request	ffffff	255.255.255.255
IPX SAP	ffffff	network.ffffff
Route update	ffffff	network.ffffff network.255

Understandably, the telephone system does not support a broadcast approach to information transfer. The telephone system infrastructure would be overwhelmed by the amount of telephone calls that the broadcast approach would create.

So how does the data network system handle broadcasts? The next sections explain how switches handle broadcasts, how routers handle broadcasts, and how endstations are affected.

HOW SWITCHES HANDLE BROADCAST TRAFFIC

As each broadcast is transmitted through the network, it is intercepted and forwarded through the network devices. The first intercept is at the Layer 2 switch (such as an Ethernet switch). When the broadcast reaches the Layer 2 switch, the switch only looks at the MAC destination address, not at the protocol destination address, as illustrated in Figure 3–10.

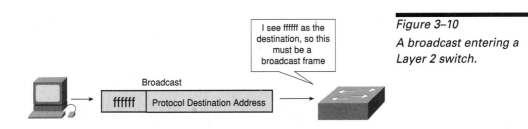

Figure 3–10

A broadcast entering a Layer 2 switch.

Layer 2 switches, by definition, do not have the intelligence to understand network (protocol) layer information; they are only capable of understanding MAC layer information. As a result, the switch doesn't know how to restrict where the broadcast goes. Because it only sees the "ffffff" as the MAC destination address, the switch understands the instruction to be "send me to everybody," and it sends the broadcast frame out all of its ports.

Figure 3–11 shows the behavior of the switch after it receives a broadcast. This behavior, which occurs at all switches on the network, is called *broadcast propagation*. As long as the broadcast travels through switches, it continues throughout the network and reaches all endstations.

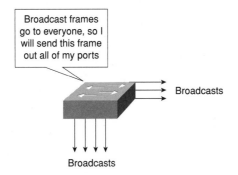

Figure 3–11

Switch propagating broadcasts.

The next interception point is at Layer 3, where the routers operate. If the broadcast enters a Layer 3 device, such as a router, then a more complex action is taken.

HOW ROUTERS HANDLE BROADCAST TRAFFIC

When a broadcast frame reaches a router on the network, the router takes a specific action. The router has the intelligence to determine what type of broadcast frame has arrived (such as an IP ARP request, a DHCP request, or an IPX SAP). After the router learns the nature of the broadcast frame, it takes one of several actions:

- Turns the broadcast into a *unicast*, a transmission sent to only one receiver

- Builds a table and stores the broadcast information for future requests

- Builds a table and periodically sends out broadcasts

- Drops the broadcast frame

The following sections describe each of these scenarios in more detail.

Generating Unicasts

The router can turn the broadcast into a unicast and send it to the appropriate device that can respond to the original broadcast.

For example, when a station first connects to the network, it does not have an IP address and must ask for one. If the network is running DHCP, the station sends out a DHCP Discover/Request broadcast frame to ask for an address from the DHCP server.

Figure 3–12 shows the router's response to a DHCP request. When the router receives a DHCP broadcast request from a station, it turns the DHCP request broadcast into a unicast with the DHCP server's destination address. The router then sends the request to the DHCP server as a unicast frame, as shown in Figure 3–13..

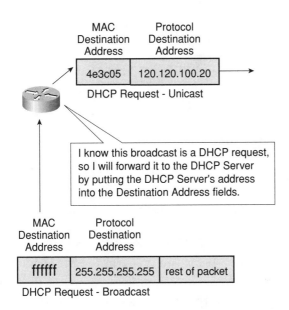

Figure 3–12
Router responding to a DHCP request.

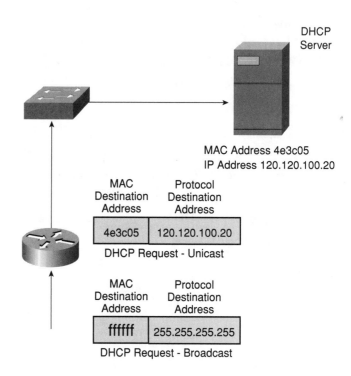

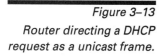

Figure 3–13
Router directing a DHCP request as a unicast frame.

Storing Broadcasts

The router can store the information contained in the broadcast frame in a table, or cache, that it builds. The router can then respond to future requests for the information.

An example of this process is with IP ARP, or more specifically, proxy ARP. As the router learns the MAC address associated with a particular IP address, it stores that MAC/IP address pair in its IP ARP cache. The next time a station sends out an ARP request for Station A, the router can respond to this request directly by sending an ARP response back to the originator with station A's MAC/IP address pair. Figure 3–14 illustrates the router's response to an IP ARP request.

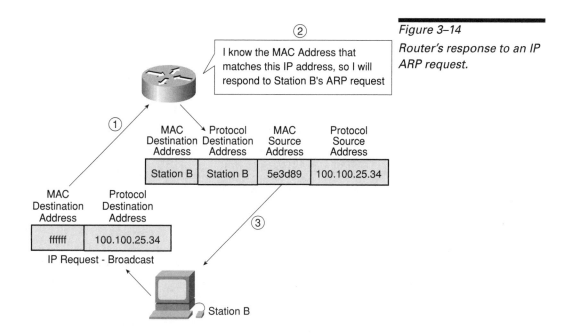

Figure 3–14

Router's response to an IP ARP request.

Generating Broadcasts

The router can build a table and send out broadcasts periodically. For example, when a router maintains an IPX SAP table, it learns the SAPs from the IPX server and builds a table. Then, using a MAC broadcast destination address and an IPX network broadcast address, it sends the table to the other routers on the network in the form of broadcasts every 60 seconds. All routers are thereby kept informed about what services are available on the network. Figure 3–15 shows the IPX SAP update frame coming from a router.

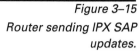

Figure 3–15
Router sending IPX SAP
updates.

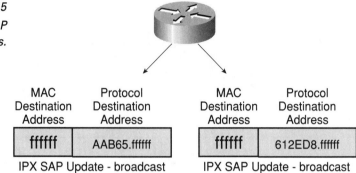

Dropping Broadcasts

In many instances, a router may drop the broadcast and not do anything with it. This is a perfectly normal operation for a router to do, and in fact, a major benefit of placing routers in a network . This is commonly known as controlling the broadcast domain. For instance, if a router sees an ARP request with a particular IP address, but the router does not have a matching ARP cache or route entry, the router will simply drop the packet without forwarding the packet or responding to the originating station. In this case, the station which matches the destination IP address may respond directly to the ARP request, or possibly another router on the network with a route to the destination subnet will respond that has a specific MAC destination address, the router receiving the IP ARP looks in its ARP cache table to find the MAC/IP address pair. If the MAC address is not in the ARP table, the router drops the frame because it does not know the MAC/IP address pair and therefore cannot help with this ARP request.

In traditional networks, the router is the only device that can terminate a broadcast and prevent it from traveling throughout the entire network. Because a router can understand the protocol layer and because it is the gateway between different networks or subnetworks, it creates broadcast domains and controls what traffic passes between networks. The broadcast frame can travel within and throughout the broadcast domain in which it originated, but it cannot traverse into other broadcast domains, as shown in Figure 3–16.

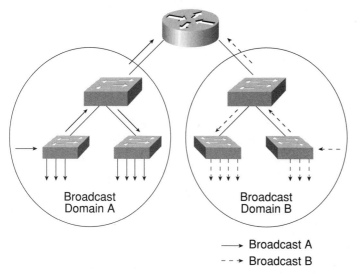

Broadcast
Domain A

Broadcast
Domain B

⟶ Broadcast A
- - ⟶ Broadcast B

Figure 3–16
Broadcast frames traveling in a network.

We've described how broadcasts propagate throughout the network, and shown how switches and routers handle the broadcast frames. But how do the endstations handle broadcast traffic?

HOW BROADCAST TRAFFIC AFFECTS ENDSTATIONS

What happens when endstations receive broadcasts can be quite dynamic. Tests have shown that if the endstation has a Pentium 120 MHz chip and receives 1,000 broadcasts-per-second, 15 percent of the CPU is used just handling those broadcasts. At 3,000 broadcasts-per-second, 28 percent of the CPU is used handling broadcast traffic. A Sparc5 station behaves similarly. Machines with slower processors are affected even more; some lock up when they have to process 3,000 broadcasts-per-second.

Processing broadcast frames translates into a lower percentage of available CPU power for the endstation. When a user is working on a database application or creating a document, the percentage of CPU that is used to process broadcasts is not available for the user's tasks.

Keep in mind that the number of broadcasts-per-second is significant relative to the protocols and applications you're running on your network. If you're running IP only or if you have just a few IPX servers, then 3,000 broadcasts-per-second is certainly a high number of broadcasts. However, if you're running applications that are broadcast-intensive, such as NetBIOS, or if you have 75 or more IPX servers, then you can see upwards of 10,000 to 20,000 broadcasts-per-second.

Likewise, some applications operate through broadcast frames. If one of these applications is crucial to the business, then you will probably see more than 3,000 broadcasts-per-second during the peak times of the day. It is important to relate the numbers of broadcasts on the network to the protocols and applications that run on that network. The number of broadcasts-per-second may put an unacceptable burden on an endstation's processing capacity. The question of how much broadcasting is too much for an endstation is discussed further in the section "Controlling Broadcast Traffic," later in this chapter.

As mentioned earlier and shown in Figure 3–9, broadcast frames can contain broadcasts in the protocol and MAC destination addresses. It is logical then for a broadcast sent by an IPX server announcing its services to go only to IPX endstations.

However, when it comes to broadcast traffic, that's not necessarily the case. When an IPX server broadcasts its services via SAPs to the network, the switches on the network send it out through all ports, regardless of whether the receiving endstation is running the IP, IPX, or AppleTalk protocol. Remember, this is because switches do not recognize protocol addresses.

For the IPX endstations on the network, responding to the IPX broadcast is straightforward. The endstation receives the IPX SAP broadcast, processes the frame, and either uses it or discards it.

For IP endstations, the response is not so straightforward. All of the IP hosts that connect to the same switch as the IPX endstations also get the broadcast. The MAC broadcast destination address is the same for both IP and IPX, so each IP endstation needs to process the broadcast in order to recognize that the frame isn't an IP broadcast and throw it away.

Even though the frame being sent is an IPX broadcast, the IP endstations need to interrupt their processing tasks to check the nature of the broadcast and, ultimately, throw it out, which is a waste of valuable CPU. Figure 3–17 shows an IPX endstation and an IP endstation responding to the same IPX SAP broadcast.

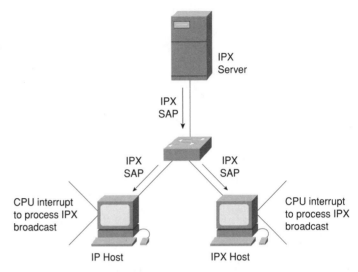

Figure 3–17

IP and IPX endstations responding to the same IPX SAP broadcast.

The reason that the IP endstation must process the IPX broadcast has to do with the way broadcasts are sent and handled on the NIC card in the endstation. Because the MAC broadcast destination address is the same in IP and in IPX—they both use the same destination address of ffffff—the NIC card cannot tell what protocol the broadcast frame is. The endstation needs to bring the broadcast frame up to the CPU. The CPU must strip the MAC address header off of the frame and take a look at the protocol address to determine which protocol it is and to then decide whether or not the frame is useful for the endstation.

This behavior occurs with protocols that use the MAC broadcast destination addresses. Other protocols, such as AppleTalk, use multicast frames, which have a slightly different MAC destination address. An AppleTalk endstation can discard the broadcast frame immediately upon receiving it because the NIC card does not recognize the MAC broadcast address.

CONTROLLING BROADCAST TRAFFIC

We've seen that broadcasts can be important and can contain useful information that needs to traverse the network. However, when broadcast traffic runs unchecked, it can have a devastating effect—especially on the endstations—if they lock up and the users can't use them for their work. The most effective network design balances the pros and cons of broadcast traffic and keeps broadcasts in check.

How do we control how much broadcast traffic occurs on the network? The following steps are generally helpful:

1. Take a look at the applications running on the network and check how many of those applications are sending out broadcast-intensive data frames.
2. Consider the protocols you're running on your network (for example, NetBIOS runs very broadcast-intensive applications; IPX sends out SAPs every 60 seconds).
3. Divide up the devices that generate most of the broadcasts into different subnets across the network so that their broadcasts can be terminated by a router and won't travel everywhere on the network. The goal is to prevent the broadcast traffic from adversely affecting endstation performance.
4. Try to reduce the protocols and applications that are causing a majority of the broadcast traffic (especially if they are not critical to your business). Given the obvious trend of networks migrating to the IP protocol, maybe it's time to stop running NetBIOS as well as other less common protocols on your network.

5. Be aware of the new applications that are being introduced into the network and find out their potential
impact on endstation performance with respect to
broadcast traffic.

How much broadcast traffic is too much? If the people in
your company are getting faster responses from the applications they are running by unplugging their computers from
the network, then your broadcast traffic is certainly too high
and you have a network performance problem. But, unplugging from the network is a drastic step you'd like to prevent.

Monitor the broadcast traffic so that you can see where the
"heavy hits" are coming from. Unfortunately, it's not easy to
monitor broadcasts. To do so, you need, at the minimum, to
attach an analyzing tool such as a *sniffer*, and watch the network. This should be done for an hour during peak traffic
times and for an hour during slower times to baseline the
amount of broadcast traffic that is traversing the network.

On the surface, this task appears to be reasonable and not
too difficult, especially if you're just monitoring the backbone or a few subnets. However, if you need to do more than
just minimal monitoring, such as monitoring at the endstation level, it can require a substantial amount of work for the
network administrators and the network support team. The
network team has to monitor multiple endstations on each
switch for all of the subnets on the network as well as the
backbone. This takes a lot of time and manpower. Certainly,
end users can monitor their stations with software, but that
means that they spend time doing an extra job, which doesn't
make them very happy or productive.

Designing your network so that it is flexible enough to handle new applications and emerging technologies while keeping standard broadcast traffic in check can be tricky, but it's not impossible. It's tricky because there are no set formulas or industry standards on how broadcast-intensive each application is, and an application's impact varies from network to network.

SUMMARY

You now have an understanding of what broadcast traffic is, how it propagates through a network, and ways to keep it under control. When a new application is needed on your network, you should analyze its likely impact on broadcast traffic in advance and integrate it in such a way that its traffic patterns don't overwhelm the network.

One newly popular application that is already having a tremendous impact on networks is multimedia. It, too, can be broadcast-intensive, so it needs to be carefully scrutinized and understood by the network designer. We cover the effects of multimedia in the next chapter.

The following design considerations are relevant to broadcast traffic:

- Broadcasts are useful and necessary traffic, but too much broadcast traffic can cause network performance problems. Managing broadcast traffic is a critical aspect of campus LAN design.

- Switches propagate broadcasts throughout the network.

- Using routers to create subnets and to process broadcasts intelligently is an effective way of controlling broadcast traffic.

- Endstations may receive broadcast traffic that is not pertinent to them but which they must still process and throw away. Effective network design is needed to minimize this waste of CPU.

- Reducing the protocols and/or applications that generate a lot of broadcast traffic is one way of controlling broadcast traffic.

- New applications should be evaluated for their impact on broadcast traffic before they are put on the network. Anticipating such impact is generally easier than monitoring the system after it is already suffering the effects of too much broadcast traffic.

This chapter covers the following topics:

- Multimedia application types

- Multimedia traffic characteristics

- IP multicast operation

- Multicast network requirements

- Routing methods for multimedia

- How the switch handles multimedia

CHAPTER 4

Factoring in Multimedia Traffic

Multimedia applications provide an exciting new media because they offer so much—the integration of sound, graphics, animation, text, and video. It's no wonder then that multimedia applications have become extremely popular and that everyone wants these applications to be available on the campus.

For the network designer, however, setting up the network to handle these applications takes some thought and planning. Multimedia, by its very nature, is multifaceted, and it requires several specific items to be preset on the network before it can operate successfully. We therefore devote an entire chapter to covering multimedia so that you can prepare the network for these applications.

We begin this chapter by defining typical multimedia application types and the ways they may travel across your network. We then explore the various protocols that the designer can use to transfer multimedia applications from the sender to the receiver, and define these protocols in terms of their effect on network traffic.

MULTIMEDIA APPLICATION TYPES

Multimedia applications are quite diverse. One popular application is distance learning, which allows more than just the "local" classroom students to take courses. Although users are at other locations, the application is interactive so that the users at distant sites can ask questions, answer questions, and so forth, just as local classroom students can. Distance learning is a multimedia application because the application travels over the data network, as opposed to television programs, which travel via transmitter or satellite signals.

Real-time imaging is another example of a multimedia application. In this application, images are updated on the screen at the same rate that they occur in the real world. Real-time imaging allows dynamic involvement by users because the computer can accept and incorporate keystrokes or controller movements while the image appears. For example, doctors in different locations can study x-rays at the same time during a critical operation and note their areas of concern to each other via computer. Another example is a complicated flight simulator program that makes use of real-time animation to translate the user's airplane course movements into onscreen actions.

Other popular applications include videoconferencing and shared whiteboard applications. Videoconferencing is similar to distance learning in that participants can interact via the data network using video, voice, and text. Shared whiteboard applications let users see and work on the same file at the same time.

As you would expect, blending several media into one and sending this combined media over a data network can be a complicated process. And it can bring with it the potential for high bandwidth use on the network. We explore these issues in the following sections.

MULTIMEDIA TRAFFIC CHARACTERISTICS

Multimedia traffic can work its way through the network in one of several ways—as unicast traffic, broadcast traffic, or multicast traffic. Each method has a different effect on network bandwidth, which is explained in the sections that follow.

Multimedia as Unicast Traffic

Unicast traffic is a point-to-point application; it doesn't go out to everyone on the network. In the past, users who subscribed to a video conference logged into a central video server. The video server validated each user and presented all of the conferences that the user was authorized to view. The server acted as a focal point and distributed the video streams to each user, as shown in Figure 4–1. As each new user connected to the server, a new video stream was set up.

The downside of this operation is that the video server sent out multiple streams of the same data frame across the network. For example, if 20 users connected to the video server to view the same video conference, 20 streams of the same data were sent over the network. Because of this characteristic, the multimedia traffic quickly used all of the bandwidth on the network, slowing the network dramatically.

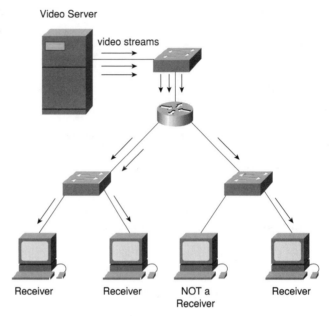

Figure 4–1

Multimedia sent as unicast traffic.

Because the network designer now has other choices for sending multimedia traffic, unicast multimedia is used today on a limited basis, primarily when only a few people want to have a video conference. For instance, if you and a coworker in another building have a "network meeting" type of multimedia application on your computers, you can have a video conference instead of using the telephone.

Multimedia as Broadcast Traffic

Broadcast multimedia traffic is a point-to-multipoint application. Here the video server sends out one data frame (instead of multiple streams), which goes to everyone. This point-to-multipoint operation is shown in Figure 4–2.

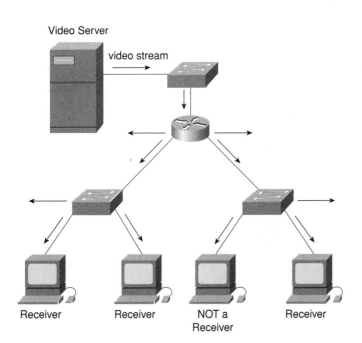

Video Server

video stream

Receiver   Receiver   NOT a   Receiver
                                Receiver

Figure 4–2
Multimedia sent as
broadcast traffic.

Broadcast multimedia is dispersed throughout the network just like normal broadcast traffic. And, just as with normal broadcasts, every client has to process the broadcast multimedia data frame. However, unlike standard broadcast frames, which are generally small, multimedia broadcasts can reach as high as 7 MB or more of data. If an endstation is not using a multimedia application, it still needs to process the broadcast traffic, which can use up most, if not all, of the allocated bandwidth. For this reason, the broadcast multimedia method is rarely implemented.

Multimedia as Multicast Traffic

Multicast traffic, like broadcast traffic, is also point-to-multipoint. However, instead of sending the data stream out to everyone on the network, the video server only sends the traffic to those stations that want to receive it. And unlike the unicast method, the video server sends out a single data stream to multiple clients or multiple endstations (instead of sending out a separate data stream to each client that requests it). Figure 4–3 shows a multicast operation.

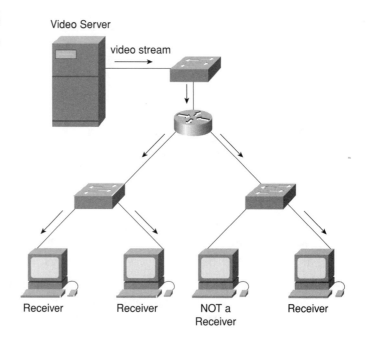

Figure 4–3
Multimedia sent as multicast traffic.

Because of the multicast method's unique capability, application developers have quickly adopted it for sending multimedia traffic. This multicasting method is defined in Host Extensions for IP Multicasting (RFC 1112), which was standardized in August 1989. Among other things,

RFC 1112 reserves a range of addresses at the MAC layer and at the IP protocol layer that can be used only for IP multicasting. An overview of the standard and of the way IP multicasting travels through the network is described in the following sections.

IP MULTICAST OPERATION

In general, the Internet standard defines *IP multicasting* as the transmission of an IP data frame to a host group, which is identified by a single IP address. Because of the host group and the single IP address rule, the IP multicast contains a specific combination of the destination MAC address and a destination IP address. Here's how it works:

Host groups are identified by class D IP addresses. At the protocol layer, the multicast host group must have a class D IP address, which fits into the range of 224.0.0.1 to 239.255.255.255 (IP address 224.0.0.0 is guaranteed not to be assigned to any group). The host group represents all of the users of the multicast application. Instead of sending separate data frames out to each member of the host group (which would be unicast point-to-point traffic), the server sends a single multicast data stream to the host group. Figure 4–4 shows a host group address.

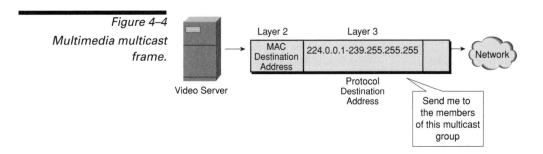

Figure 4–4
Multimedia multicast
frame.

The IP protocol address, 224.0.0.1, is used to address all of the multicast hosts that are directly connected to the same network as the multimedia server. Figure 4–5 shows endstations on the same local network as the multimedia server.

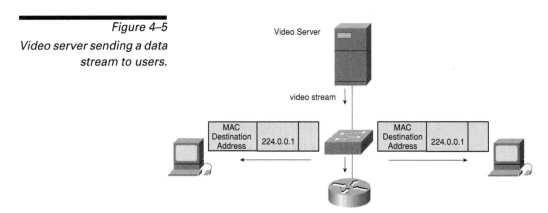

Figure 4–5
Video server sending a data
stream to users.

For the MAC layer, the destination MAC address always begins with 01-00-5E, followed by the IP group address. These addresses combine to form a single multicast group address: 01-00-5E-*xx-xx-xx* ("*xx-xx-xx*" specifies the IP group address). For example, if the destination IP protocol address for a multimedia group is 224.10.10.10, the destination MAC address becomes 01-00-5E-10-10-10. Figure 4–6 shows this example.

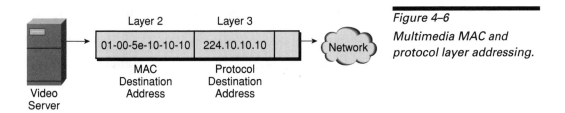

Figure 4–6

Multimedia MAC and protocol layer addressing.

Because only the last half of the MAC address is used for the IP host group address, there can be some overlap. For example, the IP host group addresses 224.10.10.10 and 230.10.10.10 both have the same MAC address: 01-00-5E-10-10-10. The groups remain separate, however, because they have different IP host group (protocol layer) addresses.

Aside from multicast addressing, the Internet standard also specifies additional requirements that the network devices must support in order to operate successfully with multimedia applications.

MULTICAST NETWORK REQUIREMENTS

As you might expect, sending and receiving multimedia require coordination from all network devices—the server, the host, the router, and the switch. Additional protocols are also required so that each device can understand and support multimedia applications. The sections that follow describe the requirements and the way each device needs to operate in order to support multimedia applications.

How the Server and Host Handle Multimedia

The multimedia server and the host (also known as the end-station) must be able to support the multicast-addressing scheme as well as the Internet Group Management Protocol (IGMP) that is specified in RFC 1112. IGMP defines the methods by which multimedia messages are passed among the devices in a LAN.

When a host—let's call it Host A—wants to receive a multimedia application, it sends a message to the server asking to become a member of the multimedia host group receiving the application. This step is required because the transmission of multimedia data frames can only go to a host group. The message from Host A, known as an IGMP JoinHostGroup message, is illustrated in Figure 4–7.

Figure 4–7
Host sending an IGMP Join message.

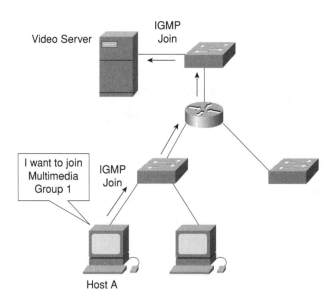

The video server running multimedia applications sends data frames out only to members that belong to a multimedia host group. Host A, through its IGMP Join message, becomes a member of the desired group and can receive the multimedia data stream, as shown in Figure 4–8.

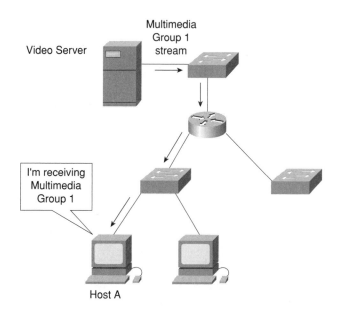

Figure 4–8

Host receiving a multimedia data stream.

The membership of a host group is dynamic—that is, hosts may join and leave groups at any time. Further, there are no restrictions on the location or number of members in a host group. Let's take another look at this process, but this time let's include the specifics of the group address.

Host A wants to join a video conference, which is identified as multimedia group XYZ. The group has an address of 230.1.1.1. Host A sends an IGMP Join for multimedia group

XYZ to the video server. Figure 4–9 shows the joining process. The video server responds by adding Host A to the multimedia group XYZ.

Figure 4–9
IGMP Join request going to a video server.

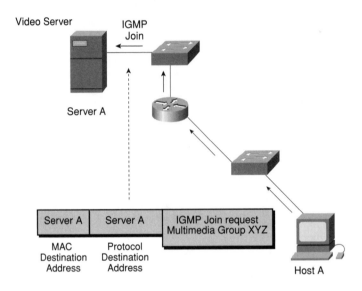

The video server sends the video conference traffic for multimedia group XYZ out to the network. As shown in Figure 4–10, the video conference is sent to the IP multicast group address 230.1.1.1, which contains the MAC group address 01-00-5E-01-01-01. Because Host A is now a member of the group, it can participate in the video conference.

When Host A wants to leave the video conference (multimedia group XYZ), it sends an IGMP Leave to the server, and the server removes Host A's address from the group XYZ membership. Figure 4–11 shows the IGMP Leave process.

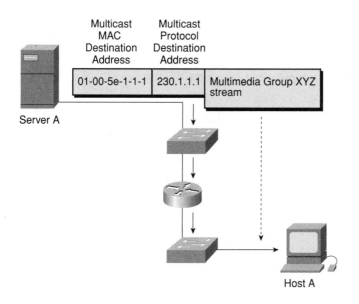

Figure 4–10

IP multicast group-addressing scheme.

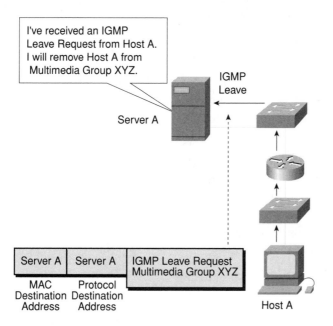

Figure 4–11

IGMP Leave request to a video server.

The server is responsible for accurately keeping the members of each multimedia group that it supports. It is also responsible for sending out the data traffic onto the network. The host is responsible for sending Join and Leave messages to the server so that it can start and stop receiving the multimedia traffic. The host is also responsible for sending IGMP Reports back to the router, which we discuss in the next section.

How the Router Handles Multimedia

IP multicasts and IGMP must also be understood by the routers in order for multimedia applications to successfully traverse the network. First, let's look at the way the router handles IGMP, and then we will show the methods that the routers use to perform multicast routing.

As described in the previous section, a host sends its IGMP Join message to the server when it wants to join a multimedia group. This message must go through a router (unless the host and the server are on the same subnet, which is highly unlikely). The router must know it is an IGMP Join message. When the router intercepts the message, it looks at its IGMP table and adds the network information for the host (if the network is not already in the table) so that it knows to send multimedia multicast packets out to the host's interface. The router typically adds the host's IP network address, not the host's specific IP address, to the table. Figure 4–12 shows an example of the IGMP table.

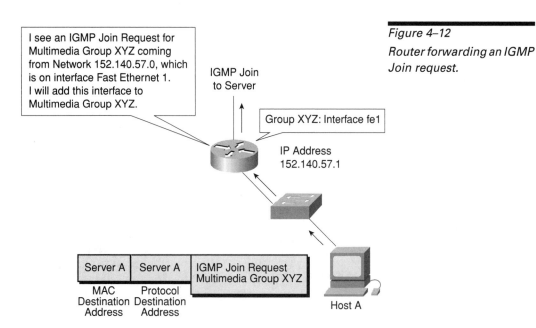

I see an IGMP Join Request for Multimedia Group XYZ coming from Network 152.140.57.0, which is on interface Fast Ethernet 1. I will add this interface to Multimedia Group XYZ.

IGMP Join to Server

Group XYZ: Interface fe1

IP Address 152.140.57.1

Server A | Server A | IGMP Join Request Multimedia Group XYZ

MAC Destination Address

Protocol Destination Address

Host A

Figure 4–12

Router forwarding an IGMP Join request.

The router then forwards the IGMP Join to the video server that is responsible for the specified multimedia group. In order to do this, the router must understand all of the IGMP instructions in the messages; otherwise, it could not direct them to the appropriate multimedia server.

Routers also send out IGMP Queries periodically to keep their group membership tables current. A router sends out a query on each network for each multimedia group, as shown in Figure 4–13.

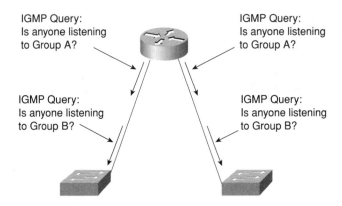

Figure 4–13
Router sending update
messages to the network.

Hosts respond to the query by sending an IGMP Report back to the router. Only one report is sent for each multimedia group on each network; therefore, only one host from each multimedia group needs to respond to the query. The router is not concerned about which host actually sends the report back. The details of this method are explained in RFC 1112. Figure 4–14 shows hosts sending IGMP reports back to the router.

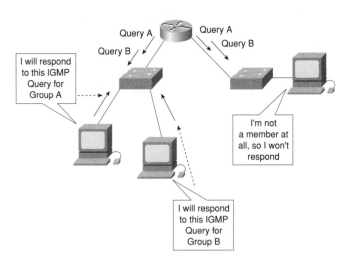

Figure 4–14
Hosts responding to a
router update request.

The router does not need to know who all of the members in the multimedia groups are. For example, if the router sees an IGMP Report come back from network 150.150.150.0 for the multimedia group address 230.1.1.1, the router continues to keep network 150.150.150.0 as a member of 230.1.1.1 group in its IGMP table, as shown in Figure 4–15.

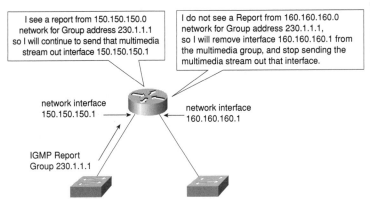

Figure 4–15
Router response to a host update report.

If the router does not receive a report back after several queries to the 160.160.160.0 network for the same multimedia group address 230.1.1.1 at the same time, it removes network 160.160.160.0 from the IGMP table for the group address 230.1.1.1, as can be seen in Figure 4–15.

As long as the router receives IGMP Reports back, it continues to keep those networks in the IGMP table for each multimedia group.

ROUTING METHODS FOR MULTIMEDIA

The routers in the network are responsible for knowing which networks can receive and which networks do not receive the multimedia traffic (IGMP keeps the router up-to-date). Multicast routing is the method used to direct the traffic to the appropriate networks.

In general, multicast routing protocols are extensions of unicast routing protocols—they take advantage of the unicast single-network destination operation and build on it in order to precisely send data frames to multiple destinations.

The network designer currently has several choices of multicast routing protocols:

- Multicast Open Shortest Path First (MOSPF)

- Distance Vector Multicast Routing Protocol (DVMRP)

- Protocol Independent Multicast (PIM)

  ○ dense-mode

  ○ sparse-mode

Multicast routing protocols can have very complex operations. Because our focus is on the way multimedia affects network traffic, the following discussion provides details of network design and traffic flow. Definitive information about each protocol's architecture can be obtained by reading the RFCs or the Internet draft which we reference in the text and in Appendix A.

As with any protocol, there are advantages and disadvantages to each, depending on the relative size, complexity, and internetworking scheme of your network. We provide an overview of the way each protocol operates within the network in the following sections.

Multicast Open Shortest Path First

Multicast Open Shortest Path First (MOSPF, defined in RFC 1584) works in tandem with IGMP. It is an extension of the OSPF routing protocol. OSPF features include multipath routing, load balancing, and least-cost routing. It is this last feature that MOSPF builds upon. OSPF determines the shortest (least-cost) path between a source and a destination by using a link-state algorithm. MOSPF performs this same function for multicast data frames. The protocol creates shortest-path trees that branch out to the multicast receivers. This feature is important from a network design aspect because it reduces the traffic load traversing the network. MOSPF operates best when many members belong to each multimedia group.

MOSPF does have a drawback, however, which is due to the OSPF Autonomous Systems feature. Because Autonomous Systems are collections of networks divided into areas, full trees (end-to-end paths) cannot be created from the source to the destination if the networks are in different areas. Only partial trees to the area boundaries can be created.

It's the same as wanting to travel from Arizona to Nevada using an Arizona map. The states may be grouped into an area named Western States, but when you reach the Arizona border, you have no instructions about where to go next.

In the campus network, this drawback is typically not a problem because you're working within a LAN. However, if the campus is running a protocol other than OSPF, such as the Routing Information Protocol (RIP), then MOSPF is probably not an optimal solution. Using RIP means that MOSPF needs to create its own routes and could potentially conflict with RIP.

Distance Vector Multicast Routing Protocol

The Distance Vector Multicast Routing Protocol (DVMRP, defined in RFC 1075), a derivative of RIP, also works in conjunction with IGMP.

DVMRP combines parts of RIP, such as the distance vector algorithms, with the Truncated Reverse Path Broadcasting (TRPB) algorithm. This combination forms what is referred to as reverse-path forwarding. As the name implies, the router receives instructions via information coming back from the devices (the reverse path).

When the video server receives a IGMP Join request from a host, it sends that multimedia group's multicast data out to the network. The routers receiving the multimedia traffic from the server initially flood the multicast out all of the ports, as shown in Figure 4–16.

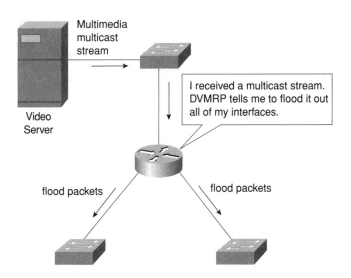

DVMRP assumes that all of the routers are in multicast for-warding mode, meaning that the routers are configured for multicast routing. If a router is receiving the multicast stream from the server and it has other routers connected to it, we call that router an *intermediate router*. The intermediate router continually receives data frames from the server. The intermediate router assumes that the routers it is connected to are in multicast forwarding mode, and it forwards the multicast out to the other routers. Figure 4–17 shows an example of an intermediate router.

Figure 4–17
Multimedia data stream
traveling through an
intermediate router.

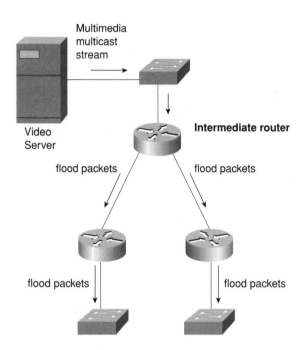

The router that connects to end-user subnets is called the *end router*. When the end router detects that no group members are on one of its interfaces (through the IGMP Query/Report method), then it stops sending that multicast stream out that interface, an action known as *pruning back*. Figure 4–18 shows an example of an end router pruning back the multicast stream.

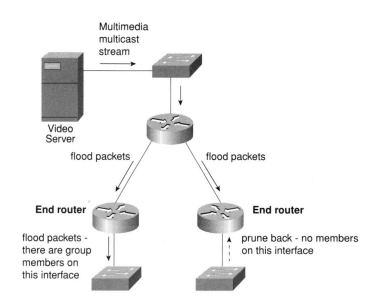

Multimedia
multicast
stream

Video
Server

flood packets   flood packets

End router   **End router**

flood packets -
there are group
members on
this interface

prune back - no members
on this interface

Figure 4–18
Response by end routers to
a multimedia data stream.

If an end router has no interfaces (remember, each interface represents a different network) with group members, it sends a prune message to the intermediate router directly above it. In the prune message, the end router tells the intermediate router not to send the multimedia group multicast packets to it. The intermediate router then stops sending multicast packets out that interface.

One of the unique characteristics of DVMRP is that it continually checks for new group members to keep its member table current. On a regular basis, generally every 60 seconds, DVMRP instructs each intermediate router to flood the multicasts out all of its ports and to wait until the end router sends a DVMRP prune message. For this reason, the DVMRP multicast routing protocol works best when numerous members belong to each multimedia group. That way, there is little need for the router to constantly send prune-back messages. Figure 4–19 shows the operations of the DVMRP protocol.

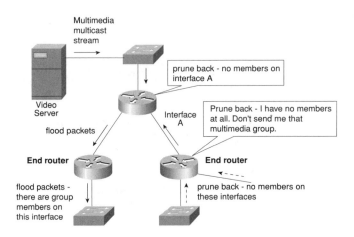

Figure 4–19
DVMRP query and
prune-back operations.

Although periodically sending queries keeps the member table current, a network designer should look very closely at any protocol that floods data frames out to the network. DVMRP provides a great tool: It allows devices to support multimedia applications and it limits itself to appropriate interfaces once they are known. However, it comes at a price—its flooding characteristic brings with it the potential for network traffic overload.

Protocol Independent Multicast

Protocol Independent Multicast (PIM) is the most recent method developed by the internetworking community to handle multimedia traffic.

Like the previous two multicast-routing techniques (MOSPF and DVMRP), PIM works alongside a unicast routing protocol, which could be OSPF, RIP, or the Enhanced Interior Gateway Routing Protocol (EIGRP). Like the others, it works in conjunction with IGMP. PIM comes in two forms, however: dense-mode and sparse-mode.

PIM Dense-mode

PIM dense-mode (Internet-draft name draft-ietf-idmr-pim-dm-05.txt) is very similar to DVMRP. It uses the reverse-path forwarding mechanism, which means that it floods out the multimedia packet and then prunes back in places where no members belong to a group. It also works best when there are numerous members belonging to each multimedia group, which limits the router's need to send prune-back messages on the network. Figure 4–20 shows PIM dense-mode operating in a network.

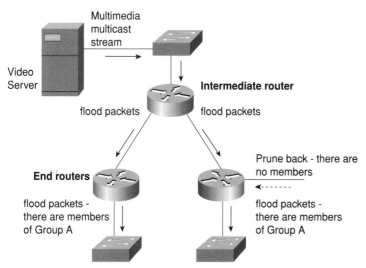

Figure 4–20
PIM protocol dense-mode operation.

The main difference between DVMRP and PIM dense-mode is that DVMRP calculates its own route paths and tables, whereas PIM dense-mode uses the existing route paths and tables, which the unicast routing protocol (RIP, OSPF, or EIGRP) has already created.

PIM Sparse-mode

The next form of PIM, PIM sparse-mode (defined in RFC 2117), is very different from PIM dense-mode. It works with IGMP and a unicast routing protocol, like the other methods mentioned previously. However, PIM sparse-mode is designed to make optimum use of "small membership" environments. As shown previously, PIM dense-mode (as well as MOSPF and DVMRP) operates best when there are lots of members belonging to each multimedia group. PIM sparse-mode, however, works best in situations where there are several multimedia groups, and a small number of members within each group. Figure 4–21 shows PIM sparse-mode operating in a network.

PIM sparse-mode provides a unique way of operating with routers to get multimedia traffic to the endstations. Instead of using reverse-path forwarding, in which traffic is sent out everywhere and then pruned back where there are no members, PIM sparse-mode utilizes a "rendezvous point" mechanism. A rendezvous point is configured on a router for each of the multimedia groups. The multimedia groups do not need to use the same router as the rendezvous point. For example, you can have one router as the rendezvous point for multimedia Group A, then select another router as the rendezvous point for multimedia Group B, as shown in Figure 4–22.

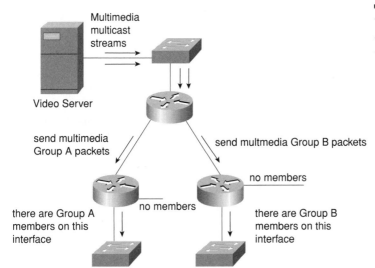

Figure 4–21
PIM protocol sparse-mode operation.

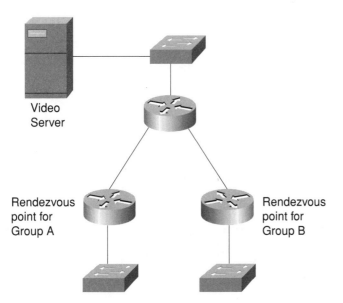

Figure 4–22
PIM rendezvous points.

When the host sends out its IGMP Join, the end router sends the Join request to the rendezvous point router, as we see in Figure 4–23.

Figure 4–23

PIM rendezvous point routers forwarding an IGMP Join request.

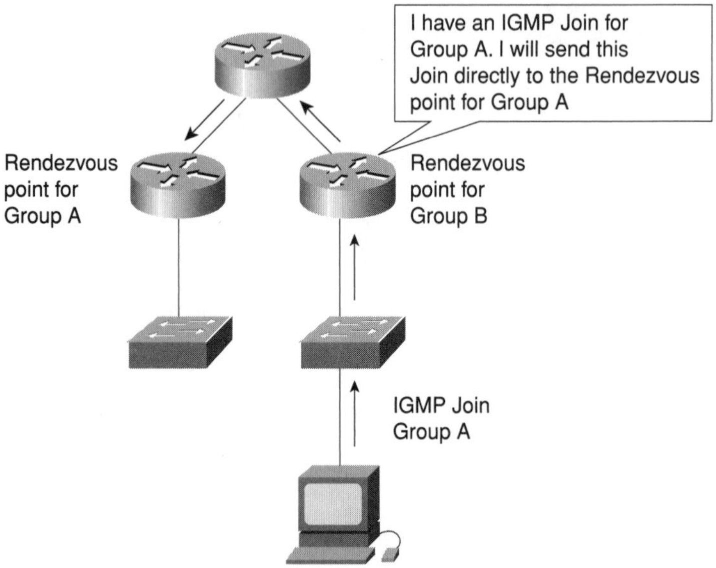

The IGMP Join message is first registered with the rendezvous point. The rendezvous point router then sends the Join message to the video server. Figure 4–24 shows the actions of the rendezvous point router.

When the video server starts sending out the multimedia traffic, the server sends it to the rendezvous point first, as shown in Figure 4–25, and the rendezvous point router sends the multicast traffic on to the end router. The end router then forwards it out the interface that the group member is connected to, as we see in Figure 4–26.

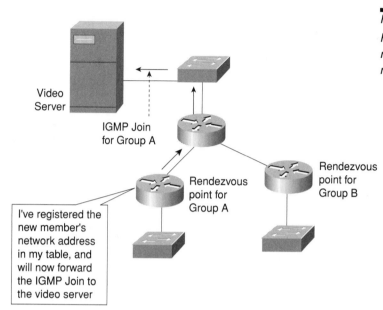

Video
Server

IGMP Join
for Group A

Rendezvous
point for
Group A

Rendezvous
point for
Group B

I've registered the
new member's
network address
in my table, and
will now forward
the IGMP Join to
the video server

Figure 4–24

*PIM rendezvous point
routers registering Join
requests.*

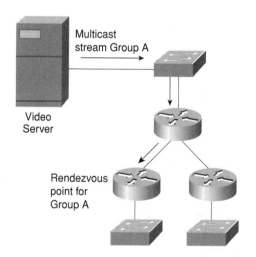

Video
Server

Multicast
stream Group A

Rendezvous
point for
Group A

Figure 4–25

*Server sending multimedia
data stream to PIM
rendezvous points.*

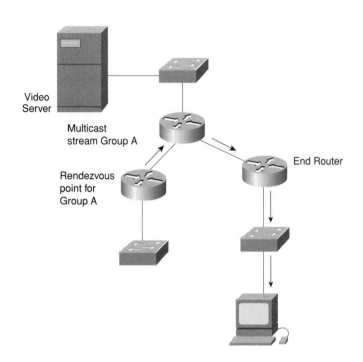

Figure 4–26

PIM end router response to a multimedia data stream.

Once this path is established from the video server to the host (that is, the multimedia group member) through the rendez-vous point, the routers then optimize the path and create a shorter path across the network (through RIP, OSPF, or EIGRP), as shown in Figure 4–27.

Remember, however, that the multimedia traffic must initially go through the rendezvous point router before the data path to its group members can be optimized.

With PIM sparse-mode, the reverse path forwarding and pruning actions are not needed to prevent the routers from sending the multimedia traffic to hosts who don't want it.

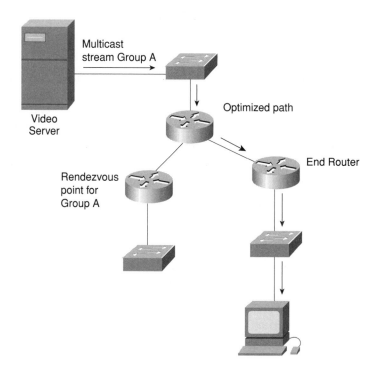

The intermediate routers don't flood the traffic out all of their ports, because PIM sparse-mode lets them create an optimized path throughout the network.

HOW THE SWITCH HANDLES MULTIMEDIA

Compared to routers, the behavior of switches with respect to multimedia applications is much simpler.

The switch does not need special networking tools in order to support multimedia. When multimedia traffic is sent via unicast, the switch acts as a "pass-through" device; it simply sends it along to the receiving device. When it's sent via broadcast, multimedia traffic is handled like any other broadcast and sent out of all the switch's ports. A multimedia multicast transmission is handled in the same manner—the switch sends the traffic out to all devices. This is because multicast instructions reside at the protocol layer, which the switch is unable to recognize. The switch therefore sends the traffic out all of its ports.

To help the network operate in a more efficient manner, however, there are some things that the network designer can and should configure on the switches. First, we'll describe how the network operates without anything configured on the switch, then show how switch operation can be optimized for multimedia traffic flow.

Switches without Configuration

When the switch sees a multicast packet, it treats it like a broadcast, meaning that it sends the packet out all of its ports. This operation is shown in Figure 4–28.

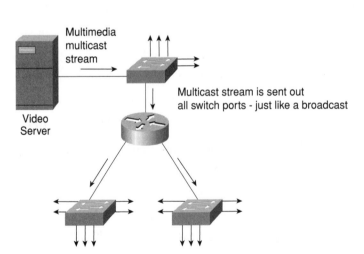

Figure 4–28

Switch response to a multimedia data stream.

Technically, multimedia can travel across the network without special operation from the switch. But from a network performance and scalability perspective, the switch should be able to have some sort of intelligence to prevent multicast flooding.

As an example, let's suppose your company is enthusiastic about in-house video training and does a lot of it. Video training sessions can run upwards of 4 MB of data, which is data that will cross the network and form a multicast.

If you're not one of the people watching the training, your endstation is getting taxed because it still needs to process that 4 MB of data, which is shown in Figure 4–29.

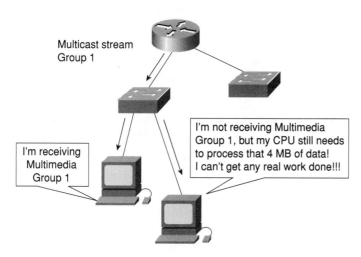

Multicast stream
Group 1

I'm receiving
Multimedia
Group 1

I'm not receiving Multimedia
Group 1, but my CPU still needs
to process that 4 MB of data!
I can't get any real work done!!!

Figure 4–29

Endstation response to a multimedia data stream coming from a switch.

As we've described in the previous sections, the routers in the network send multicast traffic to specified host groups, thereby reducing network traffic overhead. Keep in mind, however, that the multicast traffic leaving the router usually travels through at least one switch before reaching the end device and the switch floods multicast traffic out all of its ports.

Switches with Filters

To optimize network performance, you can use a filtering mechanism at the switch. This can be done in two ways:

- You can manually configure a filter for each switch port

- You can use dynamic filtering

The first option, manually setting up multicast address registration at the switch, can be an arduous task, especially considering that a switch can have upwards of 24 or more ports.

As for the second option, each vendor today is setting up some type of proprietary dynamic filtering, so that the switch can filter out multicast traffic and send it only to the ports that are members of a multicast group. Some vendors design the switch to understand IGMP packets, thereby giving the switch some network layer intelligence. Other vendors set up a Layer 2/Layer 3 linkage so the switch can do dynamic filtering without having to understand Layer 3 IGMP packets.

Dynamic filtering seems to be the best way to filter at the switch, but all vendors currently use a different, proprietary method. Because most networks use a mix of vendor products, the result would be a mix of switch filtering methods—a potential nightmare to keep track of from a network administration point of view.

Manual configuration of filtering is administration-intensive and takes up a lot of time, but it is still better than doing nothing at all.

SUMMARY

For multimedia applications to traverse the campus successfully, the network designer must set up and install specific items on the network. First, the designer must decide which enterprise server will hold the application. Next, IGMP must be configured on the endstations, the multimedia server, and the routers. The designer next must choose an appropriate multicast routing protocol (MOSPF, DVMRP, or PIM dense-mode or sparse-mode). And finally, to optimize network performance, a filtering mechanism should be placed on the switches to prevent them from flooding multimedia multicast traffic throughout the network.

The traffic generated by multimedia applications is considered to be cross-campus traffic because users at various locations want to use them. We describe how multimedia and other forms of traffic flow through the network in the next chapter.

The key things to remember for designing a campus network that can accommodate multimedia applications are as follows:

- Because of its unique capability to send out a single data stream to multiple clients or endstations, the multicast method has become the transmission method of choice for most multimedia applications.

- IGMP is required on the network so that endstations can join and leave multimedia application sessions.

- You have a choice of routing methods for multimedia, and you should choose one based on the amount of multimedia traffic you anticipate will be traversing the campus.

- The DVMRP routing protocol is appropriate when numerous members belong to a multimedia group.

- PIM dense-mode is also appropriate when numerous members belong to a multimedia group. In addition, it takes advantage of and uses existing route paths and tables set up by the unicast routing protocol running on the network.

- PIM sparse-mode is appropriate when the network has only a few multimedia groups and a small number of members within each group. It also lets routers optimize the path between the multimedia sender and receiver through its rendezvous mechanism.

- Configuring a filter for multicast traffic on each switch port, either manually or dynamically, provides efficient network operation.

This chapter covers the following topics:

- Local traffic

- Cross-campus traffic

- Effects of Internet traffic on the campus

- Broadcast and multimedia traffic through the campus

- Determining how much traffic is local versus cross-campus

CHAPTER 5

Looking at Local versus Cross-Campus Traffic

Anticipating where traffic will go on the network is another design element that must be taken into consideration when planning for optimal network performance.

Previous chapters described traffic in terms of its type, such as broadcast and multicast. In this chapter, you will look at traffic in terms of what portions of the network it traverses—that is, whether certain traffic is local or cross-campus.

We begin with general descriptions of local and cross-campus traffic. Although the terms may seem self-explanatory, it's helpful to define them in terms of network operations, because each type affects the campus differently.

LOCAL TRAFFIC

Local traffic is traffic that remains within a small part of the network; it does not enter the network backbone or cross a router. Typically, local traffic is confined to data that travels between a server, a switch, and an endstation client, as shown in Figure 5–1.

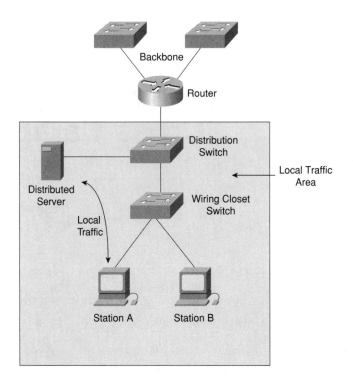

Figure 5–1
Local traffic on the network.

As we discussed in Chapter 2, "Server Placement," distributed servers need only to support a certain group of users. When the distributed server is placed at the distribution or wiring closet switch, and the users it supports are also connected to this switch, then the traffic going to that distributed server is local traffic.

To look more closely at the path that the traffic takes from an endstation to the distributed server and back again, consider Station A and Server B in Figure 5–2.

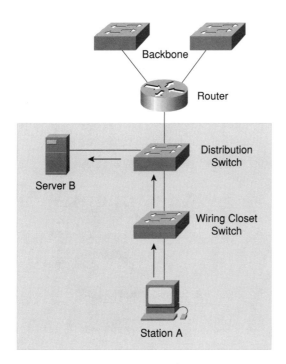

Figure 5–2
Traffic sent from Station A to Server B.

The endstation, Station A, sends a request to download a file from the distributed server, Server B. The request sent from Station A travels through the wiring closet switch and up to the distribution switch. The request then travels directly to Server B. Notice that the traffic generated by the request does not need to go to the router or across the backbone. Figure 5–2 shows the request traveling from Station A to Server B.

Server B receives the request and begins to transfer the requested file. The traffic goes to the distribution switch and then down to the wiring closet switch. It then goes directly to Station A without crossing the router or the backbone. Figure 5–3 shows the traffic traveling from Server B to Station A.

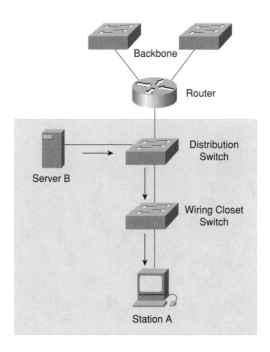

Figure 5–3
Server B sending a file to Station A.

Traffic between endstations and servers, as in this example, is known as client/server traffic, which is one of the most common forms of traffic in campus networks today.

Another example is data traffic passing between clients, such as a shared whiteboard application between two users. Because this type of application is becoming more popular, it is worthwhile to study its impact on the network's traffic pattern.

Let's assume that Stations A and B in Figure 5–4 want to work on a single document by using a shared whiteboard application. Although these two stations are not connected to the same wiring closet switch, they do share the same distribution switch.

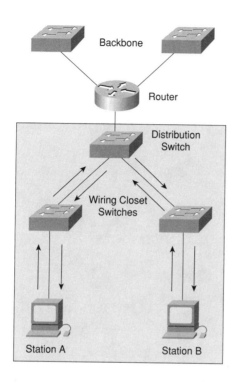

Figure 5–4

Traffic between Stations A and B.

When Stations A and B run the whiteboard application, traffic is sent point-to-point between the two stations. Whenever a change is made on the document, traffic is sent. Figure 5–4 highlights the parts of the network this traffic traversed.

The traffic from the shared whiteboard application is considered local traffic because it only crosses the wiring closet switches and the distribution switch—not the router or the backbone.

CROSS-CAMPUS TRAFFIC

Cross-campus traffic is traffic that crosses the backbone of the network, travels through a router, or does both. Typically, cross-campus traffic is data that travels from endstations to enterprise servers or between endstations on other subnets. Figure 5–5 shows the cross-campus traffic area.

Figure 5–5
Cross-campus traffic area.

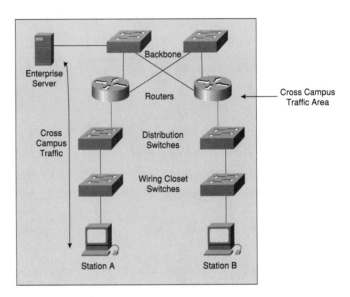

Just as local traffic involves the distributed server, cross-campus traffic involves the enterprise server. Because everyone needs to access the enterprise server, it's placed close to the backbone of the network. Therefore, all traffic going to that enterprise server needs to cross the backbone, as shown in Figure 5–5.

A typical example of cross-campus traffic is shown in Figure 5–6. Station A downloads e-mail from the e-mail server; the figure shows the path that the traffic takes. The request to download e-mail travels through the wiring closet switch and the distribution switch, and then enters the router. The router sends the request across the backbone to the e-mail server.

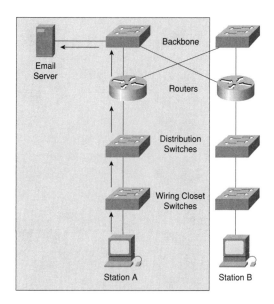

Figure 5–6

Cross-campus traffic to the e-mail server.

When the e-mail server sends the download back to Station A, it follows the same path through the network, as highlighted in Figure 5–6. Like the local traffic example in Figure 5–2, this traffic is considered client/server, but this time the traffic is cross-campus traffic because it goes through the backbone.

A simple file transfer can be cross-campus traffic as well, and it can involve the distributed server instead of an enterprise server. For example, suppose that Station C wants a file from Server B, as illustrated in Figure 5–7.

As Figure 5–7 shows, Station C and Server B do not connect to the same distribution switch. Figure 5–8 shows the path that the traffic follows from Station C to Server B.

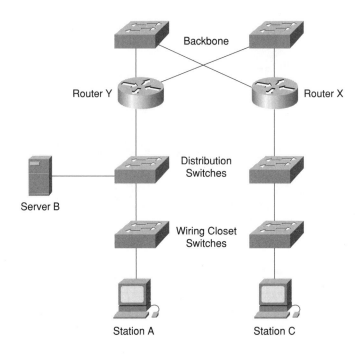

Figure 5–7
Network location of Station C and Distributed Server B.

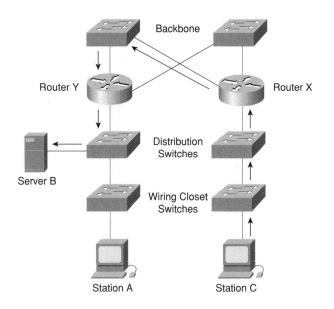

Figure 5–8
Traffic path from Station C to Server B.

Station C sends the request to Server B. The request travels through the wiring closet switch and the distribution switch that are local to Station C. It then travels through Router X, which sends the request over the backbone to Router Y. The request then travels from Router Y through the distribution switch to Server B.

The path that the data must travel shows that this traffic is cross-campus traffic, even though it involves a distributed server. The data that travels from Server B to Station C is also cross-campus traffic because it crosses the backbone of the network.

As can be expected, cross-campus traffic includes traffic between endstations that reside on different areas of the campus network. Let's look at the shared whiteboard example again, but first move the users. Figure 5–9 shows where the two endstations that share this application are now located on the network.

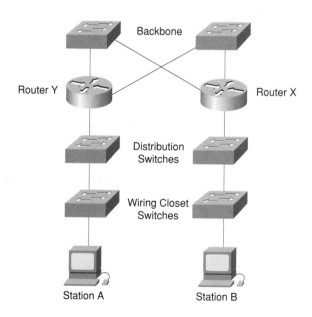

Figure 5–9
Two endstations sharing an application.

Previously, the stations connected to the same distribution switch (refer to Figure 5–4). In Figure 5–9, the stations connect to different distribution switches.

Consider the traffic between the two endstations for this application. Station A makes a change to the document. Figure 5–10 shows the path that the traffic takes across the network.

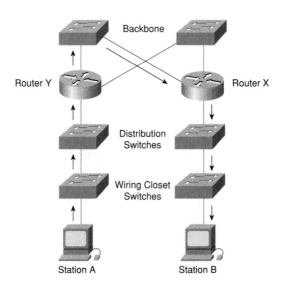

Figure 5–10

Traffic path between Stations A and B.

The traffic leaves Station A and travels through the local wiring closet switch and distribution switch. It crosses through Router Y onto the backbone to Router X. Router X sends the traffic down through the distribution switch and wiring closet switch that are local to Station B. This traffic is cross-campus traffic because it crosses the backbone. The same is true for traffic from Station B to Station A.

A final example of cross-campus traffic involves endstations that connect to the same distribution switch but are on different networks, as shown in Figure 5–11.

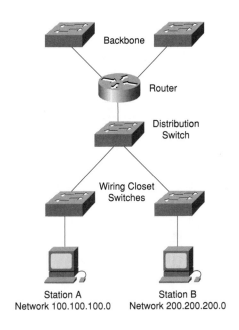

Backbone

Router

Distribution
Switch

Wiring Closet
Switches

Station A
Network 100.100.100.0

Station B
Network 200.200.200.0

Figure 5–11

Endstations on different networks that connect to the same distribution switch.

If Stations A and B are using the shared whiteboard application in this scenario, is the traffic between them local or cross-campus? Figure 5–12 displays the traffic path through the network for this situation.

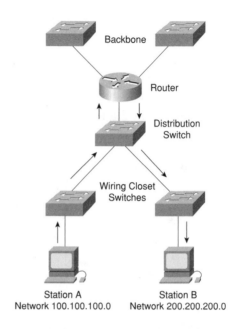

Figure 5–12

Traffic path between Stations A and B.

Station A makes a change, and that change travels out through the wiring closet switch and distribution switch. Because Stations A and B are on different networks, the switch cannot send the traffic directly to Station B; it must send the traffic up to the router, and the router must route it to Station B's network. The router then sends the traffic down to the distribution switch, through the wiring closet switch, and out to Station B.

Because this traffic must go to the router, it is considered cross-campus traffic. Remember, cross-campus traffic is traffic that crosses the backbone or a router or both.

Thus far, you've learned about traffic that originates and ends on the campus, but there is another type of traffic that must be considered—Internet traffic. At first glance, Internet traffic may seem to fall outside the scope of a text concerned with campus LAN design. But the traffic that goes out to the

Internet and comes into the campus from the Internet (also known as the wide area network, or WAN) has an extremely important effect on the LAN.

EFFECTS OF INTERNET TRAFFIC ON THE CAMPUS

Internet traffic is becoming more crucial to businesses and is growing by leaps and bounds. Network designers need to start observing how this traffic impacts the campus network, especially how it affects the servers and users residing on the campus.

Traffic going out to the Internet from the campus and the traffic coming into the campus from the Internet affect the campus network differently, as we'll show in the sections that follow.

Campus-to-Internet Traffic

When we take a look at the traffic going out to the Internet, we focus on people at different companies or at home who are connecting to our local network via the Internet. These users are accessing our campus enterprise servers and possibly distributed servers on the campus network to get information.

Let's look at several situations that involve traffic going from the campus LAN out across the Internet or wide area network.

The first example focuses on e-mail, primarily because it is so prevalent in today's business world. If your company has field support offices, branch offices, or employees who telecommute, your users need to log into the e-mail server on the campus network and download their e-mails across the wide area network or the Internet. Figure 5–13 shows how the e-mail server on the campus sends the traffic out to the wide area.

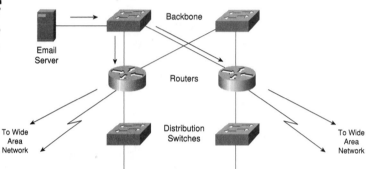

Figure 5–13
E-mail traffic going out to the wide area network.

E-mail servers can be considered to be enterprise servers because so many users from various locations need to access them. The part of the campus network that is affected by e-mail traffic is the backbone. As you can see in Figure 5–13, e-mail traffic leaves the e-mail servers, crosses the backbone (thereby becoming cross-campus traffic), and exits the campus network through a wide area router.

File servers also play an active role in generating cross-campus Internet traffic. When people outside of the campus network are downloading or transferring a file (a process known as FTP), the data travels from the file server on the campus network out across the Internet. These file servers can be enterprise or distributed servers. Figure 5–14 shows an enterprise file server sending data out across the Internet.

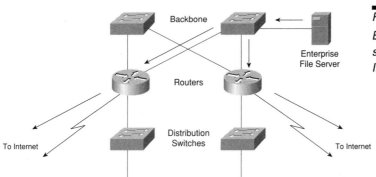

Figure 5–14
Enterprise file server sending data out to the Internet.

The enterprise file server, just like the e-mail servers, sends the traffic across the backbone to the Internet router. A distributed server, however, sends a file out to the Internet in a different manner, as shown in Figure 5–15.

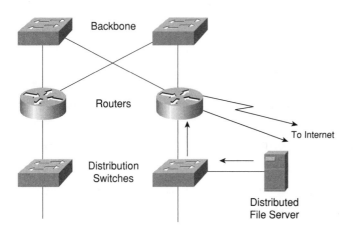

Figure 5–15
Distributed server sending a file out to the Internet.

Notice that the distributed server does not send data across the backbone. However, the data does not stay local to the distributed server's subnet. Rather, it must go through the router to get to the wide area network, which means that it meets the definition of cross-campus traffic.

Let's now consider the traffic leaving the campus to go to the World Wide Web. Again, this traffic involves enterprise servers—this time, Web servers—that can be accessed by numerous people at various locations. Web servers reside on the campus, and as users browse the Web, they are accessing the Web servers. All of the traffic that is downloaded from the Web servers has to cross the campus to get onto the Internet—that is, the Web traffic must travel across the backbone of the campus to reach the wide area router.

The location of servers on the network determines the way the traffic shown in preceding examples affects network performance. Campus traffic going out to the Internet affects either the campus backbone or the area where the distributed servers reside. In both cases, the traffic affects network performance by using some of the bandwidth and router processing power.

Internet-to-Campus Traffic

Network performance is also affected by traffic coming into the campus from the Internet. For example, if a user on the campus is browsing the Web, transferring a file from another company's file server, or downloading an application from another company's Web server, traffic is coming onto the campus network from the Internet. Figure 5–16 shows where the traffic goes across the Internet during a Web-browsing session.

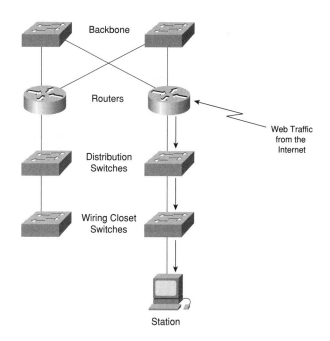

Figure 5–16
Traffic from the Internet onto the campus.

The traffic comes in through the wide area router, then passes through the campus network to reach the user's workstation. Notice in Figure 5–16 that although this traffic does not cross the backbone, it does cross the router; therefore, it is cross-campus.

This traffic pattern changes when the workstation is placed in a different location on the campus network, as shown in Figure 5–17.

In this situation, the traffic must cross the backbone of the network—in addition to the router, distribution switch, and wiring closet switch—to reach the workstation. In contrast, the traffic pattern in Figure 5–16 affects only a router and two switches.

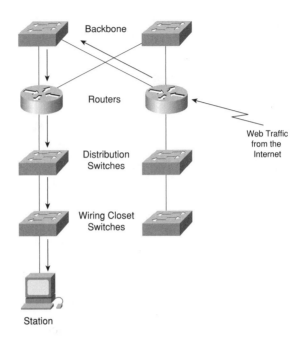

Figure 5–17

Internet traffic entering the campus network.

Let's consider what can happen with a multimedia application. Suppose you are involved in a video conference that includes people from different companies. Your multimedia traffic is coming into the campus network from the wide area or Internet. As with the Web browsing example, this traffic goes to the endstation, and it might or might not cross the backbone. Regardless of whether it crosses the backbone, however, the traffic will always go through at least one router; therefore, it is cross-campus.

Now look at the e-mail example again. Most environments that support an e-mail application let users send and receive e-mail outside of their own company. When you download e-mail, you download it from the e-mail server. The e-mail that comes in from other companies across the wide area and the Internet goes to the e-mail server on the campus, not directly to an endstation. Figure 5–18 shows e-mail coming into the campus.

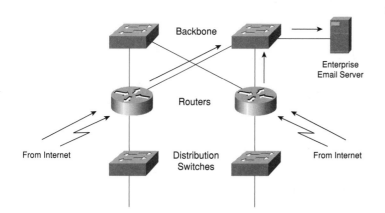

Backbone

Enterprise
Email Server

Routers

From Internet

Distribution
Switches

From Internet

Figure 5–18
E-mail coming into the campus from the Internet.

In this situation, the traffic always travels across the backbone because the e-mail servers are enterprise servers.

These three examples show that traffic coming in from the Internet or the wide area can impact the backbone of the network as well as the area where the endstations are connected.

To summarize, traffic going out to the Internet mainly affects the core—the backbone of the network and the enterprise servers that are being accessed. The traffic also can impact the area where the distributed servers are located, but to a much smaller extent. When Internet traffic is coming into the campus network, it's impacting both areas of the network, the backbone and the local user areas, but to a lesser degree the network backbone. In all cases, this traffic is considered cross-campus traffic.

So far, we've discussed the differences between local and cross-campus traffic in terms of the traffic source and destination—that is, client/server traffic, client/client traffic, and Internet traffic. However, as you know from reading Chapter 3, "The Effects of Broadcast Traffic," and Chapter 4, "Factoring in Multimedia Traffic," the type of traffic and how bandwidth-intensive it is plays a big part in network design and network performance. Let's extend the discussion of local versus cross-campus traffic to include the effects of broadcast traffic and multimedia traffic.

BROADCAST AND MULTIMEDIA THROUGH THE CAMPUS

Recall the broadcast examples used in Chapter 3, "The Effects of Broadcast Traffic": IP ARPs, IPX SAPs or routing updates, and DHCP requests. Are these forms of traffic local or cross-campus?

An IP ARP request originates at the endstation as a broadcast. It travels as a broadcast through the network until it reaches a router or the destination station, as shown in Figure 5–19.

In almost all cases, the IP ARP request will not pass through the backbone; it will instead stop at the router. Switches A, B, and C, however, will propagate the broadcast. Because the ARP request encounters a router, it can be considered as cross-campus traffic. Note, however, that in this scenario the biggest impact is on the local part of the network. The broadcast travels freely throughout the two wiring closet switches and the distribution switch. It is important to recognize that although traffic is considered cross-campus, it still affects the users on the local area of the network.

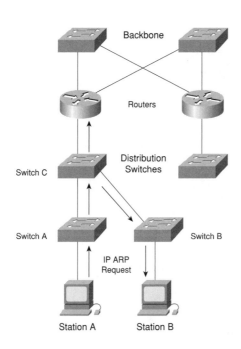

Figure 5–19
IP ARP request traveling through the network.

In the case of an IPX SAP broadcast, the frame begins at the IPX server. Because the IPX server is probably an enterprise server, the IPX SAP travels through the backbone, as shown in Figure 5–20.

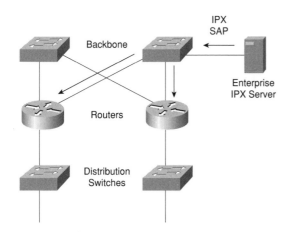

Figure 5–20
IPX SAP crossing the backbone.

This broadcast traffic is clearly cross-campus. If the server is connected to a router, as shown in Figure 5–21, the IPX SAP is still considered cross-campus traffic because the router sends the SAPs out as broadcast routing updates, which travel across the network backbone.

Figure 5–21
Router sending SAP
routing updates.

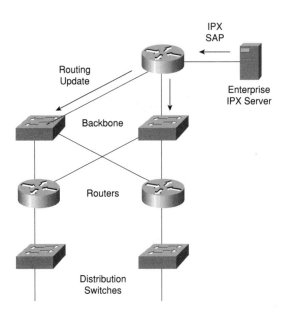

The last example in this discussion is the DHCP request, which, like the IP ARP requests, begins at the endstation. The endstation sends out the DHCP request, which travels through the network as a broadcast until it reaches a router, as shown in Figure 5–22.

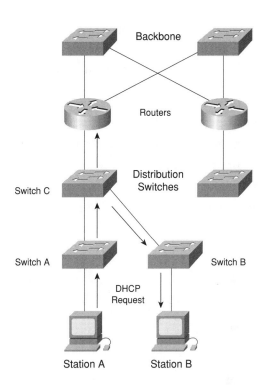

Just as in the IP ARP request example, the broadcast propagates through Switches A, B, and C. The router terminates the DHCP broadcast and sends it over the backbone to the DHCP server as a unicast. Although the DHCP request broadcast does not travel through the backbone, the router still must process it, which makes the broadcast cross-campus traffic. The router then sends the unicast across the backbone, so the unicast is cross-campus as well. The DHCP broadcast also impacts the local network because it is propagated through the switches.

These examples do not depict all of the kinds of traffic that generate broadcasts, but they do give a representative picture of the local and cross-campus effects of broadcast traffic.

You can generalize by saying that all broadcasts are cross-campus traffic, while keeping in mind that many broadcasts also affect local parts of the network.

Multimedia traffic is also predominantly cross-campus traffic. In most cases, the multimedia servers reside on the network as enterprise servers. Therefore, as the multimedia servers send out the multicast data, it is sent across the backbone to reach the appropriate endstations. Clearly, this is cross-campus traffic, as shown in Figure 5–23.

Figure 5–23

Multimedia traffic crossing the backbone.

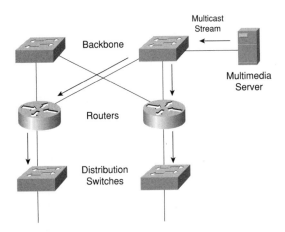

The multimedia IGMP Join and Leave requests that are created by the endstations are sent as unicast traffic. The endstations send these frames to the multimedia server. The traffic generated by these requests must cross the backbone as well, which results in more cross-campus traffic, as shown in Figure 5–24.

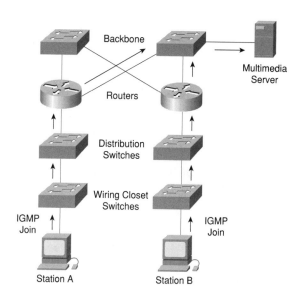

Figure 5–24
*IGMP Join requests
crossing the backbone.*

When the router updates its group membership table by sending out IGMP Queries to the networks, this traffic is considered cross-campus as well because it originates at the router.

Multicast routing is clearly cross-campus traffic because the routers do the routing. Whether running DVMRP, PIM dense-mode, or PIM sparse-mode, the router must direct the multimedia traffic through the network. Figure 5–25 shows an example of traffic flow for PIM dense-mode, and Figure 5–26 displays traffic flow for PIM sparse-mode.

Figure 5–25

PIM dense-mode sending cross-campus traffic.

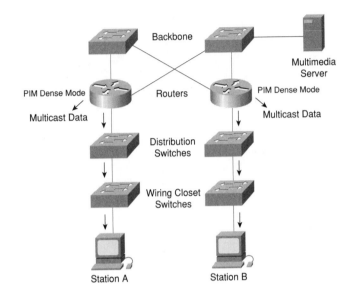

Figure 5–26

PIM sparse-mode sending cross-campus traffic.

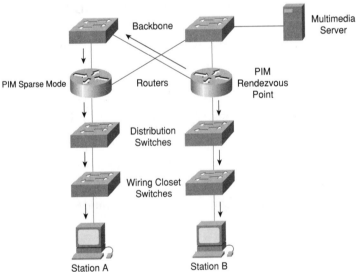

PIM dense-mode instructs the router to flood the multicast traffic down to the users. Because the router does this, the traffic is cross-campus.

The rendezvous point mechanism for PIM sparse-mode sends the multimedia traffic through the network to each group member. As shown in Figure 5–26, this is also cross-campus traffic.

As with broadcasts, multimedia traffic is cross-campus. The multimedia traffic certainly impacts local end users on the network, but because it crosses the backbone in almost all cases and certainly passes through a router, it is characterized as cross-campus traffic.

An important aspect of network design is to know which type of traffic is local and which is cross-campus. Even more important is to figure out the percentages—how much of your network traffic is cross-campus and how much is local.

DETERMINING HOW MUCH TRAFFIC IS LOCAL VERSUS CROSS-CAMPUS

As your campus LAN grows and evolves, you need to determine how much of the traffic can stay local and how much of it needs to be cross-campus so that you can allocate bandwidth in adequate amounts at the appropriate places.

One way to do this is to use the method described in Chapter 3, "The Effects of Broadcast Traffic." Put a network-monitoring tool on different parts of the network and monitor how much traffic crosses each network segment. In doing so, you can obtain a baseline of the traffic pattern on your network.

Once you create your baseline, you can see where your traffic is traveling on the network and determine what percentage is local and what is cross-campus. As the traffic patterns on the network change, you can determine where the changes are occurring and what impact they are having on the network.

Establishing a baseline can also help you understand the impact that new applications will have on network performance.

SUMMARY

Traffic is considered local when most of it stays off the backbone and remains local to the distributed server. If your traffic is local, you can concentrate on how much bandwidth needs to go to the distributed server. Because local traffic does not cross the whole network, you can probably operate a less complex network.

Cross-campus traffic involves enterprise and distributed servers, as well as routers. It places a greater load on the network because it travels across the backbone. If your traffic is cross-campus, you need to concentrate on how much bandwidth you need to go to the enterprise servers, distributed servers, and routers. You will probably have a more complex network infrastructure.

The important design concepts to remember from this chapter are:

- Local traffic is traffic that does not enter the network backbone and does not cross a router.

- Cross-campus traffic is traffic that crosses the network backbone or travels through a router or does both.

- Internet traffic, whether to or from the network, is cross-campus traffic. Because of the pervasiveness of Internet traffic, especially e-mail, network designers almost always need to plan for this type of traffic and for its effects, which are felt throughout the network.

- Broadcast and multimedia traffic are predominantly cross-campus, although they often have a strong local impact as well.

- Use network-monitoring tools to establish baseline percentages of local and cross-campus traffic, and to allocate bandwidth appropriately.

Part II

Essential Elements of Design

- **Chapter 6**—Network Reliability and Resiliency

- **Chapter 7**—Setting Traffic Priorities

- **Chapter 8**—Addressing Security Issues

- **Chapter 9**—Designing for Change and Growth

In Part 1, we discussed the importance of traffic patterns on the network. In Part 2, we cover ways to optimize and protect this traffic by using network design elements.

The need for these design elements is closely intertwined with making your network scalable for future growth and changes. The objective is to plan so that as your network changes and grows, you can add people, equipment, connections, and even traffic, easily and seamlessly. For example, network growth will probably result in higher redundancy requirements. You must consider how to provide reliability and resiliency for users in case of failure. An increase in applications also may require taking a look at how traffic is prioritized, if at all. Which traffic needs to get across the network first? Is some traffic delay-sensitive? Your network must effectively support this high-priority traffic.

Another crucial area to examine as your network grows is network security. An increase in the number of users may mean that you need to reconsider your security applications. How much security do you have in place on your network and is it sufficient? Determining the level of security your network needs is critical for successful network operation.

Also, as your network changes due to increasing user mobility, you must think about how to provide network scalability through the use of dynamic protocol addressing, and possibly VLAN implementation.

The chapters in Part 2 will help you to analyze your network in terms of how much and what kinds of redundancy, traffic prioritization, security, dynamic addressing, and VLANs are required to ensure network scalability as your network grows and changes.

This chapter covers the following topics:

- The meaning and importance of redundancy

- Minimal need for redundancy

- Median need for redundancy

- High need for redundancy

- Redundancy methods

- Component redundancy

- Server redundancy

- Network link and data path redundancy

- Software redundancy

CHAPTER 6

Network Reliability and Resiliency

As you design your network, you no doubt want to ensure that it is reliable and has a certain amount of resiliency should something go wrong. The cornerstone of building a reliable network is to protect it as best as you can from unforeseen disruptions.

This chapter describes where and why a backup plan may be necessary and provides information on the tools that you can use to keep your network up and running.

THE MEANING AND IMPORTANCE OF REDUNDANCY

Redundancy refers to the use of reliable backup methods to protect against network failure. Network design includes determining when the network needs to be operational and which portions are critical for the day-to-day operation of the business. Some companies, such as catalog centers, use their network on a 24-hour basis. For them, most portions of the network are critical at all times, which means that the network design must include extensive redundancy. Other companies, such as manufacturing firms, may need the assembly line computers operating on a 24-hour basis and the business office computers operational from 8 a.m. to 7 p.m. In this case, complete redundancy is needed for the assembly line, while the business office can operate sufficiently with less redundancy.

The level of redundancy that you design into your network will depend on several factors, including network "uptime" needs and costs in terms of user productivity and business operations.

For example, when you place a server on the network, you're aware of the function it performs. You now need to consider when that server needs to be operational and how critical it is to your business. If the server fails for some reason, how will it impact your business profitability? If the answer is a lot, you'll need to design a backup plan. Additionally, have you factored in when that server needs to be taken offline for software or hardware upgrades, or for general maintenance?

To clarify these aspects of network uptime and business cost and productivity, we have categorized redundancy needs into three separate levels: minimal redundancy, median redundancy, and high redundancy. Each of these is briefly explained in the sections that follow. After that, we'll describe different redundancy methods to use in your network.

Minimal Need for Redundancy

Minimal redundancy fits for networks in which unexpected downtime will not impact the user's productivity or affect the company's business significantly. In this case, if the network goes down, the company can still function and conduct its daily tasks without losing money or otherwise disrupting its business affairs.

In general, minimal redundancy is used on networks that meet the following criteria:

- Network needs to be operating for only one shift per day.

- Downtime is easily scheduled after working hours.

- Minimal loss of business due to network failure.

- Network failure does not significantly diminish users' productivity.

At the minimal level, redundancy can be accomplished within the hardware devices by using *component redundancy*, which refers to the use of additional hardware to back up or duplicate parts for a network device. You can limit and help prevent network downtime by using redundant power supplies, redundant processors, or redundant interface modules. This level of redundancy provides a baseline of reliability; if a component fails, the network device still continues to operate.

If during your network survey you find a specific area of the network that needs resiliency more than the others do, you can expand the network's component redundancy. This includes, for example, adding a backup switch that comes into operation if the primary switch fails, thus keeping that portion of the network up and running. Similarly, you can install a backup router to a primary router.

For networks with minimal resiliency needs, a selection of component redundancy may suffice. There are, however, many methods of adding redundancy via software. These methods are generally used for networks requiring median or high-level redundancy, but can be used as well on networks with minimal needs. We cover the software approach in the "Redundancy Methods" section later in this chapter.

Median Need for Redundancy

Median redundancy is used for networks that need to operate and to continue to operate correctly during business hours. In this case, if a portion of the network goes down, the company loses some important functions and user productivity decreases.

In general, median redundancy is used on networks that meet the following criteria:

- Network requires operation for at least two shifts
- Centralized servers need to be up 24 hours a day
- Downtime needs to be scheduled on the weekends
- Loss of business results if critical parts of the network fail
- User productivity suffers with network failure

At the median level, redundancy should begin at the hardware level, especially for critical devices. In addition, some form of network link and data path redundancy, as well as software redundancy, should be used to assure resiliency and limit network downtime. These additional forms are described in the "Redundancy Methods" section of this chapter.

High Need for Redundancy

High-level redundancy is used on networks that need to successfully operate around the clock: 24 hours a day, seven days a week. In many cases, 80 percent of the network needs to be operational only Monday through Friday, with Saturday or Sunday reserved for scheduled downtime to perform upgrades or maintenance. But the other 20 percent of the network must operate all the time to keep critical portions of the business running.

In general, high-level redundancy is used on networks that meet the following criteria:

- Network needs to be operating 24 hours per day, seven days per week.

- Downtime needs to be scheduled well in advance and completed according to a guaranteed schedule so that network operation can resume on time.

- Major loss of business occurs if network fails.

- User productivity drastically suffers with network failure.

At the high level, a blend of redundancy methods is used to assure network resiliency at all times. This combination includes component redundancy, network link and data path redundancy, various forms of software redundancy, and server redundancy. The network usually contains redundant power supplies, redundant processors, or redundant interface modules. In addition, network-level redundancy (such as hot backup links and parallel routes) are included for critical operations, and backup servers are used as well. We cover these additional approaches in the "Redundancy Methods" section that follows.

REDUNDANCY METHODS

Several redundancy methods are available that you can use to keep your network running. These range from hardware options such as redundant power supplies to complex software operations such as duplicate network links. We describe a selection of these options in the following sections.

Component Redundancy

As noted earlier, a basic approach to network redundancy is component redundancy—the use of additional equipment that can replace failed devices. Component redundancy encompasses the use of additional hardware to provide duplicate or backup parts for a network device, such as power supplies, fans, and processors. Component redundancy also includes having spare components on hand to replace a failed device so that the network can remain operational.

Server Redundancy

As we described in Chapter 2, "Server Placement," when discussing server placement, most traffic in the campus network goes to the servers. It makes sense then that those servers should be operational all the time, unless they are deliberately brought down for maintenance. There are two parts of server redundancy: the data that is stored on the server and the servers themselves.

Having backup data storage is critical in many environments. Can you imagine banks not having backup data storage for account information, for example? If some of the bank's devices shut down, the bank wouldn't know how much money customers have in their account. If a server fails, we still want to be able to retrieve the information that was on the server so that we haven't lost everything.

How critical the information on each server is dictates how often data storage backup occurs for these devices. Some servers are not critical and can be backed up once a week with no problems. Other servers need to be backed up two or three times a day because they are crucial to the business and productivity. It is important to evaluate each server and implement the appropriate data-storage backup schedule.

The servers themselves also need redundancy. Data storage keeps the data safe, but it doesn't protect the applications that need to run on the network. If there are a few critical applications running on one server, and that server fails, how will this affect the network? One option is to have multiple servers that are capable of running these applications. In case of failure, the users can log onto a different server and run the applications. They lose some work in the process, but can still get work done.

For highly critical applications, it may make sense to have a backup server that continuously backs up the data from the primary server and can support the same applications. That way, if the primary server goes down, end users won't necessarily lose the majority of their work because the redundant server has most of the work backed up.

In both cases, it is important to not have the redundant or backup servers on the same part of the network as the primary servers. Should the data center lose power, the backup servers can also lose power if they are residing next to the primary servers in the data center. To prevent the backup servers from also shutting down, you would want them to be at different locations on different power circuits. For this reason, it is important to study your network and determine where the best location is for backup servers.

Network Link and Data Path Redundancy

Network link and data path redundancy involve two forms of redundancy that are dependent upon each other. *Network link redundancy* refers to the physical redundant connections between network devices. *Data path redundancy* refers to the software protocols that determine how the data travels over these network links. First we'll briefly discuss network link redundancy, and then we'll delve into how the protocols send the traffic over these redundancy links.

In general, you design for network link redundancy in your network architecture by providing more than one link from each component to the rest of the network. Figure 6–1 shows network link redundancy in the campus network.

Figure 6–1

Network link redundancy in the network.

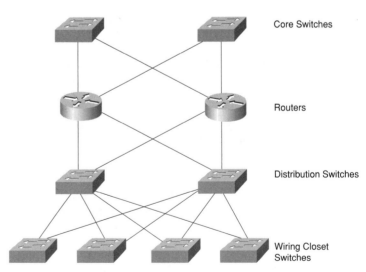

Core Switches

Routers

Distribution Switches

Wiring Closet Switches

As we can see from Figure 6–1, the wiring closet switches connect to both distribution switches. The distribution switches connect to two routers, and the routers connect to more than one core switch. These multiple physical links make up network link redundancy.

The way that these multiple links are used is determined by the software protocols—more specifically, the Spanning Tree Protocol and the routing protocol running on the network.

The operation known as data path redundancy determines how to send data across the multiple network links. If one network link fails, other paths are available for data to travel over the network.

Data path redundancy comes in two forms: hot backup and parallelism. *Hot backup* means that the physical link is already in place, ready to activate through Spanning Tree without manual intervention. Hot backup and Spanning Tree are used by the Layer 2 switches. *Parallelism* uses the routing protocol that runs on the network (such as RIP, OSPF, or EIGRP). The Layer 3 routers in the network use parallelism. Either one or both forms can be used for data path redundancy.

Spanning Tree

Spanning Tree is an IEEE standard (IEEE 802.1d). When implemented, Spanning Tree uses the physically redundant network links so that if a data path becomes unavailable, Spanning Tree automatically reconfigures the data path to ensure continued network communication. To do this, one primary path is activated. The other redundant connections are placed in standby or blocking mode, then activated when the primary link fails. If the primary path goes down, the second backup path becomes primary, and all other redundant paths are placed in backup mode. By doing this, Spanning Tree prevents data path loops in the network, which maintains data integrity and data path direction. Figure 6–2 shows switches with redundant network links; the primary data path and the backup path are illustrated.

Figure 6–2

Primary and backup data paths.

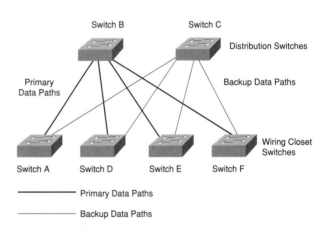

As you can see, the primary link allows only one path for the data to travel in order to get from any of the wiring closet switches to a distribution switch. The other links are in backup mode and do not forward any data.

If a link failure occurs, as shown in Figure 6–3, the data path must change.

Spanning Tree automatically activates the backup path and makes it the primary path. Likewise, the original primary path becomes a backup path, as displayed in Figure 6–4. This process is known as Spanning Tree *reconvergence*.

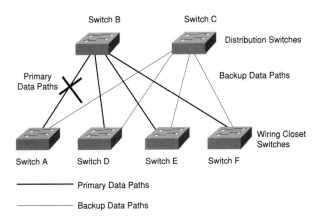

Figure 6–3

Link failure.

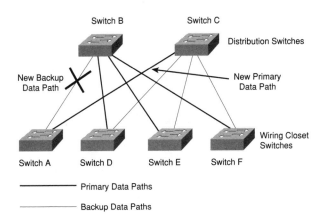

Figure 6–4

Spanning Tree reconvergence.

The data now travels on the new primary path across the network.

Why do we need a protocol such as Spanning Tree to operate over Layer 2 switches? Let's take a look at what happens instead if there are multiple active links between switches. Figure 6–5 shows the same network link redundancy between switches, but they are now all active. If a broadcast is sent out by Station A, it enters Switch A, and Switch A sends the broadcast out all of its other ports.

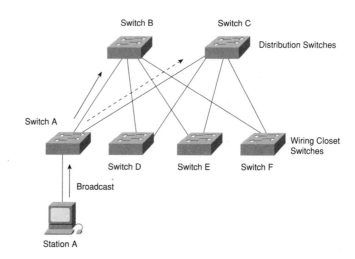

Figure 6–5
Broadcast propagation over multiple active links.

The broadcast enters Switches B and C, and those switches in turn send the broadcast out all of their ports, as shown in Figure 6–6.

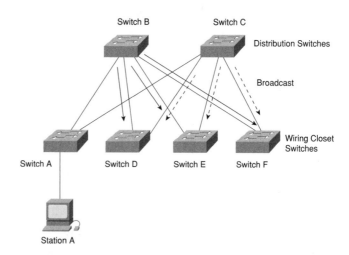

Figure 6–6
Switches B and C sending the broadcast.

As the illustration shows, both Switches B and C are sending the broadcast; so Switches D, E, and F each receive the broadcast from both switches. In turn, Switches D, E, and F forward the multiple broadcasts via all their ports, as shown in Figure 6–7.

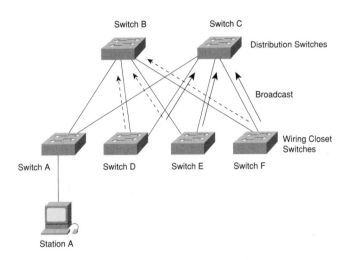

Switch B   Switch C

Distribution Switches

Broadcast

Wiring Closet
Switches

Switch A   Switch D   Switch E   Switch F

Station A

Figure 6–7

Switches D, E, and F sending the broadcast.

Then, as shown in Figure 6–8, the broadcast goes back to Switch A from Switches B and C. A never-ending loop occurs, and the broadcast continues to bounce between the switches and out to the endstations. Because of this behavior, it is impossible to allow more than one path in the network. Spanning Tree resolves this problem by automatically allowing only one primary path to be active, and designates all other paths as backup paths.

Figure 6–8

Switches B and C sending
the broadcast back to
Switch A.

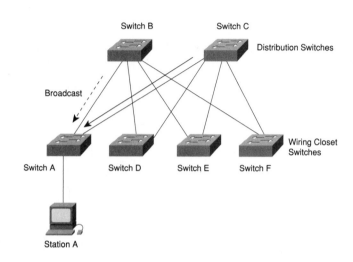

Spanning Tree does, however, take time to reconverge the data paths. By default, it is 50 seconds for the reconvergence to occur in simple networks. In more complex networks, the reconvergence time is longer. The more loops there are in the network, the longer it will take for the network to recover from a link failure. This can be manipulated a bit by changing some default timing values, but cannot be changed drastically.

To learn more about Spanning Tree and how it's used for data path redundancy, we recommend that you read the IEEE 802.1d standard.

Parallelism

Spanning Tree is the hot backup form of data path redundancy, and it is used for redundant links between Layer 2 switches. The other form of data path redundancy is parallelism, which is used by routers at the Layer 3 level. Here, multiple paths from the router to other network devices can be established that allow the traffic to traverse all paths. Parallelism is also commonly referred to as *data load sharing*. Figure 6–9 shows the redundant links between routers and switches.

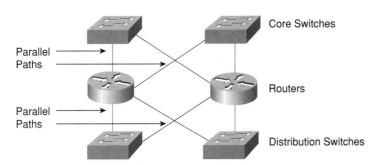

Figure 6–9
Redundant links between routers and switches.

When parallelism is implemented at Layer 3, all redundant paths can be used to send traffic over the network. This works because each interface on the router represents a different network, or subnet. Therefore, the redundant links do not reside on the same network, as is the case with Layer 2 devices. Keep in mind that loops are created when multiple paths reside on the same subnet. Figure 6–10 represents the network links on the router and shows the interfaces by distinct network addresses.

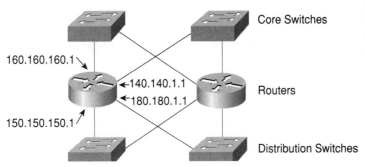

Figure 6–10
Redundant links on different networks.

The following example clarifies the notion of parallelism. In Figure 6–11, Station A wants to send data to Server B. Station A sends out the data, the data passes through Switch A and Switch B, and goes up to Router X. Router X has the option of sending the data onto network 100.100.100.0 or 200.200.200.0.

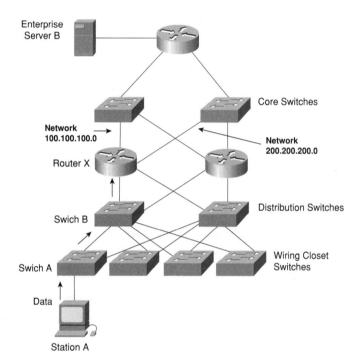

Figure 6–11
Sending data through the router.

The network that the router sends the data onto is determined by the routing protocol that is running on the network, such as RIP, OSPF, or EIGRP. The routing protocol determines which path is optimal and instructs the router to send the data out that path. (The method that the routing protocols use to determine the best path is unique to each routing protocol, and will not be discussed in this book. For in-depth information on routing protocols, please check the references listed in Appendix A, "Technical References.")

In our example, the router sends the data out network 100.100.100.0, which crosses the backbone to reach Server B, as shown in Figure 6–12.

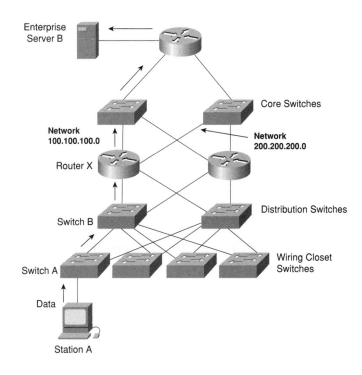

Figure 6–12

Router sending data across network 100.100.100.0.

When the data comes back from Server B, Router Y needs to decide which path to send the data. This time, Router Y decides to send the data across the 200.200.200.0 network, as shown in Figure 6–13. Router X receives the data across this path.

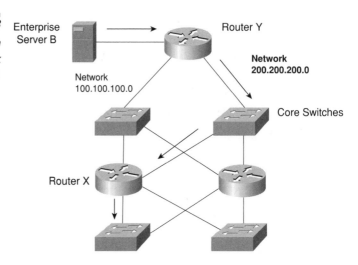

Figure 6–13
Router Y sending data
across network
200.200.200.0.

Router X then forwards the data down to Station A. As this example shows, the routers used both links to send data—in other words, parallelism.

Parallelism provides more usable bandwidth than Spanning Tree does because all of the data paths and network links can be used at the same time to send data across the network. If one path fails, the other paths are already operational, so there is less reconvergence time. Again, the reconvergence time depends on the routing protocol used, but by default, it is less than the Spanning Tree 50 seconds in all routing protocols.

Vendors support network redundancy in a variety of software forms. Unfortunately, most of these methods are proprietary, and there is not a standardized way of supporting software across different vendors' platforms. We can, however, discuss these software redundancy forms in general and provide an example of software redundancy using a method being considered by the Internet community that is currently an Internet draft.

Software Redundancy

Software redundancy aims at helping to recover the network without manual intervention and with the least amount of network downtime. For example, Spanning Tree automatically recalculates a new data path when the primary path fails. This is one form of software redundancy. Users are affected for only a limited time, because the network recovers by itself without manual intervention. And routing protocols automatically find another path to direct the traffic if one path goes down. There are, however, other areas that need software redundancy besides the data path—these include services that are necessary to make the network run.

For example, consider the service provided by a default gateway. When the network is running IP, end users need to have an IP address and an IP default gateway. Without these two things, the end user cannot gain access to the network. When the endstation sends data across the network, it goes through the default gateway or router. If the default gateway fails, the endstations can no longer get out onto the network. In this case, it is ideal to have software redundancy that protects the default gateway address without network interruption for the end user.

Let's look at possible ways to protect the IP default gateway from network failure. Figure 6–14 shows a network that has the IP default gateway for a set of endstations that operate successfully. Figure 6–15 shows a failure that keeps these endstations from communicating across the network.

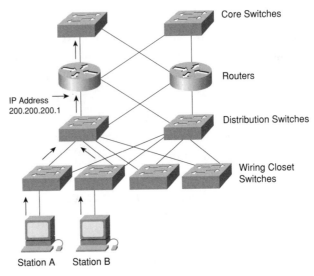

Figure 6–14
Network with IP default gateway operating.

Core Switches

Routers

IP Address
200.200.200.1

Distribution Switches

Wiring Closet
Switches

Station A   Station B

IP Default Gateway 200.200.200.1

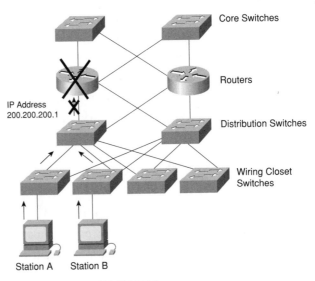

Figure 6–15
Network with IP default gateway failure.

Core Switches

Routers

IP Address
200.200.200.1

Distribution Switches

Wiring Closet
Switches

Station A   Station B

IP Default Gateway 200.200.200.1

The routing protocol (RIP, OSPF, or EIGRP) can automatically recalculate a new path to bypass the failed link. However, this does not protect the default gateway address; users are affected for a limited time, depending on how quickly the protocol can perform reconvergence.

In response to this concern, a new method to protect the default gateway address from failing has been developed, which is currently an Internet draft. It is called *Hot Standby Routing Protocol*, or HSRP. HSRP helps to maintain network operation by having two routers share the same virtual IP and MAC addresses, thus creating a "phantom" or virtual router. Figure 6–16 shows this operation.

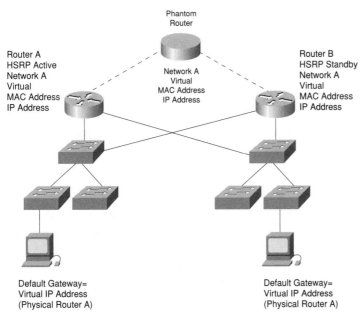

Figure 6–16

HSRP on two routers.

In our example, Router A is the primary HSRP router for network A, and Router B is the backup. If Router A fails, as shown in Figure 6–17, then Router B becomes the primary HSRP router and takes over the virtual IP and MAC addresses.

Figure 6–17
Router A failure.

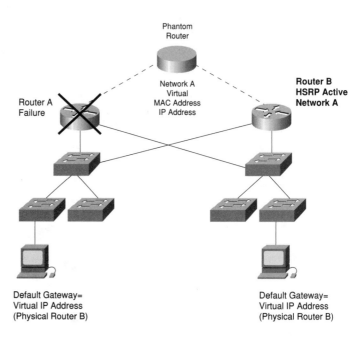

Because the routers are sharing the same virtual IP and MAC addresses, the endstations can keep their same IP default gateway address (which is the virtual IP address) and do not lose connectivity to the network. The endstations do not care if they are going through a different physical router, and they won't be affected by the change.

Figure 6–18 shows that Router B is the primary HSRP router for Network B and Router A is the backup router for Network B. Similarly, Router A is the primary router for Network A and Router B is the backup router for Network A.

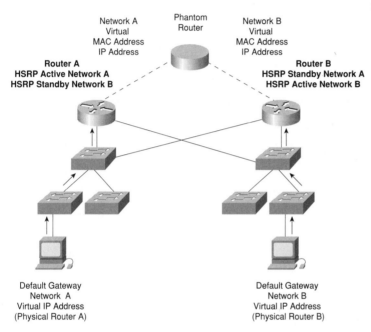

Network A
Virtual
MAC Address
IP Address

Phantom
Router

Network B
Virtual
MAC Address
IP Address

Router A
HSRP Active Network A
HSRP Standby Network B

Router B
HSRP Standby Network A
HSRP Active Network B

Default Gateway
Network A
Virtual IP Address
(Physical Router A)

Default Gateway
Network B
Virtual IP Address
(Physical Router B)

Figure 6–18

Routers A and B as primary and backup HSRP routers.

By having both routers as the primary HSRP router for a different network, they can both be used at the same time to route traffic. Each router is not limited to being just a backup router that doesn't operate unless a failure occurs; they both can be running parallel instead. For more details on HSRP, the Internet draft title is draft-li-hsrp-00.txt.

Another way to view the importance of software redundancy is to look at an *ATM LAN Emulation* (LANE) network. For ATM LANE, there are several services that are interdependent and must be operational for this network to work.

Because this type of network relies heavily on services, it provides one of the best examples of the importance of software redundancy.

ATM LANE needs to have three services running smoothly for data to travel successfully across the network. The first service is the *LAN Emulation Configuration Server* (LECS). There is one LECS for the entire ATM network. The LECS tells each LANE client that logs onto the network which LAN Emulation Server it should contact for an ATM address. Once the LANE client has its ATM address, it does not contact the LECS again. If the LECS fails, no new LANE clients can gain network access. (The LANE clients that are already on the network, however, are not affected.)

The second service is the *LAN Emulation Server* (LES). There is one LES for each Emulated LAN (referred to as the ELAN). The LES is responsible for allocating ATM addresses to the LANE clients in that ELAN. If the LES fails, new LANE clients cannot gain access to the network. (Again, existing LANE clients are not affected.)

The third and final service is the *Broadcast and Unknown Server* (BUS). There is one BUS for each ELAN, and the LES and BUS reside on the same network device in each ELAN. The BUS handles all broadcast traffic in that ELAN, as well as requests for destination addresses, such as an IP ARP request.

When an endstation sends out a broadcast, it first goes to the BUS, and the BUS then sends it out to the rest of the ELAN. Similarly, when a station needs to find the ATM address of another station, it sends the request to the BUS first.

The BUS plays a critical part in the operation of a LANE network—if the BUS fails, all endstations on the network are adversely affected. Because the LES and BUS reside on the same device, new LANE clients cannot get their ATM address if the device fails. Further, existing LANE clients can only send data to the addresses that they already know, and the broadcasts that they send out go nowhere because the BUS is not operational.

It's apparent that if just one of these three LANE services is down, the network is affected. It is definitely important to have some sort of backup services for the primary services here.

Many vendors offer ways to have backup LECS and LES/BUS automatically become active if the primary one fails. Currently, there is no standard way of doing this, and most vendors are staying within the ATM LANE specification guidelines for their implementation. As with all of the other network resiliency methods, the key is to have an automatic fail-safe mechanism without manual intervention. Please refer to the LANE 1.0 or 2.0 specification for details on ATM LAN Emulation.

SUMMARY

Every network designer wants the network running whenever it is needed. This may be only eight hours per day, or around the clock for seven days per week. In either case, a level of redundancy needs to be installed to ensure that critical parts of the network operate correctly at critical times.

Without redundancy, disruption of network functions and services can occur, which may impact business production and profitability. It is especially important to provide redundancy for those services that must get through the network in a timely fashion. If your network relies on a certain application, or if it will include time-sensitive applications such as voice or real-time imaging, the portion of the network that those applications travel through should have redundant systems in place. We discuss ways to prioritize this type of traffic in the next chapter.

The key things to remember for designing network redundancy are as follows:

- Component redundancy refers to the use of backup or duplicate hardware in a network, and to the practice of keeping spare components on hand in case they are needed. Whether a network requires minimal, median, or high redundancy, component redundancy is recommended.

- Server redundancy refers to the backing up of both data and applications. Networks that must maintain high levels of redundancy generally include server redundancy.

- The purpose of network link redundancy is to provide alternate physical pathways through the network in case one pathway fails. Generally, networks that have median or high redundancy requirements need network link redundancy.

- The purpose of data path redundancy is to direct traffic across the active physical pathways. Data path redundancy is needed wherever network link redundancy has been implemented because the two work in tandem.

- Spanning Tree uses hot backup links, and only the primary active link is used for data transfer. Parallelism uses all links to forward data.

- The goal of software redundancy is to help recover the network in the least amount of downtime, without manual intervention. Networks requiring median or high redundancy generally need to implement software redundancy.

This chapter covers the following topics:

- What needs to be prioritized

- Using a software approach

- Using a hardware approach

- How ATM networks prioritize traffic

CHAPTER 7

Setting Traffic Priorities

The entire topic of where and how to prioritize traffic plays a more relevant role for the wide-area network and the Internet than for the campus, primarily because the WAN network links become oversubscribed and congested much more easily than those in the campus. The congestion on the WAN and Internet is typically caused by slow link speeds, which can be as low as 12.2 Kbps, and sometimes only as high as T-1 (1.54 Mbps) or E-1 (2.048 Mbps) speeds. The campus network avoids this problem because it runs at far quicker speeds (10 Mbps for Ethernet; 4 or 16 Mbps for Token Ring; and up to 100-155 Mbps for Fast Ethernet, FDDI, or ATM).

Additionally, bandwidth is expensive in the wide-area network because it entails leased lines and access premiums, whereas it is relatively inexpensive in the campus. Once the campus network cables are purchased and installed, that's the end of it; there are no additional charges to deal with, and costs can be controlled.

So why should the campus LAN designer be concerned about setting priorities for network traffic? Because new and emerging technologies coming onto the campus—such as voice-over-data, real-time imaging, and multimedia applications—have to follow strict time-delay requirements in order to operate successfully. In addition, some of these new applications are huge, often requiring more bandwidth than a standard campus network can provide. If this is the case, you can go to the expense of adding more lines and bandwidth or use the existing bandwidth more efficiently by setting traffic priorities.

This chapter describes traditional and new methods for prioritizing network traffic and gives an overview of the tools you can use to establish traffic priorities in the campus network.

WHAT NEEDS TO BE PRIORITIZED

When you set priorities, you are essentially guaranteeing which traffic gets across the network first. There are two cases in which this is important: when network devices or the network itself becomes oversubscribed and when you have delay-sensitive traffic.

Should devices or the network become congested, the devices decide which traffic is most important and send that traffic first. For example, an executive video conference takes precedence over a Web-browsing session, and a real-time imaging application gets priority over file transfers.

In designing for prioritization, you need to keep several questions in mind:

- How much bandwidth does the high-priority traffic need?

- Is the high-priority traffic constant or intermittent?

- Can the network infrastructure support the high-priority traffic successfully?

Answering these questions helps you decide which methods of prioritization to apply. Network designers can meet traffic priority requirements in the campus via a software solution such as queuing or via a hardware solution—by adding bandwidth to specified devices. These solutions, which can be used separately or in conjunction, are detailed in the sections that follow.

USING A SOFTWARE APPROACH

Most network devices use a "first-in, first-out" (FIFO) rule to keep traffic moving. However, you can use software methods to change the rules so that traffic is "first out" because of its higher priority, not because it was "first in." One software approach to prioritize traffic is to set network devices to use a mechanism called queuing. Another is to use a Quality of Service (QoS) mechanism that guarantees, via software parameters, which data traffic receives priority over other data traffic.

Queuing Methods

Queuing, as its name suggests, is a way of lining up network traffic so that it flows according to the prioritization preferences set by the network designer. Queuing is set up at the router level for campus networks because LAN switches generally do not understand queuing methods. The exception is the ATM switch, which uses special methods that we'll describe later in this chapter.

Queuing at the router can take place in a variety of ways. The most typical forms are:

- Priority queuing

- Bandwidth-percentage queuing

- Shared queuing

- Dedicated bandwidth queuing

The following sections describe these queuing methods in more detail.

Priority Queuing

This method instructs the router: "If there is any prioritized traffic at all, send that out, and everything else will have to wait." Figure 7–1 shows an example of priority queuing.

Figure 7–1

Priority queuing.

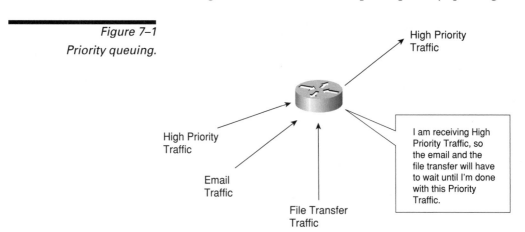

High Priority Traffic

High Priority Traffic

Email Traffic

File Transfer Traffic

I am receiving High Priority Traffic, so the email and the file transfer will have to wait until I'm done with this Priority Traffic.

The priority queuing method works best for networks that have sufficient bandwidth available at all times and rarely have delay-sensitive traffic going through the campus.

The drawback to this queuing method is that if there is fairly constant prioritized traffic (such as a real-time imaging data stream), it can use up the available bandwidth, which causes all of the other traffic to be blocked and to not be sent through the network at all.

Bandwidth-Percentage Queuing

This method of queuing allocates a certain percentage of bandwidth for high-priority traffic and gives the remaining bandwidth to the other traffic. The network administrator typically configures this bandwidth percentage. The router processes the high-priority traffic first, up to its available bandwidth, and then sends the remaining traffic.

Let's assume that high-priority traffic is allocated 50 percent of the bandwidth and the remaining traffic is allocated the other 50 percent. The high-priority traffic gets 50 percent of the available bandwidth, and the rest of the traffic is processed in a FIFO manner, as shown in Figure 7–2.

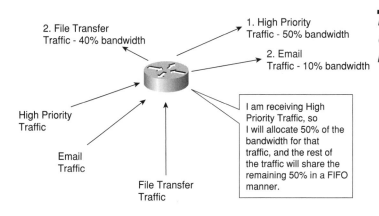

2. File Transfer
Traffic - 40% bandwidth

1. High Priority
Traffic - 50% bandwidth

2. Email
Traffic - 10% bandwidth

High Priority
Traffic

Email
Traffic

File Transfer
Traffic

I am receiving High
Priority Traffic, so
I will allocate 50% of the
bandwidth for that
traffic, and the rest of
the traffic will share the
remaining 50% in a FIFO
manner.

Figure 7–2

Queuing by bandwidth percentage.

When there is no prioritized traffic, all network traffic can use all of the available bandwidth. The bandwidth-percentage queuing method works well for networks that have occasional high-priority traffic.

This queuing method does, however, have two drawbacks. When high-priority traffic is being sent, all other traffic is restricted to the non-allocated bandwidth until the high-priority traffic is processed, thereby causing traffic congestion. This method also imposes limits on prioritized traffic; it can only use up to its allocated percentage of bandwidth. If the high priority in our example needed 55 percent of bandwidth, five percent of the traffic would experience higher delays than it should.

Shared Queuing

This method incorporates a shared approach to moving traffic through the router. With shared queuing, both high-priority and other traffic can be processed by the router bandwidth at the same time. For example, if the prioritized traffic is multimedia traffic that does not need all of the allocated bandwidth, the router can send traffic such as e-mail messages while it is sending multimedia traffic. This is accomplished by borrowing some of the bandwidth from the prioritized traffic, as shown in Figure 7–3.

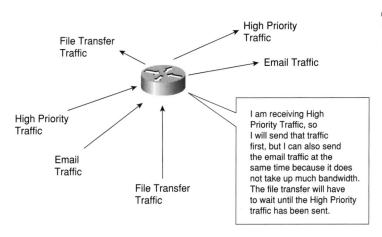

Figure 7–3
Shared queuing.

The shared queuing method allows prioritized traffic to get the bandwidth it needs, and it allows other traffic to be processed without waiting. However, high-priority traffic is still limited to its allocated amount, and normal traffic won't be interleaved should prioritized traffic require its total allocated bandwidth. The shared queuing method works best for networks that have occasional or fairly constant high-priority traffic.

Dedicated Bandwidth Queuing

This method allocates a dedicated amount of bandwidth for the prioritized traffic at all times. The prioritized traffic can use the bandwidth whenever it needs to. The dedicated bandwidth method works well for networks that have constant high-priority or delay-sensitive traffic, such as videoconferencing. A drawback to this method is that when there is no prioritized traffic going across the network, other traffic cannot use the guaranteed bandwidth set aside for high-priority traffic, as shown in Figure 7–4.

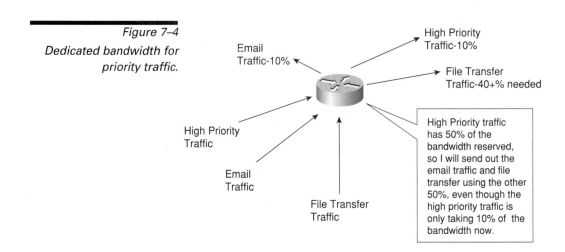

Quality of Service Methods

Quality of Service (QoS) is another software solution to setting traffic priorities. QoS is similar to queuing in that it designates bandwidth requirements (service availability) for high-priority traffic. But QoS goes beyond queuing in that it reflects the performance requirements (transmission quality) of such traffic. Specifically, QoS is intended for applications that need a firm guarantee that a datagram will arrive no later than a certain time after it is transmitted by its source. For example, some audio and video "play-back" applications are intolerant of any datagrams arriving after their play-back time. QoS works in conjunction with one of the queuing mechanisms described earlier in this chapter.

Several Internet drafts and working documents tackle the issue of how to deliver a guaranteed service (guaranteed delay and bandwidth) in networks. Of these, the most promising for campus applications is an Internet draft entitled the Resource Reservation Protocol (RSVP).

A host uses RSVP to request specific qualities of service from the network. RSVP is not a routing protocol, but it is designed to operate in tandem with a routing protocol. Routing protocols determine where packets are forwarded; RSVP, which is only concerned with the QoS of those forwarded packets, typically executes in the background.

To ensure optimum performance, RSVP must be supported on several network devices, including the routers and the application server. In addition, the application running on the endstation should support RSVP. Here's how it works:

The application first determines how much bandwidth it needs to run successfully. The application then uses RSVP to send out a request-for-bandwidth message to the network.

The message asks the network to guarantee that it gets the bandwidth it needs (in our example, one megabyte) when it is running. The entire network does not need to guarantee the bandwidth; rather, the devices in the path between the endstation running this application and the application server must be able to guarantee it. The request for bandwidth and the path it takes are shown in Figure 7–5.

The first device the RSVP request reaches is a switch. Because it does not understand or care about RSVP, the switch simply forwards the packet to the destination. The switch does not block the data, but it does not guarantee the bandwidth that the application needs. Figure 7–6 shows the switch's behavior toward the RSVP request packet.

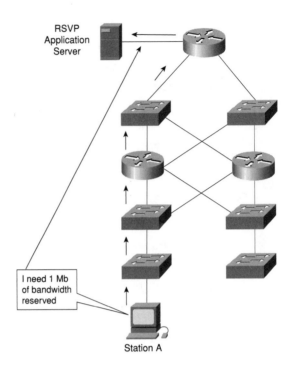

Figure 7–5

Path from the RSVP endstation to the RSVP application server.

RSVP Application Server

I need 1 Mb of bandwidth reserved

Station A

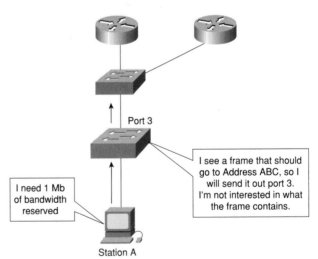

Figure 7–6

RSVP request packet in the switch.

Port 3

I need 1 Mb of bandwidth reserved

I see a frame that should go to Address ABC, so I will send it out port 3. I'm not interested in what the frame contains.

Station A

A router receiving the request-for-bandwidth message under-stands the message and processes the request and then deter-mines whether it can guarantee the requested one megabyte of bandwidth for the application on the specified interface. If it can, it forwards the request along the network path, as shown in Figure 7–7.

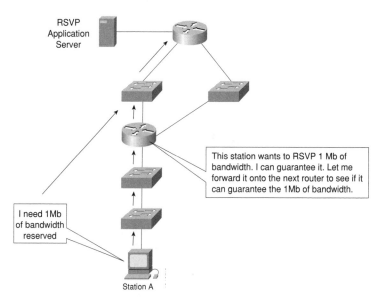

Figure 7–7

Router propagating the RSVP request through the network.

If the first router (or any subsequent router along the path) cannot guarantee the bandwidth, it sends a message back to the endstation refusing the request for bandwidth, as shown in Figure 7–8.

Figure 7–8
Router refusing the RSVP
request.

Figure 7–8
Router refusing the RSVP
request.

RSVP Application Server

This station wants to RSVP 1 Mb of bandwidth. I cannot guarantee it. I will refuse this request.

I need 1Mb of bandwidth reserved

Station A

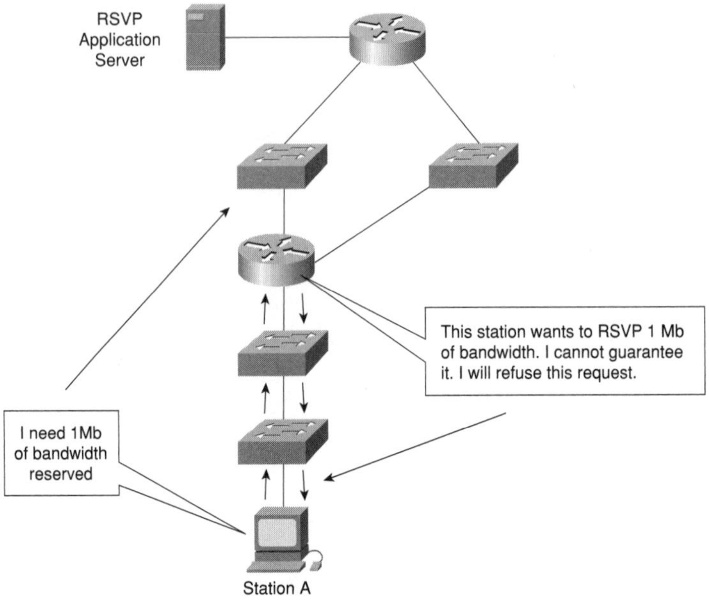

The RSVP request-for-bandwidth message propagates all of the way through the path to the server that is supporting the RSVP application. If the router and the server in the path can support the one-megabyte-of-bandwidth requirement, then a guaranteed one-megabyte link is set up for the application across these devices. An acknowledgment is sent from the server back to the endstation that initiated the request stating that the requested bandwidth can be guaranteed. Each router in the path reserves one megabyte of bandwidth for that application, as shown in Figure 7–9.

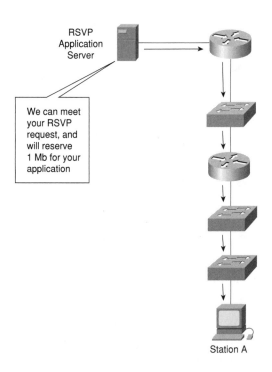

RSVP
Application
Server

We can meet
your RSVP
request, and
will reserve
1 Mb for your
application

Station A

Figure 7–9

Server sending acknow-ledgment back to the endstation.

The endstation can now run the application on the network. The one megabyte of bandwidth is guaranteed to the server while the application runs. When the application is restarted, the RSVP process must begin again. While the application is running, other network traffic, which uses the remaining bandwidth, can be processed simultaneously.

The amount of bandwidth needed, whether it is one megabyte or three megabytes, is determined at the application level on the endstation. It is configurable based on the application software. If, for example, the network cannot support a requested one megabyte of bandwidth, the user can reduce the amount to 500 kilobytes of guaranteed bandwidth for the application and send out a new RSVP request to the network.

To gain more in-depth knowledge about this protocol, consult the "Resource ReSerVation Protocol (RSVP) Version 1 Functional Specification" (draft-ietf-rsvp-spec-16.txt).

For some networks and some applications, using a software approach to obtain needed bandwidth may not be sufficient. In these cases, you can add bandwidth via hardware.

USING A HARDWARE APPROACH

Some devices become oversubscribed or cannot process delay-sensitive traffic due to bandwidth bottlenecks in the campus network. Let's say that an endstation wants to run a video RSVP application that needs 5 megabytes of bandwidth, and the endstation is connected to a concentrator that provides 10 megabytes of bandwidth. There is certainly enough bandwidth to run the application. However, the network may not be able to *guarantee* that the application gets 5 megabytes because there is not enough bandwidth at the concentrator to support the request and to run tasks for the other endstations connected to it. This potential bottleneck is shown in Figure 7–10.

When users run applications that require high priority, the network designer has to make sure that the network infrastructure, including the bandwidth, can support the needs of those applications. In the previous example, if we replace the concentrator with a switch, the change might provide enough bandwidth to support the video application. We show this change in Figure 7–11.

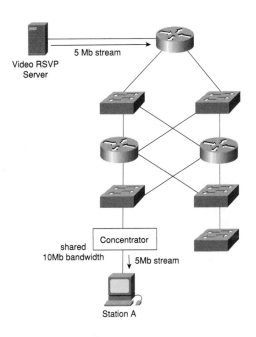

5 Mb stream

Video RSVP
Server

Concentrator

shared
10Mb bandwidth

5Mb stream

Station A

Figure 7–10

*Not enough bandwidth for
the priority application.*

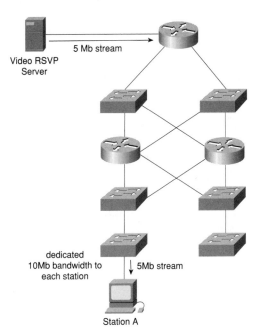

5 Mb stream

Video RSVP
Server

dedicated
10Mb bandwidth to
each station

5Mb stream

Station A

Figure 7–11

*Replacing the concentrator
with a switch.*

A hardware solution, such as the previous solution, may take care of the requesting endstation's needs, but you also have to consider the bandwidth requirements of the supplying side—the server. The server sending the high-priority application must have a high enough bandwidth connection to the network to support the required amount of megabytes for the application, *plus* the needed bandwidth for the other applications it supports. If the server in the previous example is connected via the Ethernet to the network, and one application needs 5 megabytes of bandwidth, the server does not have enough bandwidth to perform all of its functions. It needs more than a 10-megabyte Ethernet connection to the network. The solution in this case can be to provide a 100-megabyte Fast-Ethernet connection to the network.

The software and hardware methods for handling traffic priorities discussed so far are well-established and widely practiced. ATM networks take different approaches. Although many of the ATM standards are still under development, this emerging technology provides some interesting solutions for data-traffic needs.

HOW ATM NETWORKS PRIORITIZE TRAFFIC

ATM networks have the capability to support diverse quality of service requirements. They also have the capability to allow bandwidth to be assigned and shared among multiple sources. The latter capability in particular goes beyond what is possible with the queuing methods discussed earlier.

ATM uses a technique known as Class of Service to prioritize traffic, which is performed on the ATM switch. The quality of the service in ATM is determined by two main parameters: cell delay and cell loss. *Cell delay* specifies the maximum amount of time that can elapse between when the cell is sent and when it is received. *Cell loss* refers to the acceptable number of cells that can be dropped due to congestion. The QoS requirements of the application play an important part in the ATM Class of Service.

ATM combines four Class of Service types in its technology, as described in the following sections. The requirements of the application determine which of the four is used to send traffic in any given instance.

Constant Bit Rate (CBR)

CBR services support user information that originates in a continuous stream of bits. CBR typically requires a quality of service that ensures minimum delay variation in the arrival time of CBR cells. But like today's voice or video transmissions, CBR can tolerate some cell loss.

Low-delay paths are established in the network to support this service. Because CBR information arrives at a constant rate, bandwidth requirements are predictable and relatively easy to manage. CBR is desirable for real-time voice and video applications.

Variable Bit Rate (VBR)

VBR service also has a low tolerance factor (low cell loss and low delay for real-time traffic), but it allows a higher acceptable cell delay for non-real-time applications, such as packetized voice and video.

VBR negotiates a peak cell rate, a sustainable cell rate, and a maximum burst size for traffic on the ATM network. The sustained cell rate may be guaranteed. But neither the peak cell rate nor the maximum burst size is guaranteed. An example of how these values are used is the following: "I typically use 3 megabytes of bandwidth, but sometimes I need 5 megabytes for an application that lasts 10 seconds." In this example, 3 megabytes is the sustainable cell rate, 5 megabytes is the peak cell rate, and 10 seconds is the maximum burst duration. The ATM network guarantees the 3 megabytes of bandwidth only. VBR service is usually for bursty data transfer applications, such as client/server computing and LAN-to-LAN interconnection.

Available Bit Rate (ABR)

ABR service has a higher tolerance factor than CBR or VBR. It has a low cell-loss factor, but it can sustain a high cell delay for its applications, which are basically data traffic over the LAN.

ABR negotiates the peak cell rate and a minimum cell rate with the network. The network guarantees the minimum cell rate that the connection needs, but nothing more. If there is extra bandwidth available, the ABR traffic can use it until the CBR or VBR traffic needs it.

Unspecified Bit Rate (UBR)

UBR service offers no bandwidth guarantee at all. It gets the remaining bandwidth after the first three bit rates (CBR, VBR, and ABR) are satisfied. It accepts high cell loss and high cell delay for its connections. Public WAN networks typically use the UBR service.

For further information about ATM Class of Service, see the "ATM User-Network-Interface (UNI) Signaling Specification Version 4.0" (af-sig-0061.000).

SUMMARY

Although prioritizing traffic is not yet mandatory in the campus network, the growing popularity of mixed-media applications is forcing network designers to consider more efficient ways to move these applications through the network.

Network speed and bandwidth have typically not been issues for the campus, but it is becoming less desirable and somewhat costly to solve network congestion by simply adding more devices and faster connections.

Several solutions, many of which are employed by wide-area networks, can be used on the campus to efficiently transmit delay-sensitive traffic and to garner more bandwidth for large applications.

The key aspects to remember for designing traffic priorities are as follows:

- In campus networks today, the main approach to meeting the needs of high-priority traffic is to provide additional bandwidth on the network.

- To use queuing methods effectively, you must determine how much bandwidth is needed for high-priority traffic and allocate the appropriate percentage of total available bandwidth.

- Different queuing methods work better than others, depending on whether high-priority traffic occurs rarely, occasionally, or fairly constantly. You must match the optimal method with your network's circumstances.

- The RSVP method automatically requests that a certain amount of bandwidth be allocated for a specific high-priority application. But if the network denies the request, the user can manually configure a smaller amount and send another request.

- Even with software methods of handling high-priority traffic, the network may still be overburdened by it.

- In ATM networks, the quality of service parameters—cell delay and cell loss—determine the ATM Class of Service used to send traffic. The four Classes of Service are the following: Constant Bit Rate (CBR), Variable Bit Rate (VBR), Available Bit Rate (ABR), and Unspecified Bit Rate (UBR).

This chapter covers the following topics:

- How much security?

- User identity

- Security within the network

- Data security and integrity

CHAPTER 8

Addressing Security Issues

Security is one of the hottest issues in networks today. Concern about security has been fueled in large part by the increasing magnitude of electronic commerce occurring over the Internet and by the quickly evolving business trend toward telecommuting. As a result, more sensitive and critical information is crossing the wide area than ever before.

Companies are beginning to recognize that security in the campus network is also required. Without it, anyone can gain access to the campus servers and endstations, and perhaps steal valuable information. Outsiders have also been known to access a campus LAN and introduce a virus to disrupt business. Even though it may appear that your campus network is not at risk, you should carefully review the security features you currently have and plan to design more security functions for future needs.

This chapter describes the key elements of network security on the campus: identity and integrity. *Identity* refers to ascertaining who a user is. Methods of identity include basic authentication and authorization, as well as the more advanced mechanisms, known as filters and route authentication. *Integrity*, which refers to keeping the data safe as it traverses the network, is accomplished by encryption, a more sophisticated mechanism than identity methods. These are not the only security methods, but they are the most useful forms for the campus network.

How Much Security?

To make a network secure, there are three important questions to ask:

- Who is allowed to get onto the network?

- What information and devices is that person allowed to access?

- Once access is allowed, is the data safe as it transfers back and forth across the network?

The first two questions have to do with user identity. Every network needs this basic level of security. The third question refers to an additional level of security, data integrity, which may be required, depending on data sensitivity. For example, highly classified documents passing between two executives or a top-secret development project would likely benefit from this extra level of data integrity.

The following sections examine the types and mechanisms of identity and integrity that are used for security.

User Identity

As the term implies, identity refers to finding out who is trying to access the campus network. Once the "who" is known, you have the option of allowing or not allowing access, thereby providing a basic level of security.

User Authentication

The most common form of security identification is *user authentication*—that is, verification of who a user is and that the user is permitted to use the network. There are several ways to authenticate a user. The first is to enable network logon, which ensures that only valid users are allowed to access the campus network.

Typically, an endstation obtains an IP address; the user is then asked to log onto the network with a username and a password. If this logon succeeds, then the user has gained access to the network, but not necessarily to the servers. If the logon fails, however, that user cannot go anywhere on the network. Figure 8–1 shows both a successful and an unsuccessful network logon.

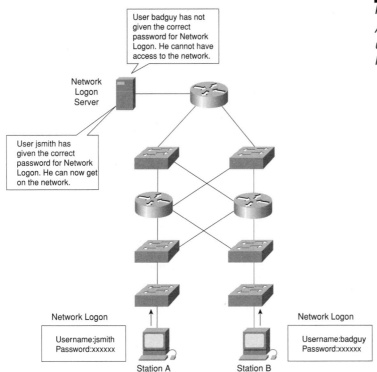

Figure 8–1

A successful and an unsuccessful network logon.

If the network does not have any form of network logon whatsoever, then anyone can gain access to the network. We show this scenario in Figure 8–2.

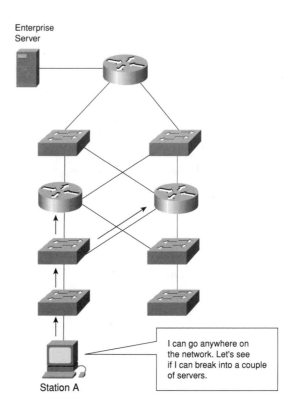

Figure 8–2

Open security: no network logon.

The absence of network logon, which is known as *open security*, is rarely implemented. If there is no network logon, then any user can travel around the network and modify devices, such as other users' endstations, routers, switches, printers, and servers. This is clearly an opportunity for a huge security breach. Therefore, network logon is considered the first security wall.

The next step in security is to provide user authentication on servers. Authentication at the server operates independently of network logon. Networks that have network logon authentication usually also have authentication security on most servers as an additional level of security. Each server has a database containing a list of users (with their passwords) who are allowed access to that server. Once the users pass the network logon, they can attempt to log into a server using similar username/password combinations. If a user fails authentication, the server's response is typically "login failed," as shown in Figure 8–3.

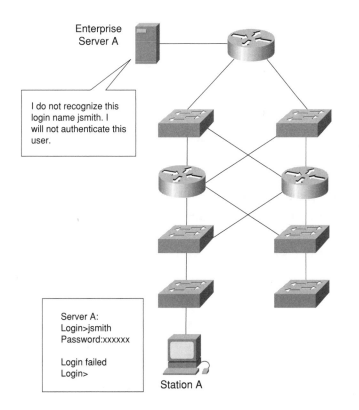

Enterprise
Server A

I do not recognize this login name jsmith. I will not authenticate this user.

Server A:
Login>jsmith
Password:xxxxxx

Login failed
Login>

Station A

Figure 8–3
Failed access to the server.

If a username passes login, but the password fails, the server is stating that it knows the user's login name, but the password that the user tried is wrong.

The username/password combination is the most common form of identification for network security. This authentication can be used as a manual (or static) entry, as a changing dynamic entry with devices such as security cards, or in conjunction with a more sophisticated form of security, such as encryption.

Manual Username/Password

Manual username/password allows users to choose their own passwords. The password stays the same until the user decides to change it. This is a common form of authentication for both network logon and server login. A typical example of this is gaining access to the network and then logging into your e-mail server. Before the e-mail server lets you download your e-mails, you are required to enter your username, which is typically your e-mail ID. You then enter the password, which does not alter unless you manually change it.

Dynamic Username/Password

In the *dynamic username/password* method, the password continually changes. It can be implemented via devices such as security cards. Security cards are sometimes employed to provide an extra level of authentication prior to allowing network access to people who want to connect to the campus remotely (individuals who need to gain access to the campus network from a wide-area network, for example).

Security cards keep the network secure by preventing network access to users who don't have them. Security cards require a username and a password. The username remains the same, but the password is temporary; it works only once and becomes invalid after a certain amount of time (such as 60 seconds). After the current password is used or expires, a new password becomes valid.

To log on with a security card, the user turns on the card and types in the username. If the username is accepted, the card displays a password for the user to enter for network access. The process is repeated every time the user needs to log on to the network, with a new password provided each time.

The passwords belonging to each security card are synchronized with a central security card server that resides on the campus. If the user types in the wrong password, the security card server does not accept the password, thereby denying network access. The user then must start over by typing in the username on the security card to get a new password. Figure 8–4 shows the dynamic security card method of username/password login.

This security method is used in addition to network authentication. After the remote user connects to the network using a security card, that user still needs to go through the network logon procedure to gain access to the rest of the network. Most campuses do not utilize security cards on the LAN; however, this security method is becoming quite popular for remote users.

Even though a user has logged on to the network, the user does not necessarily have free reign and unlimited movement throughout the campus. The next form of security identification is authorization, which works hand-in-glove with user authentication to specify what the user can do on the network.

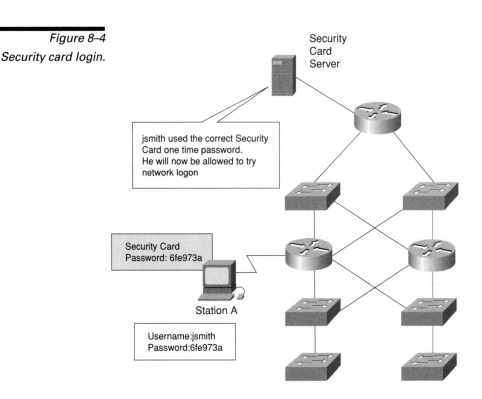

Figure 8–4
Security card login.

Security Card Server

jsmith used the correct Security Card one time password. He will now be allowed to try network logon

Security Card Password: 6fe973a

Station A

Username:jsmith
Password:6fe973a

User Authorization

User authorization refers to securing the network by specifying which areas of the network (applications, devices, and so forth) a user is allowed to access. The authorization level varies from user to user. For example, an engineer likely has access to the engineering server and the printers it supports but not to the payroll information servers. Conversely, Human Resource personnel have access to the payroll servers, but there's no need to allow them access to the engineering servers.

The devices on the network typically handle their own specific authorization processes. The following sections cover server authorization, routers, and switches.

Authorization for the Server

For a user to gain access, the server requests some form of identification, such as a username, and the unique password that matches the account. The username/password provides authentication and access to the server; it also establishes which directories that user is authorized to access on the server. For example, if you log in to your e-mail server, you can then access your home account. Your login does not, however, give you access to someone else's (such as John Smith's) home account.

A server with minimal security allows the user to make multiple attempts to enter the authorization information. A server with stricter security parameters limits the number of attempts, such as a maximum of three (to allow for typographical errors). After three unsuccessful attempts, a secure server locks the user out and does not recognize further user commands for a predetermined period of time (which is usually established by the network administrator).

Authorization for Routers and Switches

Other devices on the network also require authorization, such as routers and switches. Routers and switches require this so that only authorized personnel can change configurations. Typically, this authorization process includes a password but does not specifically require a username. And unlike server authorization, there is only one password per device instead of a unique password for each user of the device. The network manager typically chooses the password on the network devices.

SECURITY WITHIN THE NETWORK

You can augment network protection by setting up security within the network infrastructure itself, thereby taking some of the network-access responsibility and traffic load off of the servers. Two popular secure access methods are described next—filtering and route authentication.

Using Filters

Filters, which are also referred to as access lists, can be configured on routers in the campus. Filters enable the router to either accept or reject access on a per-traffic or per-subnet basis. The effect of filters is displayed in Figure 8–5.

A filter is also known as a *firewall*. It blocks out all users who are not authorized to access certain parts of the network and allows access only to authorized users. As an example, let's use the Engineering and Payroll departments again.

Engineers do not need access to the payroll servers, so it would be ideal to set up a filter on the network that keeps engineers from accessing the payroll servers. However, we do want to allow access for the Payroll department personnel.

Figure 8–6 shows that the Payroll department's IP subnet can have access to the payroll servers, but the Engineering department's IP subnet cannot.

By implementing filters on the routers, the network itself becomes another secure gateway that unauthorized users must pass through, thereby preventing access to parts of the network they're not allowed to use.

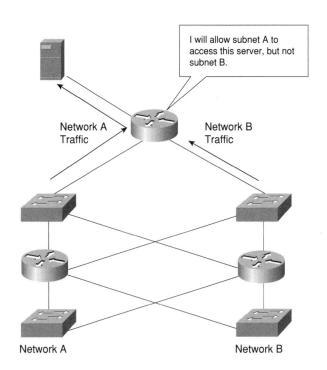

I will allow subnet A to access this server, but not subnet B.

Network A Traffic

Network B Traffic

Network A

Network B

Figure 8–5
Filtering on subnets.

Filters do not remove the authentication and authorization process inherent on the network servers; instead, they augment the server's own security. If there are servers on the campus that you want to secure, you can configure the router only to accept and pass through requests received from a specific subnet, as we've shown in the previous example.

Keep in mind that the final authentication/authorization responsibility still remains at the server, which performs the username/password verification for each individual trying to gain access who has succeeded in passing through the router's firewalls. For the users who could not get through the router's filters, however, the server does not need to perform the authentication and authorization procedures, hence saving processing power for the server.

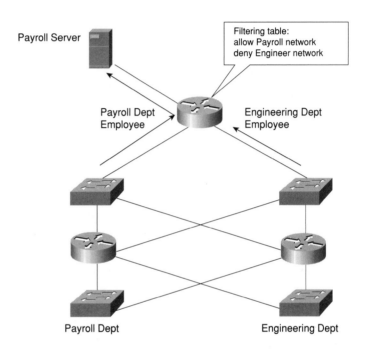

Figure 8–6

Filtering to control access to the Payroll server.

Payroll Server

Filtering table:
allow Payroll network
deny Engineer network

Payroll Dept
Employee

Engineering Dept
Employee

Payroll Dept

Engineering Dept

Using Route Authentication

Another way to provide access security within the network is route authentication. In the *route authentication* method, the routers verify among themselves that they are indeed valid routers and that they provide valid paths to the rest of the network. This method can be especially helpful when you want to protect a gateway.

For example, if a hacker can log onto the network and set up a workstation as the default gateway for a group of subnets, the hacker can tap into all of the data that is sent from the stations using this fake default gateway. In Figure 8–7, a hacker has set up an endstation as a fake default gateway (1.1.1.1). The new user's endstation believes, incorrectly, that it should use this gateway.

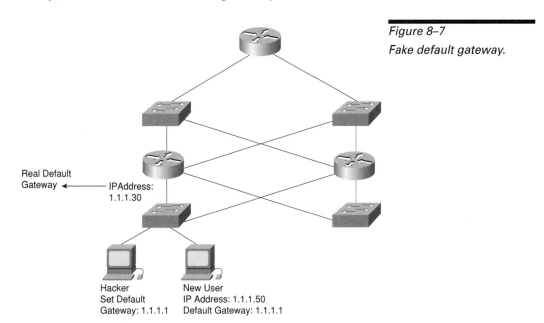

Figure 8–7
Fake default gateway.

Real Default
Gateway ← IPAddress:
1.1.1.30

Hacker
Set Default
Gateway: 1.1.1.1

New User
IP Address: 1.1.1.50
Default Gateway: 1.1.1.1

With route authentication, the routers make sure that the correct device is in fact the default gateway and that no false default gateways are created. Figure 8–8 shows the result of applying route authentication to the hacker scenario in Figure 8–7.

Route authentication is also used to verify that the routing paths available on the network are real routing paths, not paths to an unauthorized or unknown device.

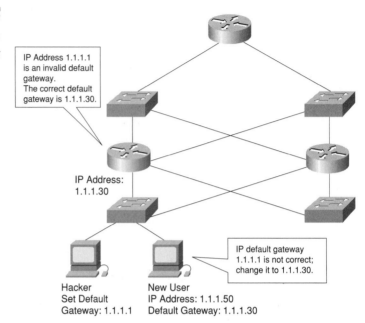

Figure 8–8

Route authentication blocks off the fake default gateway.

IP Address 1.1.1.1 is an invalid default gateway. The correct default gateway is 1.1.1.30.

IP Address: 1.1.1.30

IP default gateway 1.1.1.1 is not correct; change it to 1.1.1.30.

Hacker
Set Default
Gateway: 1.1.1.1

New User
IP Address: 1.1.1.50
Default Gateway: 1.1.1.30

DATA SECURITY AND INTEGRITY

Once a user has logged onto the network, has been authenticated, and has accessed the desired server, there is still another issue to consider. How can the network be structured to ensure that the data being transferred to or received from the user is safe when it traverses the network? Historically, the majority of file transfers in a campus network did not contain highly sensitive data. However, as more businesses rely on the network instead of traditional methods to send important data quickly, data security is rapidly becoming a significant concern.

For networks that need high data security, a method known as encryption can be utilized.

Securing Data by Encryption

Encryption is the process of scrambling data so that it cannot be read by anyone except the intended receiver. The data must be decoded or *decrypted*—that is, translated back to its original form—before the receiver can understand it. Encryption maintains data integrity on the network, and the confidentiality of the sender and the receiver from other users on the network points.

Encryption uses two mechanisms, an *algorithm* and a secret value known as a *key*. The algorithms, which are very complex, basically take the data and scramble it up. The *key* is the value that allows the sender and the receiver to actually encrypt and decrypt the data. We can relate these two mechanisms to a combination lock. The combination lock itself is the algorithm, and the actual combination to the lock, the key, is unique. Unless you know the combination, it is difficult to open the combination lock.

Several methods are used to encrypt and decrypt data. Three of the more commonly used methods are symmetric encryption, asymmetric encryption, and hash functions. We will describe each one of these security operations in general terms to show you how they work and then provide references for more in-depth information.

Symmetric Encryption

Symmetric encryption is a secret key encryption method that provides data confidentiality. When two endstations use symmetric encryption, they must agree on which algorithm to use and on which secret key to share. As the number of users of symmetric encryption increases, the number of secret keys increases as well, and keeping track of the keys becomes more complex for the end users.

Figure 8–9 shows four users sharing secret keys. Station A needs to remember three secret keys—one that goes to Station B, a different one for Station C, and yet a third one for Station D. In addition, the algorithm used to create the encrypted data may be different for each pair of users.

Figure 8–9

Symmetric encryption.

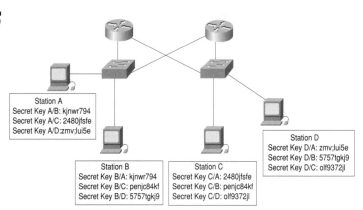

Station A
Secret Key A/B: kjnwr794
Secret Key A/C: 2480jfsfe
Secret Key A/D:zmv;lui5e

Station D
Secret Key D/A: zmv;lui5e
Secret Key D/B: 5757tgkj9
Secret Key D/C: olf9372jl

Station B
Secret Key B/A: kjnwr794
Secret Key B/C: penjc84kf
Secret Key B/D: 5757tgkj9

Station C
Secret Key C/A: 2480jfsfe
Secret Key C/B: penjc84kf
Secret Key C/D: olf9372jl

Symmetric encryption is most widely used for data integrity, which is encrypting the actual data. It is the least complex encryption method, and it requires the lowest amount of processing on the network devices, such as endstations and routers.

Some common symmetric key algorithms are the Data Encryption Standard (DES), 3DES (triple DES), and the International Data Encryption Algorithm (IDEA).

Asymmetric Encryption

Asymmetric encryption, also known as *public key encryption*, is an encryption method that utilizes both public and secret (or private) keys, and which provides data security and sender authentication. It is a bit more complex than symmetric encryption. Instead of two users sharing the same secret key, each endstation creates a public/private key pair. When two endstations want to send confidential data to each other, they agree on which encryption algorithm to use and then exchange their public keys, as shown in Figure 8–10.

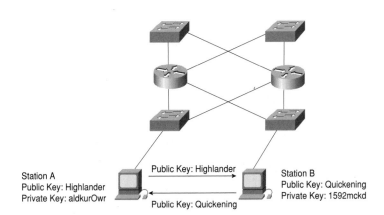

Figure 8–10
Public/private key pairs.

Station A
Public Key: Highlander
Private Key: aldkurOwr

Public Key: Highlander
Public Key: Quickening

Station B
Public Key: Quickening
Private Key: 1592mckd

When Host A wants to send information to Host B, it uses Host B's public key to encrypt the data and then sends the data to Host B, as shown in Figure 8–11.

After Host B receives the encrypted data, it uses its own private key to decrypt it, as shown in Figure 8–12.

When Host B sends information back to Host A, it uses Host A's public key to encrypt the data. Host A then uses its own private key to decrypt the data when it is received. The endstation, which knows the unique public key of each station it is sending data to, can keep a single private key for all of the information it receives.

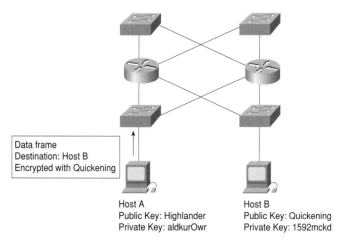

Figure 8–11

Host A sending encrypted data to Host B.

Data frame
Destination: Host B
Encrypted with Quickening

Host A
Public Key: Highlander
Private Key: aldkurOwr

Host B
Public Key: Quickening
Private Key: 1592mckd

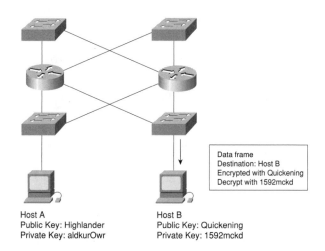

Figure 8–12

Host B decrypting the data.

Data frame
Destination: Host B
Encrypted with Quickening
Decrypt with 1592mckd

Host A
Public Key: Highlander
Private Key: aldkurOwr

Host B
Public Key: Quickening
Private Key: 1592mckd

If there is concern about who actually sent the data, the public/private pair key encryption method can help as well.

Let's say that Host B is not sure that Host A actually sent the data and wants verification that it was actually Host A before it sends information back. Host A can send Host B a message, but instead of encrypting the message using Host B's public key, Host A can encrypt the message with its own private key, as shown in Figure 8–13.

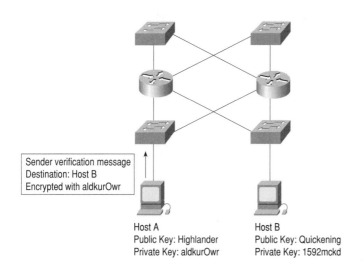

Sender verification message
Destination: Host B
Encrypted with aldkurOwr

Host A
Public Key: Highlander
Private Key: aldkurOwr

Host B
Public Key: Quickening
Private Key: 1592mckd

Figure 8–13
Host A encrypting with its private key.

When Host B receives the message, it needs to decrypt the message using Host A's public key instead of its own private key, as shown in Figure 8–14. This verifies sender authentication.

The matrix in Table 8–1 summarizes the use of public and private keys for data security and sender authentication, respectively.

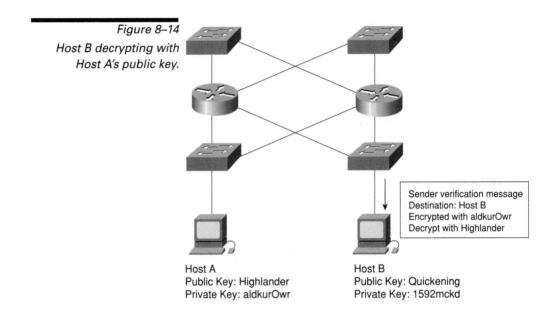

Figure 8–14
Host B decrypting with Host A's public key.

Sender verification message
Destination: Host B
Encrypted with aldkurOwr
Decrypt with Highlander

Host A
Public Key: Highlander
Private Key: aldkurOwr

Host B
Public Key: Quickening
Private Key: 1592mckd

Table 8–1   *Asymmetric Encryption Public/Private Key Relationship*

Type of Security	Sender	Receiver
Data security	Encrypts with receiver's public key	Decrypts with its own private key
Sender authentication	Encrypts with its own private key	Decrypts with sender's public key

Asymmetric encryption is not as commonly used for data security as symmetric encryption because its encryption algorithms are much more computationally intensive than the symmetric encryption algorithms. Using asymmetric encryption for data security might slow down network resources unacceptably. Instead, asymmetric encryption is generally reserved for situations in which sender authentication is needed.

Some common asymmetric encryption algorithms include Rivest, Shamir, and Adleman (RSA); and Digital Signature Standard (DSS).

There is a way to use both asymmetric encryption for sender authentication and symmetric encryption for data security. This method is known as the Diffie-Hellman algorithm, and it is useful when two endstations need to exchange keys over an insecure channel. Basically, it uses the asymmetric encryption method with public and private keys to establish a channel between two endstations. These two endstations then use this channel to exchange the symmetric encryption key, which is the shared secret key. This shared key is then used to encrypt and decrypt data.

Hash Functions

The third method of encryption is known as a *hash function*. A hash function is typically used with symmetric or asymmetric encryption to provide an even higher level of data integrity. A secure hash function takes the information (input), runs this data through the most complex mathematical computation (hash function) used for encryption, and comes out with new encrypted information (output). Figure 8–15 shows this process.

It is nearly impossible to reverse this process—to take the output, use a method of decryption, and then come up with results that are the original input. It's like scrambling eggs: after cracking three eggs in the same bowl, mixing them up, cooking them, and serving them, there is no way to take the resultant scrambled eggs and re-create the original eggs again. The same is true for the hash function. With hash functions, keys and the same algorithm are not enough to decrypt the data. You must use the same hash function that was used originally to decrypt the information. The hash function is much more computationally complex than symmetric or asymmetric encryption.

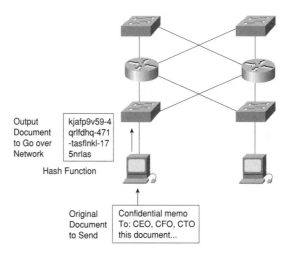

Figure 8–15

A secure hash function.

Because of its complexity, a secure hash function is typically not used on the data itself; instead, it can be used to prove the sender's identity and to ensure the integrity of the data. Common hash functions include Message Digest Algorithm 4 (MD4), Message Digest Algorithm 5 (MD5), and Secure Hash Algorithm (SHA).

Let's examine how a document is encrypted using a combination of a hash function and an asymmetric encryption. Figure 8–16 outlines the process.

Station A is sending a document to Station B; the stations have agreed on which hash function to use. Sending a document has two parts: the document itself and the identity of the sender. The document goes through the hash function, step 1 in Figure 8–16. The output of the hash function, which is now called the message digest, is encrypted using Station

A's private key (asymmetric encryption), as illustrated in step 2. After encryption, the output is called the digital signature; it provides Station A's identity. The digital signature is then appended to the original document as shown in step 3. Station A sends the resulting output document to Station B.

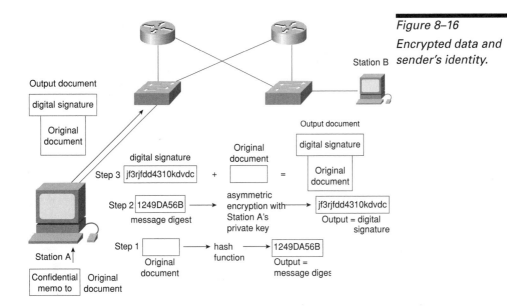

Station B

Figure 8–16

Encrypted data and sender's identity.

When Station B receives the document, it must decrypt the data as outlined in Figure 8–17. First, it uses Station A's public key to decrypt the digital signature. If the public key works, then Station B has just verified that Station A was the actual sender of the document. After decrypting the digital signature, Station B has the message digest, or the output of the hash function. Station B takes the original document, as shown in step 2, and puts it through the same hash function that Station A used. If Station B's message digest is the same as Station A's message digest (step 3), then this proves that the document has not been tampered with. Both the integrity of the document and the authentication of the sender have been verified.

The preceding process can have an even higher level of encryption added to it. The original document can be encrypted using symmetric encryption so that the sender's identity is encrypted with the hash function and with asymmetric encryption. The document is encrypted with symmetric encryption, and the integrity of the document is verified using the hash function.

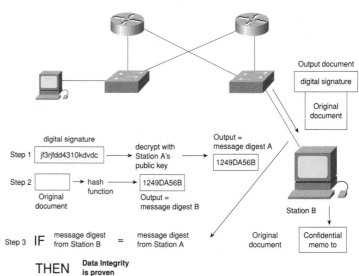

Figure 8–17

Decrypting the information.

Table 8–2 summarizes which function each encryption method supports for data integrity and sender/receiver confidentiality.

Table 8–2 *Encryption Methods and Functions*

Encryption Method	Components	Function
Symmetric encryption	Shared secret key between sender and receiver	Data integrity
	Encryption algorithm	Sender/receiver confidentiality
Asymmetric encryption	Public/private keys for sender	Sender authentication
	Public/private keys for receiver	Data integrity
	Encryption algorithm	Sender/receiver confidentiality
Hash function	Mathematical computation that can go forward to encrypt data, but is nearly impossible to reverse to decrypt data	Verifies data integrity
		Used with symmetric or asymmetric encryption

Where to Use Encryption

There are two places in the network where encryption can take place—between the sending and receiving stations (including servers), and at the router.

Encryption on the endstations and servers provides full encryption security throughout the network. Encryption on the routers provides partial encryption security on the network.

Encryption on the endstations and servers means that the data sent from the endstation is encrypted before it leaves the computer. For example, when a user sends a request to download a classified file from the server, the server encrypts the file using one of the methods we've described before it sends the file onto the network. As the file travels through the network, individuals cannot read it, even if they do succeed in looking at it. As shown in Figure 8–18, the data is garbled and unreadable.

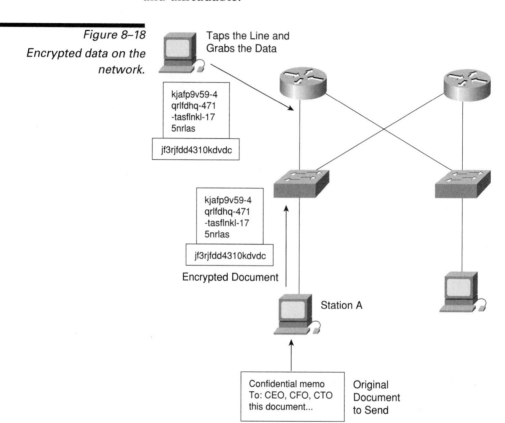

Figure 8–18
Encrypted data on the
network.

When the data reaches the endstation that requested it, the endstation decrypts it and the file becomes readable again, as shown in Figure 8–19.

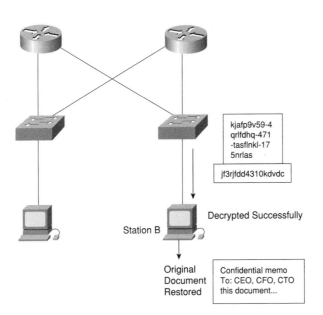

Figure 8–19
Decrypted data at the
endstation.

Encryption at the endstations and servers provides the highest level of security, because the data is encrypted the entire time that it crosses the network. If for some reason the data goes to a different endstation than the one that requested it, the other endstation cannot decrypt it properly. The file therefore remains unreadable.

Encryption can be implemented on a router for partial network data integrity. Using this method means that the data is encrypted at the first router it passes through and then decrypted at the final router it passes through, as shown in Figure 8–20.

If someone steals the data while it is traveling between the two routers, the data is encrypted and therefore unreadable. However, if someone steals the data before it gets to the first router or after it leaves the final router, the data is not encrypted, which allows it to be read by unauthorized users. Both situations are shown in Figure 8–21.

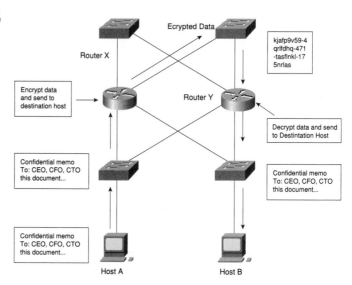

Figure 8–20
Encryption at the router.

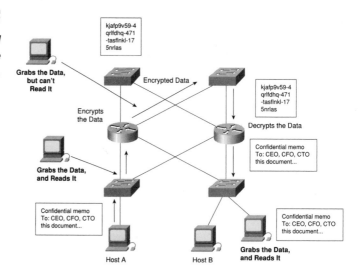

Figure 8–21
Encrypted and unencrypted data on the network.

Encryption at the router works well over the wide area or Internet, but it does not provide much benefit for the campus because most traffic does not pass through more than two routers.

Using some type of encryption on the campus network can certainly provide a level of data integrity for users. If only a few users need the level of security afforded by encryption, then it makes sense to add encryption packages to their workstations. If a majority of your network can benefit from encryption, then perhaps encryption on the workstations as well as on the routers is the best solution. By using encryption on the endstations, servers, and the network infrastructure, data integrity is safeguarded end-to-end throughout the network.

SUMMARY

Having a secure network means that there are mechanisms in place that control who can gain access to the campus network, and what information and devices are available once access is granted.

Table 8–3 summarizes the levels of security we've discussed in this chapter. Level 1 is the most basic, and Level 5 is the most advanced.

Table 8–3 *Levels of Security in the Network*

Security Level (1–most basic; 5–most advanced)	Security Method	Function
1	Network logon	Authentication/authorization
2	Server/device login	Authentication/authorization
3	Filters	Authorization
4	Route authentication	Authentication/authorization
5	Encryption: symmetric, asymmetric, hash function	Data integrity/sender-receiver confidentiality

No matter which security methods are used, some form of network security is vital to ensure that only authorized users can gain access to and operate within the campus network. Keeping security in mind becomes even more important with network changes and growth, a topic we cover in the next chapter.

The critical concepts to remember from this chapter are:

- Network logon, a common form of user authentication, is a minimum security requirement for virtually every network. Successful network logon means that a user is validated to use the network.

- User authentication on the server determines which users have access to the server. User authorization on the server goes a step further, determining what information on the server a user may have access to.

- Filters are a security method in which routers are configured to accept or reject access to certain areas of the network on a per-traffic or per-subnet basis.

- Router authentication is a security method by which routers verify that they are valid routers, providing valid paths to the rest of the network.

- Symmetric encryption is a data security method applied to data that uses private (secret) keys.

- Asymmetric encryption is an encryption method that uses public and private keys. It is used mainly for sender authentication, due to the complexity of the data encryption algorithms, but it can be used for data encryption as well.

- Hash function is an encryption method that uses a very complex scrambling method that virtually cannot be undone. It typically is used in combination with asymmetric or symmetric encryption to provide sender authentication and data integrity.

- Encryption on the network can take place at the endstation and server, and at the router. Encryption at the endstation and the server affords a greater level of security than encryption at the router.

This chapter covers the following topics:

- Addressing network rate of growth

- Looking at user mobility

- Moves, adds, and changes

- How protocols provide mobility

- Adding mobility to IP networks

- Getting help with Virtual LANs

- Types of VLANs

- Where to use VLANs

- VLAN traffic on the network

- VLAN technologies

CHAPTER 9

Designing for Change and Growth

One of the major challenges facing network designers today is how to plan for network change and growth. The capacity of a network to keep pace with changes and growth is often referred to by the term *scalability*, and it is a critical network design criterion.

We can look at network change and growth as coming from distinct, though not mutually exclusive, sources. One source is traffic, as discussed in several preceding chapters. The prevalence of broadcast and multimedia traffic may necessitate a change in network scale. Traffic prioritization mechanisms and appropriate server locations are ways of scaling the network to avoid or respond to traffic congestion due to network growth.

A second source of network change and growth is applications. The growth of multimedia and Web applications has had a tremendous impact recently on networks. Security applications have become essential as networks have become ubiquitous and internetworked.

This chapter's discussions focus more on a third source of network change and growth: network users. To emphasize the distinctions between the various sources of change and growth, the chapter begins with a brief review of some now familiar pressures on the network.

ADDRESSING NETWORK RATE OF GROWTH

It's easy for network designers to get lulled into thinking that network rate of growth is directly tied to the number of new employees hired by the company.

Network growth can also be the result of a simple change in the way business is conducted. For example, with the increasing amount of traffic going through the Internet day after day, the traffic on your campus network is increasing as well. The rate at which it is increasing directly determines and impacts the way you design your network and how you make it scalable for future needs.

Many companies can easily see an average of 20 to 30 percent network-growth rate over the course of a year. And this does not necessarily mean that the companies have hired on additional personnel—the growth rate can be the result of one or several factors, including:

- An increase in the number of client connections

- An increase in the number of servers

- An increase in the amount of traffic

- An increase in the size of the geographic region that the network must reach

- An increase in the number of supported applications

All of these factors apply when designing for network growth. Consider the example of a little company named Byzantine Manufacturing.

Byzantine Manufacturing makes copper widgets and has a staff of 100 people. They have an installed base of customers, and as customers leave, new ones are found by the field sales personnel, keeping the company on an even keel. Byzantine Manufacturing has a central enterprise server for shared applications (e-mail and word processing) and two distributed servers for confidential data (one for Human Resource records and one for administrative sales/customer statistics).

The sales manager decides that it's time to develop a Web page to garner more sales for Byzantine Manufacturing. The Web page is placed on the enterprise server to provide easy access. Here's what can happen:

- Interest in the Web page brings increased traffic into the campus network.

- Field sales personnel are now having trouble getting to e-mail because it's located on the same server as the Web page.

- A new server (enterprise) is purchased for field service e-mail.

- On-campus personnel also start using the Web, so now there is increased traffic going out from the campus.

The end result: Byzantine Manufacturing realized a 20 percent increase in network growth from one single feature—using a Web page.

Each time you add to (or subtract from) your network, you must be prepared for the potential ripple effects and plan accordingly. Otherwise, you will find that your network scheme is not scalable and performance problems will likely turn up.

What makes designing for network growth so difficult is that there is no set formula. Each of the items we've discussed in previous chapters—traffic patterns, server placement, protocols used, application types, security functions, and so forth—plays a part as your network grows. And what works for your company will not necessarily work for the company down the street.

Today, a frequent source of network change is increased user mobility. It almost takes a magic touch to be able to anticipate and react to user changes in a timely manner. You can make it easier to integrate these changes into the campus network, as we show in the next sections.

LOOKING AT USER MOBILITY

Network architects are being motivated to redesign the campus network due to an increase in user mobility. Traditionally, user mobility has resulted from companies adding new staff, promoting staff, or moving staff from one department to another. Now, however, a new aspect of user mobility must be taken into account: as more corporations implement laptop computers and as the power of the desktop becomes more portable, users are demanding more flexibility. They want to move around the campus as well as off the campus, and still be able to access their local applications as if they were sitting in their offices.

User mobility, both on-campus and off, can be segmented into distinct disciplines: moves, adds, and changes.

Moves, Adds, and Changes

Moves within the network are relatively simple to accomplish because the network already knows about the user. With *moves*, the person is physically moving but still accessing the same network services. Let's say that today you are in Building A and have access to Server X. Tomorrow you move to your new office in Building C, and still use the same Server X. Because your PC name and user ID are already known to the network, the move is a matter of adding the new switch port that you will be connected to onto the network, as shown in Figure 9–1.

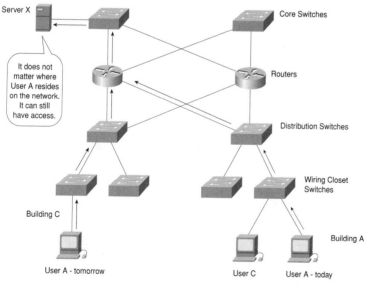

Figure 9–1

A user moves from Building A to Building C.

Adds and changes, however, are more complex. With *adds*, new users are being added for the very first time (when they log onto the network, it is the first time they have ever done so). A user ID needs to be set up, passwords need to be established, access to the appropriate servers need to be processed, an e-mail account must be created, and so on. A lot of network administration must occur before the new user can even log onto the network.

With *changes*, the person may physically stay in the same place, but now needs to access different network services. This typically happens when a staff member changes departments or gets a promotion within the same company. In this case, the user may be using Server X and be located in Building A on one day, then remain in Building A but need to access Server Y the following day, as shown in Figure 9–2.

Figure 9–2
A user accessing different servers based on change.

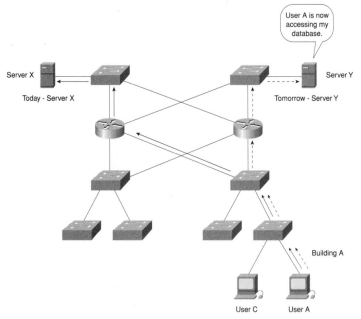

Network access for the user needs to be modified to allow for authorization to use the additional servers, access to some servers may need to be deleted, network security may have to be adjusted, and so forth.

The way in which the network designer handles these aspects of change and growth depends on the network's protocol structure. Some protocols provide inherent mobility through their addressing mechanism, while others do not, as we'll describe in the next section.

How Protocols Provide Mobility

When moves, adds, or changes occur on the network, there are specific items that the LAN administrator must set up. This starts with the LAN protocol-addressing scheme that will be used for network and server access.

Of the protocols in use today, IPX, AppleTalk, and Banyan VINES have all implemented dynamic addressing. Thus, except for implementing the drivers on the workstation, the LAN administrator does not have to specifically identify the user's workstation.

This is not the case, however, with the most widely used protocol, IP. The IP protocol still requires the identification of user (user ID) and workstation (hostname). The user's workstation and network address remain tied to each other for network identification.

Each of the network protocols uses names to identify network devices such as file servers and print servers. When a user requests a logon to another file server, for example, the protocol or network operating system will try and resolve the file server name to a network address.

In Novell's NetWare or IPX protocol, each file server contains a table that maps the file servers name to a network address.

For the IP protocol, this mapping is handled by a global server known as the Domain Name System (DNS) server. The DNS server holds a registry of all IP addresses and their associated userID/hostnames. If a workstation has an entry in the DNS server and moves frequently throughout the campus, the DNS server must be updated to reflect the change each time the user moves.

Because the IPX, AppleTalk, and Banyan VINES protocols' characteristics are inherently dynamic, these types of networks can more readily respond to adds, moves, and changes in the campus.

The IP protocol, on the other hand, uses static addressing, which places the responsibility of keeping the network current onto both the network administrator and the end-user client. Static addressing requires the network administrator to allocate an available address for the user and manually update the DNS server database to include the user and matching IP address. The user configures the IP address, the IP default gateway, the DNS server address, and any other user-specific information.

For example, if an IP user has an address of 1.1.1.10 in Building A, and tomorrow the user moves to Building B, that user will get a new network address. In our example, the new address is 2.1.1.100, as shown in Figure 9–3.

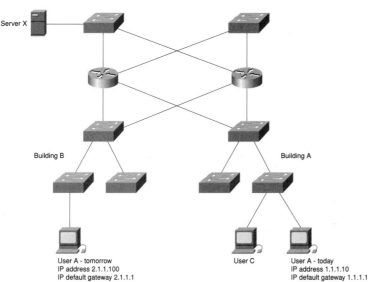

Figure 9–3
Address changes for a
moved user.

Server X

Building B

Building A

User A - tomorrow
IP address 2.1.1.100
IP default gateway 2.1.1.1

User C

User A - today
IP address 1.1.1.10
IP default gateway 1.1.1.1

The address change is not done automatically: the network administrator must make all the changes to the DNS database, give the user a new available IP address (in this example 2.1.1.100), and give the correct default gateway (2.1.1.1) for that network. The client must then change the IP address (from 1.1.1.10 to 2.1.1.100) and also change the IP default gateway (from 1.1.1.1 to 2.1.1.1) on the workstation.

Numerous scalability problems can crop up with this type of scenario, especially if there are a lot of adds, moves, and changes that occur within in the company. Because many users don't understand the network and what's required to support it, they can try to make network connections without knowing what they need to do first. This situation opens a Pandora's box of network administration problems, especially in terms of troubleshooting user-connectivity issues.

IP networks can be made more scalable by using the Dynamic Host Configuration Protocol (DHCP). We've mentioned DHCP in Chapters 3 and 5 when describing how routers handle broadcast traffic and how DHCP travels through the network. The next section describes how DHCP can make client-to-server connections dynamic.

Adding Mobility to IP Networks

DHCP allows the IP protocol to become more mobile by providing automatic IP address configuration.

To run DHCP on the network, three components are required:

- The network must contain at least one DHCP server.

- The routers must be able to forward DHCP requests (similar to forwarding BOOTP requests).

- A DHCP client must be configured on the endstation.

Once these requirements are met, DHCP dynamically assigns IP addresses in the following manner: a user turns on the endstation, and then the endstation sends out a DHCP Discover frame to the network asking for an IP address, as shown in Figure 9–4.

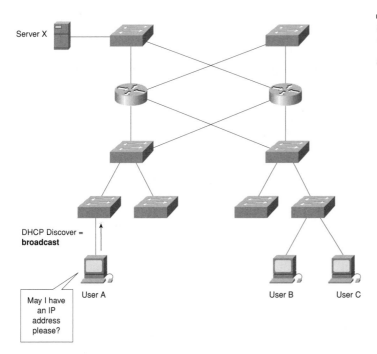

Server X

DHCP Discover =
broadcast

May I have
an IP
address
please?

User A   User B   User C

Figure 9–4
*The endstation sending out
a DHCP Discover frame.*

Because the DHCP Discover is a broadcast frame, the two destination address fields consist of broadcast addresses: ffffff and 255.255.255.255. The source MAC address field is that of the client sending the DHCP Discover. The source IP address field is 0.0.0.0 because it has not been assigned, and the gateway IP (GI) address field is also 0.0.0.0 because the default gateway address is unknown. Figure 9–5 shows the pertinent fields in the DHCP Discover frame.

The DHCP Discover broadcast floods throughout the endstation's local subnet. Other endstations on that subnet treat the frame as a broadcast and discard it after processing it.

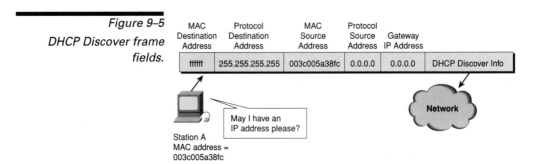

Figure 9–5
DHCP Discover frame
fields.

When the DHCP Discover broadcast reaches the router, the router understands that it is a request to discover an address. The router fills in the Gateway IP (GI) address field using the IP address of the incoming interface, as shown in Figure 9–6.

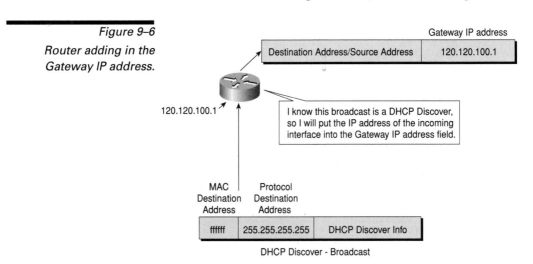

Figure 9–6
Router adding in the Gateway IP address.

The router then directs the DHCP Discover to the DHCP server by putting in the DHCP server's MAC and IP destination addresses. The frame is now relayed to the server as a unicast, as shown in Figure 9–7.

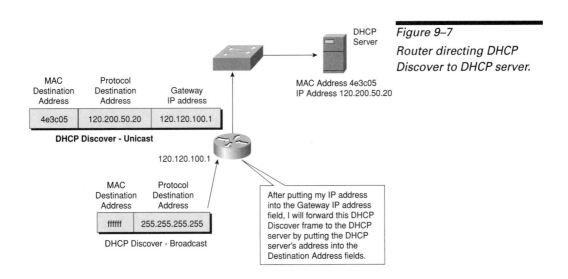

Figure 9–7

Router directing DHCP Discover to DHCP server.

When the DHCP server sees the request for an address, it registers the gateway IP address in the DHCP Discover frame and allocates an IP address for the client that fits into the correct subnet, as shown in Figure 9–8.

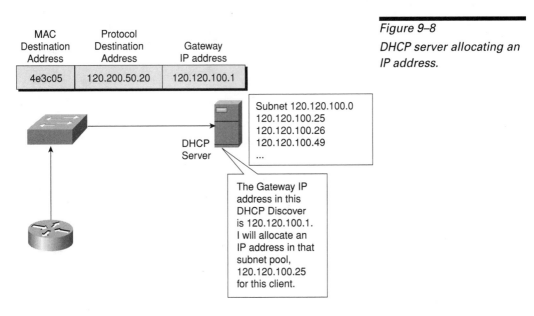

Figure 9–8

DHCP server allocating an IP address.

The DHCP server then sends a DHCP Offer frame back to the client with an IP address in the Your IP (YI) address field, as shown in Figure 9–9. Figure 9–10 shows the fields in the DHCP Offer frame.

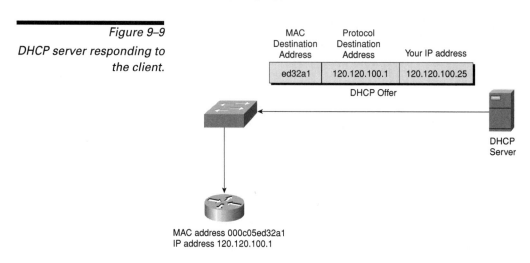

Figure 9–9

DHCP server responding to the client.

Figure 9–10

DHCP Offer frame fields.

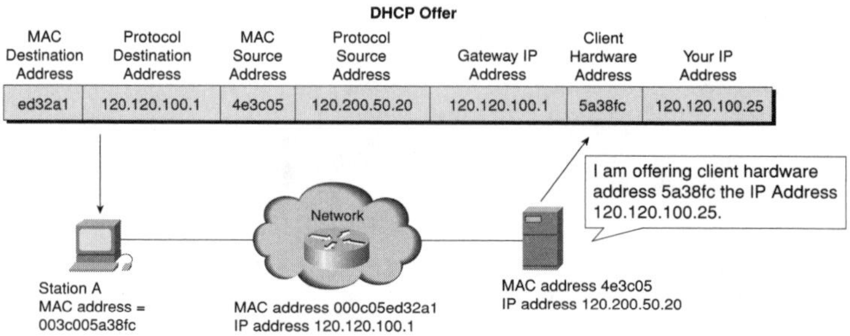

The DHCP server is offering the IP address to the client. It is directed to the router first because the router has an IP address and the server knows how to reach it, whereas the client does not have an address yet. The router then forwards the DHCP Offer back to the client.

If the client accepts this IP address, the client sends out a DHCP Request frame in the form of a broadcast asking to use the IP address, the same way it sent the DHCP Discover. The router behaves in a similar manner as well, and forwards the DHCP Request to the DHCP server.

The DHCP server will receive the DHCP Request, and send a DHCP Acknowledge back to the client through the router. The DHCP Acknowledge allocates the IP address to that client, and the DHCP server makes that IP address unavailable to other clients. The DHCP server also matches the client's IP address with the client's MAC address that it learned through the DHCP Discover process.

When the client receives the DHCP Acknowledge, it accepts the address configuration, and can now gain access to the network.

For networks that use DHCP, the IP address responsibility is placed on the network administrator instead of on each and every client. The network administrator must maintain enough available addresses for each subnet on the DHCP server and must update the DNS server with the allocated addresses and corresponding userID/hostname. Some DHCP/DNS products do this automatically; others require addresses to be updated manually.

The IP address assigned to the client by the DHCP server is dynamic, in that the client does not permanently own the assigned address (as is the case with static addressing). Rather, the client "leases" the address for a given amount of time. The time can be very short (per connection, per day, per week, and so on) or almost permanent (up to 100 years). The lease time is part of the DHCP Acknowledge frame sent by the DHCP server and is configured by the network administrator.

When a client receives its IP address, it keeps that address until one of two things occurs: either the client releases the IP address when it shuts down, thereby giving the IP address back to the DHCP server to make it available for another client; or the DHCP lease time runs out. If the DNS server needs to be manually updated by the network administrator, then the DHCP address lease time becomes important to the network, as we'll show in the following examples.

Let's say that the network manager wants to set the address lease time for one year. The network manager configures the DHCP server to allocate IP addresses for one-year leases. Because the DHCP client receives the lease time as part of its configuration in the DHCP Acknowledge, it does not release its IP address when it shuts down for the day. When the client boots up the next day, it will ask the DHCP server, using the DHCP Request frame, to allocate the same IP address that it had yesterday instead of assigning a new one. A DHCP client making this type of request is displayed in Figure 9–11.

The DHCP server will refuse to assign the requested address if the lease time has expired, or alternately, if the client has been moved to a different subnet or has changed MAC addresses (perhaps because the network interface card failed and was replaced). The DHCP server will then send a DHCP No Acknowledge (NAK) to the client, which states that it will not allocate that IP address to the client.

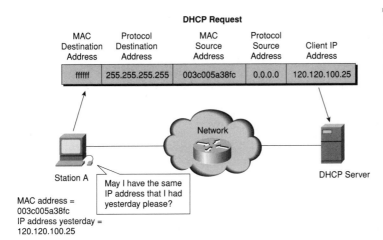

DHCP Request

MAC Destination Address	Protocol Destination Address	MAC Source Address	Protocol Source Address	Client IP Address
ffffff	255.255.255.255	003c005a38fc	0.0.0.0	120.120.100.25

Network

Station A

MAC address = 003c005a38fc
IP address yesterday = 120.120.100.25

May I have the same IP address that I had yesterday please?

DHCP Server

Figure 9–11

Client requesting a specific IP address through a DHCP Request.

When the client receives a DHCP NAK, the client must start the entire process again by asking for a new address with a DHCP Discover.

Scalability is much easier to achieve using DHCP for an IP addressing scheme than with the static addressing method. DHCP allows the automatic reuse of an address that is no longer needed by the workstation to which it was assigned. This makes it ideal for assigning an address to a user that will be connected to the network only temporarily or for users that telecommute (provided that the DHCP client software is configured to release the IP address when the user logs off the network). DHCP can also be a good choice for sharing a limited pool of IP addresses among clients who do not need permanent IP addresses or when IP addresses are sufficiently scarce that it is important to reclaim them to allow new users onto the network.

However, just as in static addressing, the network administrator must always be aware of how many addresses are available on each subnet and how many users will try to use each subnet. If a DHCP server runs out of addresses to allocate for a given subnet, then any additional users will be denied network connectivity.

Another way to obtain scalability and mobility in the network is to use Virtual LANs (VLANs). VLANs do not provide an addressing mechanism, and they must be used on top of an addressing scheme, whether it is static or dynamic addressing. VLANs do, however, provide a tool for physical moves and changes.

SCALING WITH VIRTUAL LANs

A *Virtual LAN (VLAN)* is an emulation of a standard LAN that allows data transfer and communication to occur without the traditional physical restraints placed on the network. For example, VLANs allow users to belong to the same network, such as a subnet, without needing to be located physically close together in the campus. VLANs also provide to switches the capability to support more than one subnet (VLAN) on each switch, and give routers and switches the opportunity to support multiple subnets (VLANs) on a single physical link. Like traffic-prioritization mechanisms, VLANs also help alleviate traffic congestion without adding bandwidth.

The diversity of vendor implementations of VLANs makes it difficult to capture all aspects of how and where they can be used. We can, however, describe VLAN types and common strategies in general terms to give you an idea of how they can be employed to solve scalability concerns.

Types of VLANs

VLAN types, although diverse, can be grouped into general categories. Following are brief descriptions and examples of some of these VLAN types.

Port-based VLANs

VLANs can be configured at each port on a switch. If Host A belongs to VLAN B, and connects to Port 10 on a switch, then we configure Port 10 to belong to VLAN B, as shown in Figure 9–12.

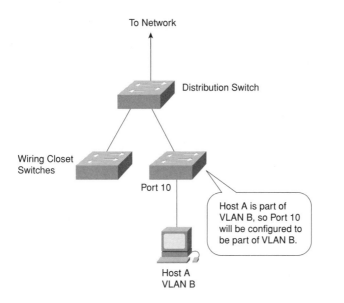

Figure 9–12

Port-based VLANs.

MAC Address-based VLANs

These VLANs are configured by the MAC address of the endstation. Host A's MAC address of 0000c3db571e belongs to VLAN B, regardless of which switch port Host A is connected to, as illustrated in Figure 9–13.

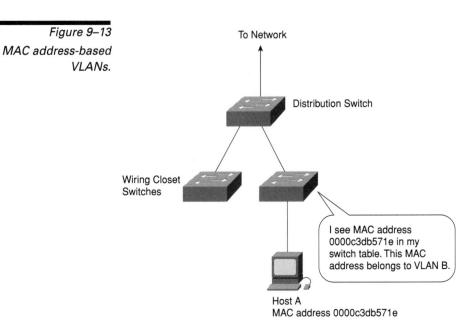

Figure 9–13
MAC address-based
VLANs.

Protocol-based VLANs

VLANs can be configured by the protocol network to which the endstation belongs. Host A belongs to IP subnet 150.150.150.0, so it is placed on VLAN B. Host A also belongs to IPX network ABCDEF123, so it is also placed on VLAN C, as we show in Figure 9–14.

Dynamic VLANs

Dynamic VLANs are configured based on a user profile and require a centralized database for profile storage. Host A logs onto the network and is automatically added to VLAN A, based on its profile in the central database, as shown in Figure 9–15.

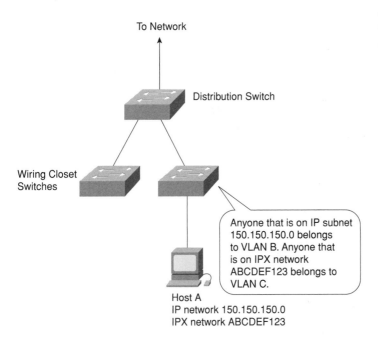

Figure 9–14
Protocol-based VLANs.

To Network

Distribution Switch

Wiring Closet
Switches

Anyone that is on IP subnet
150.150.150.0 belongs
to VLAN B. Anyone that
is on IPX network
ABCDEF123 belongs to
VLAN C.

Host A
IP network 150.150.150.0
IPX network ABCDEF123

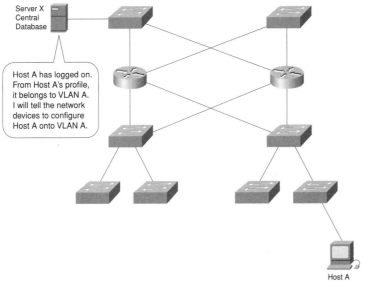

Figure 9–15
Dynamic VLANs.

Server X
Central
Database

Host A has logged on.
From Host A's profile,
it belongs to VLAN A.
I will tell the network
devices to configure
Host A onto VLAN A.

Host A

Where to Use VLANs

Before you embark on a VLAN scheme, you should completely understand your network's traffic patterns so you can get the maximum use of this tool. If, for example, your network is growing at a moderate rate and you're beginning to see network congestion on a specific enterprise server, you can set up a VLAN to improve traffic flow and provide scalability.

First, however, you must know what's causing the congestion. Is it multicast traffic coming in from another server (such as a video server)? Setting up a VLAN to separate this traffic will help. The multicast traffic stays local to that VLAN and does not cross into other VLANs, thereby reducing traffic congestion. Or, are there too many users trying to connect to the same service (such as e-mail)? Setting up a VLAN doesn't help in this situation because the same amount of users and traffic are still going to the enterprise server.

Just as with other solutions we've described in this chapter, VLANs have their limitations and may not be appropriate in all cases. Some types of VLANs (protocol-based, port-based, and so on) are used more effectively than others at various locations, again depending on your network setup, your scalability needs, and the vendor's implementation for VLANs.

VLANs can accommodate both user flexibility and traffic scalability, but there is a tradeoff in how well particular VLAN implementations balance these two sources of change. The remainder of this section describes three VLAN strategies and indicates how each VLAN strategy may work to limit scalability concerns. These three VLAN strategies are user-level VLANs, wiring closet VLANs, and distribution switch VLANs.

VLANs at the User Level

Implementing VLANs at the user level means that users belong to a specific VLAN, regardless of where they are on the network, and that they can have the same access to network services at all times. By facilitating user moves and changes in user services, this type of setup supplies user scalability, provided that most of the traffic stays local within each VLAN and that the network consists primarily of distributed servers. Figure 9–16 shows users connected to a wiring closet switch using this VLAN strategy. As we can see, the wiring closet switch must support several VLANs. This strategy can also be expanded to include most of the switches on the network.

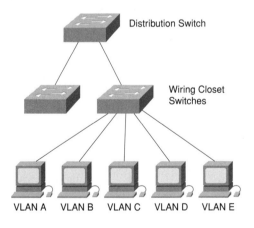

VLAN A   VLAN B   VLAN C   VLAN D   VLAN E

Figure 9–16

User-level VLANs at the wiring closet switch.

For VLANs at the user level, MAC address-based VLANs and dynamic VLANs types are good choices. As a user moves around the campus, the MAC address or user profile stays the same, and users connect to the same VLAN as before.

An example situation in which user-based VLANs work well is when there is a specific application that is run by only a certain group of users, such as a real-time imaging application. In this circumstance, the user-level VLANs keep these users in the same VLAN so that they can run this application optimally.

A user-level VLAN strategy provides high user flexibility. However, this method is ineffective from the perspective of traffic scalability because the traffic needs to stay local to the VLAN. Traffic patterns change when the users generate mostly cross-campus traffic or traffic between VLANs (such as traffic going across the backbone to the enterprise servers). The benefit of user-level VLANs disappears if all of the user traffic goes outside the VLAN (such as exclusively to enterprise servers). It doesn't matter then which VLAN the user belongs to because the traffic doesn't stay in the VLAN.

The traffic pattern on the network also becomes more volatile with the user-level VLAN strategy, due to the way VLANs handle broadcast domains.

Regardless of their physical location, users stay in the same VLAN and remain a part of that VLAN's broadcast domain. Each time they move, the scope of the broadcast domain changes, or, more specifically, the location where the traffic flows on the network changes. This is because the broadcast traffic in the VLAN travels throughout the network to wherever members of the VLAN are located. The arrows in Figure

9–17 indicate the broadcast traffic flow for User A, who is connected to Switch A and belongs to VLAN A. Figure 9–18 shows the broadcast traffic flow after User A moves to Switch D but stays in VLAN A.

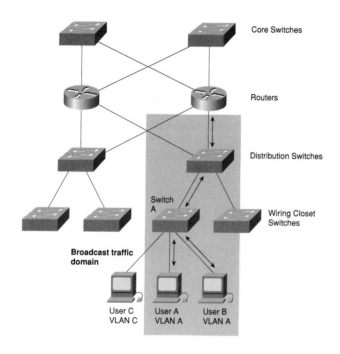

Core Switches

Routers

Distribution Switches

Switch A

Wiring Closet Switches

Broadcast traffic domain

User C
VLAN C

User A
VLAN A

User B
VLAN A

Figure 9–17
Broadcast traffic behavior in VLAN A.

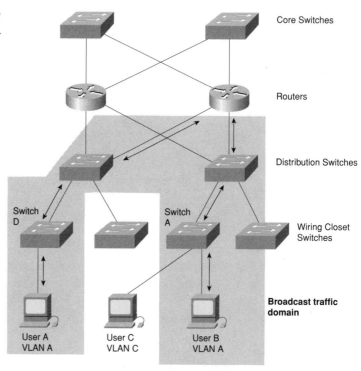

Figure 9–18

Broadcast traffic behavior
in VLAN A after User A
moves.

As you can see, every time User A moves to a different location in the network, the traffic patterns change on the network. As a result, designing for optimal network performance becomes difficult.

A user-level VLAN provides the most flexibility for user mobility and the most consistency for VLAN membership, making it ideal for user change and growth. Because a user-level VLAN creates high instability for traffic patterns and network performance, however, using it is the least optimal strategy for traffic change and growth.

VLANs at the Wiring Closet

Implementing VLANs at the wiring closet provides a method for broadcast domain control, a function traditionally performed by the router. Because a VLAN represents a single broadcast domain, using a VLAN at the wiring closet means that the VLAN controls where traffic flows on the network. Unlike user-based VLANs, which allow a VLAN to exist anywhere on the network, VLANs at the wiring closet switch provide boundaries for the broadcast traffic. As we discussed in Chapter 2, "Server Placement," broadcast traffic only travels within the broadcast domain (or in this case, the VLAN). If most of the traffic is going to enterprise servers and little of it is going to distributed servers, a wiring closet VLAN strategy works well.

Port-based VLANs or protocol-based VLANs are best for this method because these VLAN types don't tie the VLAN membership to the user. Instead, they tie VLAN membership to network characteristics, either physical port location (port-based) or to the subnet of that part of the network (protocol-based).

Typically, a wiring closet switch is configured to support only one or a select few VLANs. In addition, these VLANs most often work in conjunction with an address scheme (IP subnets, IPX, and so forth) used in your network. For traffic concerns, wiring-closet VLANs provide tighter control for both user and traffic growth and scalability on the network, as we show in the next examples.

Let's assume that a network has two wiring closet switches, Switch A and Switch B, which can support 100 users each. The network administrator decides that there can be up to 150 users per subnet, and sets up a VLAN on Switch A named VLAN A. All 100 users who connect to Switch A belong to the same VLAN or subnet: VLAN A. To handle the additional 50 users, the network administrator also sets up VLAN A on Switch B, which will support VLAN A users 101-150. This is shown in Figure 9–19.

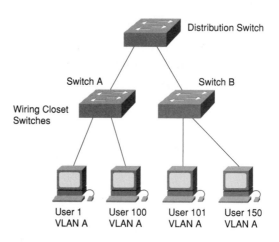

The network grows and 50 more users are added to Switch B. The network administrator now needs to set up VLAN B on Switch B to support these 50 users, as shown in Figure 9–20.

Switch A supports one VLAN (VLAN A) and Switch B now supports two VLANs (VLAN A and VLAN B). Switch A supports the 100 users that belong to VLAN A. Switch B supports the remaining 50 users that belong to VLAN A and the 50 users that belong to VLAN B.

This VLAN strategy also provides improved traffic control because the VLANs dictate where the broadcast traffic goes. The shaded area in Figure 9–21 indicates VLAN A's broadcast domain when a user (User A) is connected to Switch A.

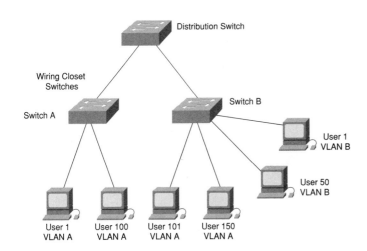

Figure 9–20
Adding 50 users to VLAN B.

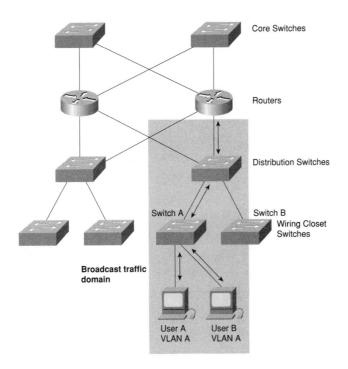

Figure 9–21
Broadcast behavior in VLAN A for User A.

When User A moves to another location, he becomes part of another VLAN. The broadcast traffic does not follow the moved user, but stays within the boundaries of the original broadcast domain, as shown in Figure 9–22. The traffic patterns on the network therefore remain predictable.

Figure 9–22

Broadcast behavior in VLAN A after User A moves.

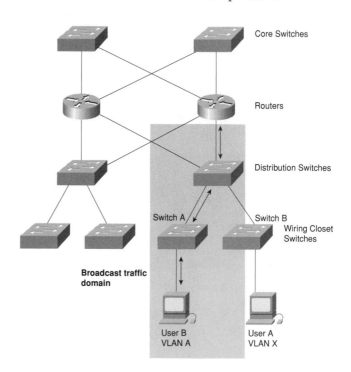

As traffic increases on the network, it is easier to maintain and scale for optimal network performance because the traffic patterns remain fairly stable. However, user flexibility and mobility are restricted because the users belonging on the same VLAN subnet must connect to the same wiring closet switch(es). This means that users must be physically close together on the campus (such as on the same floor or in the same part of the building).

If users move around a lot on the campus, they constantly change the VLAN they belong to in a wiring-closet VLAN strategy. This may adversely impact network response time for some applications, especially if users are trying to run an application from a distributed server in another VLAN.

Defining VLANs at the wiring closet provides for more controlled traffic scalability and growth management, but reduces user flexibility in terms of moving around the campus.

VLANs at the Distribution Switch

In terms of balancing user and traffic scalability, VLANs at the distribution switch represent a middle ground between the user-level and wiring-closet VLAN strategies. VLANs at the distribution switch allow more user mobility, but provide less broadcast domain control than VLANs at the wiring closet. Conversely, they provide less user mobility but more broadcast domain control than VLANs at the user level.

For traffic that goes to both enterprise and distributed servers, this VLAN implementation will work well. Port-based and also protocol-based VLANs support this method because they tie VLAN membership to network characteristics instead of tying VLAN membership to the user.

Users who connect to different wiring-closet switches yet have the same distribution switch can belong to the same VLAN, as shown in Figure 9–23.

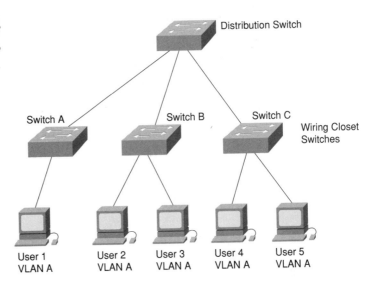

Figure 9–23

VLANs at the same distribution switch.

For the users who move and still connect to the same distribution switch (thereby staying in the same VLAN), the broadcast domain continues to include them as they move. Figure 9–24 shows the broadcast traffic behavior before User A moves, and Figure 9–25 shows the broadcast traffic behavior after User A moves.

When a user moves to another distribution switch, he must then become part of a different VLAN, as displayed in Figure 9–26. In this case, the broadcast traffic does not travel to the moved user because he's now a part of another VLAN.

Although a VLAN at the distribution switch makes it possible to predict traffic patterns, broadcast traffic can span more of the network because the VLAN can exist in a larger part of the network (as compared to wiring-closet VLANs). As a result, you have less controlled traffic scalability and growth management than you do when you implement wiring-closet VLANs.

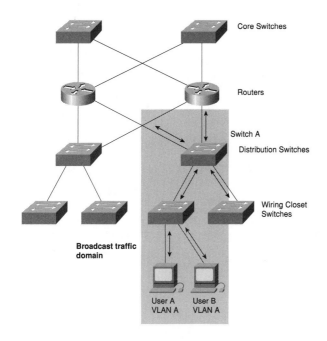

Figure 9–24

Broadcast behavior in VLAN A before User A moves.

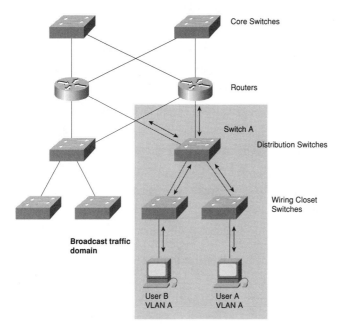

Figure 9–25

Broadcast behavior in the VLAN after User A moves.

Figure 9–26

The user moves to a different distribution switch.

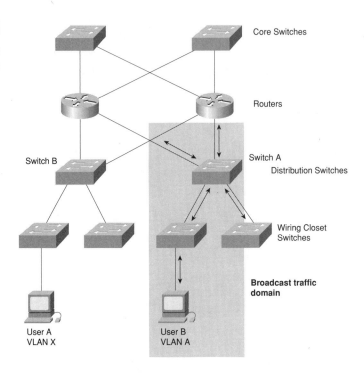

This VLAN strategy does, however, provide more controlled traffic scalability and growth management than user-level VLANs do because the VLAN cannot exist everywhere in the network. Also, it provides more user flexibility than wiring closet VLANs do. Users now are not limited to a single wiring closet, but can move among several wiring closets and stay in the same VLAN. They cannot move everywhere in the network though, making this strategy less flexible than the user-level VLAN strategy.

We've described each VLAN strategy in terms of where it is used and how appropriate it is in terms of user or traffic scalability and growth. In the next section, we look at its effectiveness in terms of overall network traffic flow on the campus.

VLAN Traffic on the Network

When viewed from a total network perspective, VLAN traffic can be categorized into two types: intra-VLAN and inter-VLAN.

Intra-VLAN communication means that all data transfers happen within the same VLAN. It is similar to local traffic, described in Chapter 5, "Looking at Local versus Cross-Campus Traffic," because data passes locally through switches and does not reach routers or Layer 3 devices, as shown in Figure 9–27.

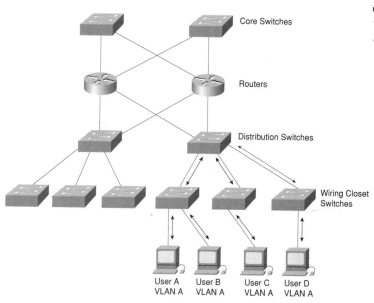

Figure 9–27
Intra-VLAN traffic.

Inter-VLAN communication means that data passes from one VLAN to a different VLAN. It is similar to cross-campus traffic because inter-VLAN traffic goes through a router or Layer 3 device, as shown in Figure 9–28. Routing between VLANs keeps each VLAN separate and unique.

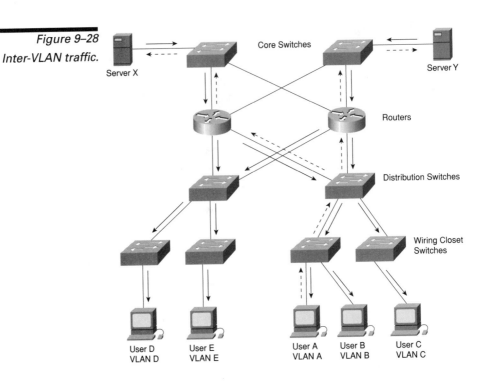

Figure 9–28
Inter-VLAN traffic.

Understanding the distinction between intra-VLAN and inter-VLAN traffic as you implement a VLAN strategy is important for three reasons: using an inappropriate strategy will decrease network performance, it makes network problems more difficult to troubleshoot and correct, and it reduces the network's capability to be scalable in the future.

Let's compare the three VLAN strategies in terms of intra-VLAN and inter-VLAN traffic scalability.

User-level VLANs allow the VLAN to exist anywhere in the network and work best when most of the traffic is local, or intra-VLAN. The network must be designed in a specific way to support this VLAN strategy. When traffic is intra-VLAN, we can assume that the bulk of the traffic goes to the distributed servers instead of the enterprise servers. Further, this traffic does not cross a router or Layer 3 device. Networks that support user-level VLANs must be designed so that the intra-VLAN traffic goes to the distributed servers across Layer 2 switches only, regardless of where the users are located on the campus. We will discuss this network design later in the design section of this book.

If the bulk of the VLAN traffic becomes inter-VLAN, either because it is going to the enterprise server or the network design cannot support user-level VLANs successfully, then the advantage of user flexibility is lost, and a user-level VLAN strategy does not add any value to network performance or scalability. If the traffic does not need to stay within the VLAN (such as traffic going to the enterprise servers), there is no need for the user to stay within the same VLAN when moving around the network.

Wiring-closet VLANs are effective when most of the traffic is inter-VLAN. In this case, users don't need to access distributed servers; instead, they access the same enterprise servers as they move around the network. Therefore, it does not matter when a user moves and joins a different VLAN because the traffic crosses a router to get to the enterprise server, regardless of which VLAN the user belongs to.

However, a wiring-closet VLAN will not be effective if most of the traffic is intra-VLAN. In this case, a user who moves from one VLAN to another may experience decreased network performance because the distributed server no longer connects to the same switch as the user. The user is on a different VLAN, which means that the traffic must be routed through the campus network.

Distribution switch VLANs work well when there is both intra-VLAN and inter-VLAN traffic. User mobility will not impact the inter-VLAN traffic network performance for the same reasons as the wiring-closet VLAN strategy.

As long as users stay connected to the same distribution switch as they move through the network, the intra-VLAN performance will not be affected. However, if the user moves to a different VLAN, the user should access the distributed server that resides on the new VLAN that the user belongs to. If the user accesses the previous distributed server, then the user may suffer some network-performance degradation because a different path on the network must be taken to reach the distributed server. By accessing the local distributed server, optimal network scalability and growth is maintained.

VLAN Technologies

The internetworking community has been developing a variety of technologies for implementing VLANs in networks. Of these, only one has been approved as a standard thus far, which is ATM LANE 1.0, designed to operate in ATM networks. For networks based on other protocols there are two Internet drafts that show promise: MultiProtocol Over ATM and IEEE 802.1q. Each of these technologies are described in the following sections.

ATM LANE

We described ATM with LAN Emulation (ATM LANE) briefly in Chapter 6, "Network Reliability and Resiliency," when discussing the importance of redundancy in the network. In this section, we'll focus on its VLAN capability.

LANE 1.0 essentially makes ATM look like a legacy frame technology, such as Ethernet or Token Ring, to the higher layers of the OSI model (the network layer and above). This is done so that protocols such as IP and IPX do not have to change their behavior and can still operate within an ATM network as if they were connected to an Ethernet or Token Ring network. The LANE 1.0 standard sets the ground rules on how ATM emulates a traditional LAN in order to make this possible. However, LANE 1.0 also removes a lot of the benefits provided by native ATM technology, such as QoS. By making this compromise, ATM LANE has been more easily adapted into existing networks.

A new version, LANE 2.0, addresses some of the QoS features that are missing from LANE 1.0 and is expected to be approved sometime in 1998. LANE 2.0 can be divided into two groups: LANE User-to-Network Interface (LUNI) and LANE Network-to-Network Interface (LNNI).

LUNI provides a more efficient distribution of multicast packets than LANE 1.0 does and allows better use of ATM QoS through Available Bit Rate support.

LNNI supports more than one LES/BUS pair per emulated LAN, which removes the single-point-of-failure issue found in LANE 1.0. It also supports LECS redundancy, which again removes the single-point-of-failure problem. LNNI can support both LUNI 1.0 and LUNI 2.0 clients for backward compatibility.

LANE 2.0 will become more important for ATM network design, especially when new technologies such as MultiProtocol Over ATM are approved, because this technology works best with LANE 2.0.

MultiProtocol Over ATM

MultiProtocol Over ATM (MPOA) is designed to forward Layer 3 packets, such as IP and IPX, directly over ATM backbones between VLANs, without using the traditional router to do the inter-VLAN routing. This is known as inter-VLAN cut-through connection. Based on LANE 2.0, a direct ATM connection is set up between sender and receiver, and traffic can be passed between the two, regardless of whether they are in the same VLAN or on different VLANs. MPOA will also allow QoS services such as RSVP to work along with the ATM Class of Services, both of which we discussed in Chapter 7, "Setting Traffic Priorities."

MPOA components include using the configuration server from LANE when first joining the ATM network; using an MPOA Client, which is similar to the LEC; and the MPOA Server, which supplies the Layer 3 forwarding information used by the MPOA client.

When the sending client is looking for the ATM destination address of the receiving client, it sends a query to the server for the ATM address. This is done through a new and yet-to-be-approved technology named the Next Hop Routing Protocol (NHRP). NHRP is expected to be finished by the IETF sometime in 1997/1998.

After the server responds to the request, the client can set up a direct ATM connection to the receiving client and the cut-through path can be established. Until this ATM cut-through path is set up, however, the data is forwarded across the network using ATM LANE mechanisms.

MPOA will likely be standardized sometime in late 1997, depending on the outcome of NHRP and LANE 2.0 technology approvals.

The IEEE 802.1q

The IEEE 802.1q, also an Internet draft, is unique because it will support all of the frame-based media, such as Ethernet, Token Ring, FDDI, Fast Ethernet, and even Gigabit Ethernet when it becomes available. It may support cell-based technology (ATM); this is yet to be determined.

The purpose of 802.1q is to provide VLAN interoperability among heterogeneous network devices. As it stands today, Vendor A's switch cannot work with Vendor B's switch if VLANs are implemented because each vendor uses a proprietary method. The 802.1q has the potential of removing this VLAN impasse from the network, and is expected to be standardized sometime in 1998.

When approved, the 802.1q standard will likely be used to support more than one VLAN on a single physical link, known as *VLAN trunking*. Other implementations may include using 802.1q to support a single VLAN, which may move VLAN configuration and control to the user and end-station level (most vendors' implementations place VLAN control at the switch, not the endstation).

SUMMARY

Designing your network so that it is scalable—so that it can keep pace with changes and growth—requires knowledge of current network patterns and, most importantly, a plan that anticipates how change and growth can be accommodated for future needs.

This chapter concludes Part II on design issues. At this point, you should have a good conceptual understanding of the types of network traffic and their practical implications, and the design parameters that shape a network. The next Part of this book moves from the conceptual to the practical. In Part III, we cover ways to meet the demands of your network based on three separate scenarios: a basic network, a scalable network, and a complex network. Keep in mind, however, that the first step is to understand what your network needs and what the challenges are before you design the optimal network.

The key concepts to take from this chapter are:

- Network growth can result from many factors, including an increase of clients, servers, traffic, or applications.

- Dynamic addressing is a central method of accommodating user changes in the campus. Many protocols, such as IPX, AppleTalk, and Banyan VINES automatically provide dynamic addressing.

- IP networks more readily support change and growth when you use DHCP.

- VLANs at the user level allow for highest user flexibility but lowest traffic scalability.

- VLANs at the wiring closet allow for high traffic scalability but low user flexibility.

- VLANs at the distribution switch allow a moderate level of both user flexibility and traffic scalability.

Part III

Campus Design and Implementation

- **Chapter 10**—Understanding the Structural Foundation of Network Design

- **Chapter 11**—Design One—A Barebone Network

- **Chapter 12**—Design Two—A Scalable Network

- **Chapter 13**—Design Three—A Complex Network

- **Chapter 14**—Preparing for the Future

The first task when designing a network is to ascertain the requirements for the critical and supporting applications in your campus. Parts 1 and 2 covered concepts and approaches for this analytical stage of network design.

Having made the necessary analysis, you can proceed to structure the network to deliver the services that the network applications demand. Part 3 presents the actual design structure, building on the concepts and approaches of Parts 1 and 2. In Chapters 10 through 13, we explain and provide design blueprints that describe which building blocks to use, how to structure the network core, and where to place servers and other devices for campus networks of varying complexity. Each design blueprint focuses on a network infrastructure that incorporates a total system approach—one that has scalable bandwidth, end-to-end service quality, and network resilience. In Chapter 14, "Preparing for the Future," we provide ideas about how you can continue to have a flexible network, with an eye toward weighing the cost of current implementations against future requirements.

This chapter covers the following topics:

- The building block

- The core block

- The server block

- Scale of campus designs

10

Understanding the Structural Foundation of Network Design

Constructing a campus LAN network begins with a general blueprint of the design. Similar to highway construction projects, creating a blueprint requires that the designer knows the specific uses of the network highway—data on-ramps and off-ramps must be placed in specific areas, traffic flows must be understood, network services must be placed at logical points, and overall network management must be provided. If the designer does not incorporate each of these elements, the campus LAN blueprint is incomplete and a totally cohesive system is not achieved.

The campus network can be separated into domains, or network foundations, to make constructing the blueprint easier. For each blueprint, we've divided the fundamental campus elements into the following network foundations: the building block, the core block, and the server block.

THE BUILDING BLOCK

Campus network designs have traditionally placed basic network-level intelligence and services at the center of the network and shared bandwidth at the user level, an implementation known as a *collapsed backbone*. Over the past few years, network design has diverged from the collapsed backbone. Instead, using distributed network services and intelligence and switching down to the user level have become the dominant technologies implemented within the campus. The prevalence of this design approach permits us to define a *building block*, which consists of the switching and routing devices required to connect users to the network. The building block provides distributed network services and network intelligence.

The building block needs to have a balanced implementation of scalable Layer 2 switching and Layer 3 services. The current generation of LAN switches are inherently Layer 2 devices. Although they are replacing shared media concentrators, they are not replacements for Layer 3 devices (routers).

As shown in Figure 10–1, Layer 2 switches in the wiring closets connect users to the network. The wiring closets merge into a distribution center, where there is Layer 2 connectivity as well as Layer 3 functionality. These two operations can be run with a Layer 2 switch, which we call the distribution switch, and an external router.

Figure 10–1
The building block.

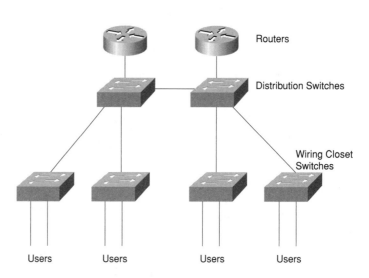

Within the building block, the Layer 2 functionality provides a central connection point for all of the switches in the wiring closets. The Layer 3 functionality provides routing and network services and creates a protection point for the building block against failures in other parts of the network.

For example, if the building block experiences a broadcast storm, the router prevents the storm from propagating into the core and into the rest of the network. Each block is protected from the other blocks when failures occur. However, the building block in which the broadcast storm occurs still experiences network problems until the device generating the broadcasts is found and removed from the network.

An alternative to using a Layer 2 switch and a Layer 3 router is to use the next generation of LAN switches, called Layer 3 switches, which integrate Layer 2 and Layer 3 functionality. These devices are being introduced now and should be widely available, beginning in 1998. A Layer 3 switch can replace a Layer 2 switch and a Layer 3 router in a real network, as long as it can provide all of the necessary network services. However, it will be awhile before Layer 3 switches can provide all of the network services that a traditional router offers. Throughout Part III of this book, the distribution center is shown as a Layer 2 switch (the distribution switch) and an external router. Visualizing two separate devices emphasizes the unique Layer 2 and Layer 3 functions being performed.

THE CORE BLOCK

The *core block* is responsible for transferring cross-campus traffic as quickly as possible without doing any processor-intensive operations (Layer 3 functionality). As we discussed in earlier chapters, all of the traffic going to and from the enterprise servers passes through the core of the network. Much of the traffic coming in from and going out to the Internet and the wide-area network passes through the core as well. Traffic going from one building block to another also must travel through the core. Because of these traffic patterns, the core handles much more traffic than either of the other blocks. Therefore, the core needs to be able to pass the traffic to and from the blocks as quickly as possible.

The core block consists of high-speed Layer 2 switches, as shown in Figure 10–2.

Figure 10–2
The core block.

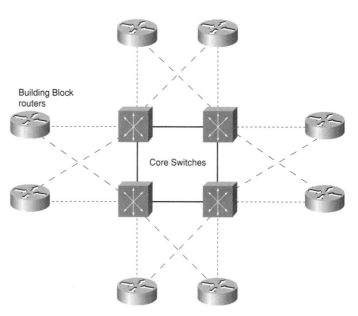

Layer 3 devices in the building blocks (and in the server blocks, as discussed in the next section) connect to the core switches, provide the network with services, and perform processor-intensive functions. Therefore, Layer 3 devices are not needed in the core block. The core can consist of any high-speed technology, such as Fast Ethernet, Gigabit Ethernet (when available), or ATM switches. You should select the technology that meets your specific network demands. Details about the features and benefits of each technology are beyond the scope of this book.

THE SERVER BLOCK

The *server block* consists of the enterprise servers in the network, and the switching and routing devices required to connect them to the rest of the network. As discussed in Chapter 2, "Server Placement," enterprise servers include e-mail servers, Web servers, multimedia servers, central database servers, and so forth—the servers that almost everyone on the network accesses.

From the data-path perspective, a design goal for the campus network is for each campus building block to be separated from the server block by an equal number of router hops. The number of router hops is more important than the physical distance between the building block and the server block. For example, it is desirable for each building block to be either one or two router hops away from the server block and for each block to have the same bandwidth connections to the server block, regardless of which building the server block resides in on the campus.

Typically, the server block is physically located in the data center, where the core block is located. We show the server block in Figure 10–3.

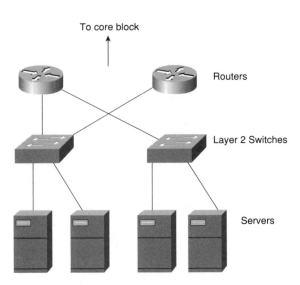

Figure 10–3
Server block.

As seen in Figure 10–3, a Layer 3 device is needed in the server block to protect the servers from failures on the network and to provide network services, such as security, multicast routing functionality, VLAN services, QoS, and so forth. If an enterprise server suffers from network performance degradation, it affects many of the users on the network. Even worse, if the entire server block experiences problems because of network instability, then everyone on the network experiences adverse effects.

The enterprise servers are the heart of the network. If the heart is not functioning effectively, then the rest of the body suffers drastically. Therefore, it is vital that the servers are protected from network problems and that they can perform their functions as efficiently as possible.

The server block generally needs only one level of Layer 2 switches; it does not need both wiring closet switches and distribution switches, as shown in Figure 10–3. If the server connections need more than a few switches, however, then it might make sense to put in a distribution switch and provide two levels of switches, as is done in the building block. Putting in a distribution switch and merging the other switches into it results in fewer physical connections to the router, as shown in Figure 10–4.

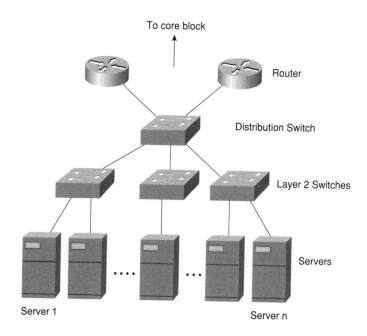

To core block

Router

Distribution Switch

Layer 2 Switches

Servers

Server 1

Server n

Figure 10–4

Distribution switch in the server block.

Another scenario in which two levels of switching makes sense for the server block is when you want to use Layer 3 switches. Layer 3 switches cost more than Layer 2 switches. Therefore, it makes sense to use Layer 2 switches at the wiring closet and a single Layer 3 switch at the distribution level, as shown in Figure 10–5. The alternative—using multiple Layer 3 switches for connection and distribution—is more expensive than using one Layer 3 switch and several Layer 2 switches.

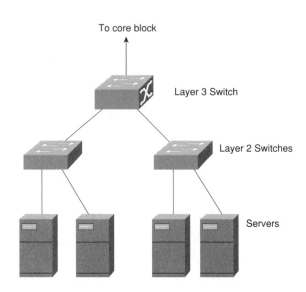

Figure 10–5
Layer 3 switch in the server block.

To core block

Layer 3 Switch

Layer 2 Switches

Servers

SCALE OF THE CAMPUS DESIGNS

Because each campus network is different, the general blueprints for network design that we provide can be used as a starting point and can be customized to meet the requirements of a specific network.

Each design we present in the following chapters has a network blueprint, and the hardware components are similar in each chapter. For example, we always recommend a Layer 2 switch in the wiring closet and a high-speed Layer 2 switch in the core, with some Layer 3 functionality separating the blocks. The specifics of each device type naturally vary based on the port count needed, the technology you are using in your network, the Layer 3 services that you require, and so on.

A typical campus network consists of one or more building blocks, a core block, and a server block, as shown in Figure 10–6.

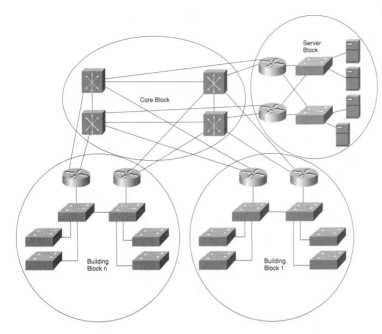

Figure 10–6
Typical campus network
structure.

The sizes of these blocks are flexible, yet we do recommend
certain ceilings. Based on geographical and administrative
constraints only, a building block can safely have up to 1,500
nodes in it (workstations, printers, distributed servers, and
so forth). This suggested maximum node count assumes that
there is more than one broadcast domain within the block,
and it does not reflect technological limitations. Constraints
posed by the particular technologies and traffic patterns on
your network may well require whittling down the number
of nodes from this maximum, perhaps to much fewer than
1,500. It's impossible to generalize a maximum node number
from a technological or traffic point of view because there
are so many different technologies and because traffic patterns vary widely from network to network. But you can use
the 1,500-node maximum as a starting point.

For example, consider a campus consisting of several buildings, including one that is four stories high. We need to estimate the number of employees and needed connections within the building. In this example, let's say that there are 200 network connections (employees, printers, and so on) on each floor. Considering that we have four floors, there would be 800 nodes in this building. Furthermore, if each floor represented a subnet, or broadcast domain, there would be a total of four broadcast domains. Thus, this example meets the recommended requirements for a building block: It does not exceed 1,500 nodes and there is more than one broadcast domain within the block. Moreover, it is a logical geographic and administrative unit to treat as a building block.

There are many examples we can use to show the size of the building block and the number of broadcast domains in it. You need to look at your specific campus environment to form the building blocks and broadcast domains that make the most sense for your network. If a building on your campus can house many nodes (not necessarily more than 1,500), then you need to decide, based on traffic patterns as well as administrative conditions, whether it can remain a single building block, or whether it needs to be divided up into more than one block.

If there is so much traffic passing through the building block routers that a bottleneck occurs at the routers, then the building block is too large. Similarly, if broadcast or multicast traffic is slowing down the switches and routers, creating bottlenecks at these devices, then the building block is too large. Additional network services on the routers, such as extra security, can also slow down the traffic passing through the routers.

If any of the preceding conditions are affecting the distribution switches or the routers that connect users to the core of the network, the people in the building block will suffer from slower network performance. If it's okay for all of these users to experience network problems, then the building block can stay large. But if users need to have higher network performance, then breaking up the large building block into two smaller blocks provides better protection and higher network performance for the users. The decision of whether or not to break up the block should be based on the traffic going across the network, rather than the specific number of nodes in a building block.

Another recommendation for safe network design is that the combined number of building blocks and server blocks attached to the core block should not exceed 20. This recommendation arises from the routing protocol that is running on the network, such as RIP, OSPF, or EIGRP.

With 20 attached blocks, you can have up to 40 routers attached to the core. These routers all share a common subnet, the subnet that the core switches belong to. Routing updates and route changes may be propagated to all of the routers on the campus, depending on which routing protocol is in use.

As the routing protocol is sending these updates and changes to the routers throughout the network, the network topology may also be changing. The more routers that are connected to the network, the longer it takes for these updates and changes to propagate through the network and change the topology. Also, be aware that one or more of the routers will connect to the wide-area network or the Internet, which are additional sources of routing updates and topology changes.

The OSPF and EIGRP routing protocols can safely handle 50 routers in a campus network, and RIP can safely handle 30. Having more than 20 building and server blocks in the campus network is feasible, but as the campus extends beyond this safety zone, the network designer must fully understand the routing protocol that is running on the network in order to predict its behavior in the larger network.

Most campus networks have at least one server block, but they might have more. For example, there might not be enough physical space for all of the enterprise servers to reside in the same building, there might be two or more geographically dispersed data centers, or traffic loads might dictate that the enterprise servers be separated among multiple server blocks. Each server block must be counted separately in order to keep the total number of blocks attached to the core to a safe maximum of 20.

SUMMARY

Each network design we discuss in Chapters 11–13 begins with a blueprint that includes the three fundamental network foundations—the building block, the core block, and the server block. Each of these designs utilizes different network services to satisfy network requirements and to enhance performance. The designs are meant to be used as a starting point; in most cases, they don't match your network requirements exactly. Instead, they are primary blueprints for you to enhance and customize according to your needs. The design you choose as a starting blueprint is up to you. Keep in mind, however, that it should address your current networking requirements and be flexible enough to accommodate change and growth in the future.

Here are important concepts regarding the structural foundation of network design:

- A building block is the unit that contains distributed network services and network intelligence. It consists of Layer 2 switches, Layer 3 routers (or integrated Layer 2 and Layer 3 devices), and sometimes distributed servers. The building block connects users to the network.

- A core block is the unit that transfers cross-campus traffic. It consists of high-speed Layer 2 switches.

- A server block is the unit that contains enterprise services and network intelligence. It consists of enterprise servers, Layer 2 switches, and Layer 3 routers (or integrated Layer 2 and Layer 3 devices).

- Based on administrative manageability and building size constraints, a recommended maximum number of nodes per building block is 1,500. Traffic patterns and technology limitations might restrict the number further, however.

- A recommendation for the total number of building and server blocks connecting to the core block is 20. This number is based on the routing protocol chosen for the network.

This chapter covers the following topics:

- Design requirements and characteristics

- Barebone blueprint

- Traffic patterns

- Designing redundancy

- Designing security

- Other network services

- Small barebone network design

CHAPTER 11

Design One—A Barebone Network

The barebone design presents a blueprint for designers who do not have many network requirements. It is appropriate for a stable campus LAN that is expected to grow or change very slowly over the next five years. This design is also appropriate for environments in which network downtime does not adversely impact users' productivity.

DESIGN REQUIREMENTS AND CHARACTERISTICS

The barebone blueprint assumes that the campus LAN has the following design requirements and characteristics:

- Small network size—no more than a few hundred nodes

- Minimizing cost is important

- Low network utilization

- Enterprise servers only

- No multimedia applications

- No bandwidth-intensive applications

- Minimal Internet connectivity

- Minimal redundancy

- Network downtime does not adversely impact users' performance

- No need to prioritize traffic

- Minimal security

- Slow growth rate

- Low user mobility

- No VLANs

BAREBONE BLUEPRINT

As we established in Chapter 10, "Understanding the Structural Foundation of Network Design," the campus network can be separated into network foundations to make constructing the blueprint easier. The fundamental campus LAN elements for the barebone design are shown in Figure 11–1 and described in the following sections.

Building Block

Only a single building block is used in the barebone design because the number of users is well below the 1,500 safety-zone level described in Chapter 10. The building block consists of Layer 2 switches in the wiring closet that connect users to the network. The number of switches needed depends on how many nodes need the connection and how many ports each switch has. The wiring closet merges into a single distribution switch for Layer 2 connectivity. The distribution switch is attached to a router for Layer 3 functionality.

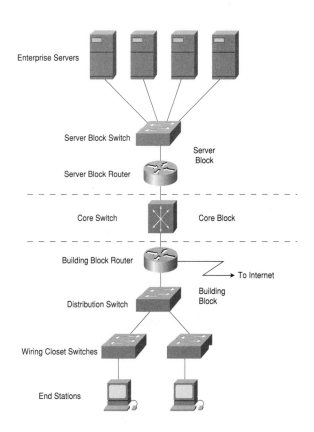

Figure 11–1
Fundamental barebone
network design.

Core Block

A single high-speed Layer 2 switch is used for the core block. Fast Ethernet is the lowest costing high-speed technology for this design.

Server Block

The server block contains the enterprise servers, which are typically located in the data center along with the core switch. In this barebone design, everyone shares the same servers (hence only enterprise servers are used), and no workgroup-specific applications reside on a distributed server.

The servers may connect to Layer 2 switches and a router, as depicted in Figure 11–1, but because minimizing cost is very important in this design, it's more likely that the servers connect directly to the core switch to save money. The server block routers and switches are thus eliminated. In this situation, the Layer 3 services that the server block router provides (broadcast domain protection) are traded off in exchange for lower cost. This alternative design is shown in Figure 11–2.

Figure 11–2

Alternative barebone server block design.

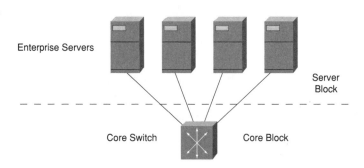

Connection to the Internet

The barebone design includes a single connection to the Internet, which is off of the router in the building block (refer to Figure 11–1). The router handles all of the traffic going out to and coming in from the Internet.

TRAFFIC PATTERNS

A small network usually requires between two and four broadcast domains, depending on the number of users and the server block design. We first show a design with only two broadcast domains and then show an alternative barebone design with four broadcast domains.

Figure 11–3 illustrates two broadcast domains. In the illustrated design, all users share a single broadcast domain. The second broadcast domain includes the enterprise servers and the core switch.

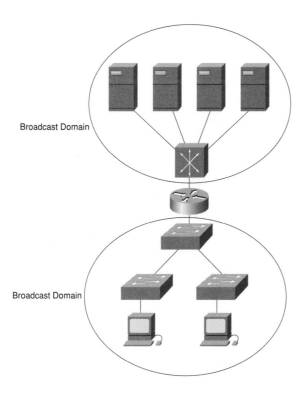

Figure 11–3

Two broadcast domains.

The number of user broadcast domains depends on the protocol and addressing scheme of the network. For example, if it is an IPX-only network, then a single broadcast domain of 300 nodes (the user's endstations, plus printers and network devices) is not a problem. If it is an IP-only network, then the number of nodes is restricted based on the class of the IP network addressing. A Class B network-addressing scheme can easily handle 300 nodes. For Class C however, the number of node connections is restricted to 253, by definition. Because many small networks use Class C, and they generally have fewer than 250 nodes to connect, a single Class C IP network address should work fine, resulting in a single broadcast domain. When a Class C network needs more than 250 node connections, however, the building block needs two Class C IP network addresses, which result in two broadcast domains.

Figure 11–3 shows that the servers are not separated from the core by a router; therefore, both the server block and the core block share a single broadcast domain.

The barebone design can also be structured to create four broadcast domains, as shown in Figure 11–4. The broadcast domains for the building block are subject to the same constraints regarding the addressing scheme and the number of node connections as they were previously. In this alternative design, however, each wiring closet switch supports a distinct broadcast domain instead of being combined into a single broadcast domain, as in the previous design.

Figure 11–4 also shows that the server block and the core block have separate broadcast domains. Because the servers interface to the core via a router and do not connect directly to the core switch, the router creates two unique broadcast domains. This design now has four broadcast domains—two for the building block, one for the core, and one for the server block.

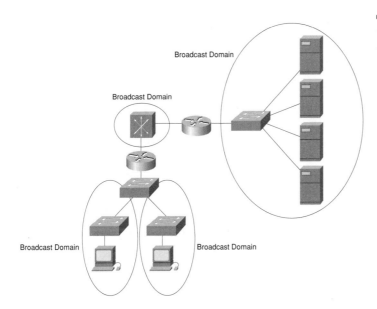

Figure 11–4
Four broadcast domains.

Broadcast Domain

Broadcast Domain

Broadcast Domain

Broadcast Domain

The traffic patterns for the barebone design are categorized as cross-campus traffic. Because only enterprise servers are used, all of the traffic to the servers from the clients crosses the core switch and at least one router. The same holds true for all of the traffic going from the servers to the clients. Because the Internet traffic proceeds through a router in the building block, it is cross-campus as well.

DESIGNING REDUNDANCY

Very little network redundancy is designed into the barebone network design. We make the assumption that network downtime does not adversely impact users' productivity. Most likely, there is some component redundancy, such as backup power supplies in the devices, but nothing more.

From a network-redundancy perspective, however, several single points of failure are worth consideration. The rest of this section explores the key points of failure that can occur when you use minimal redundancy in your network and describes the potential impact that failures can have on network operation. You can choose to increase redundancy with methods outlined in Chapter 6, "Network Reliability and Resiliency," in order to protect the network from failure. The choice is up to you.

In our barebone design, the wiring closet switches connect users to the campus network. If a wiring closet switch fails, as shown in Figure 11–5, all of the users connected to that wiring closet switch lose network operation. Users connected to the operating wiring closet switch can still use the network effectively.

Figure 11–5
Wiring closet switch failure.

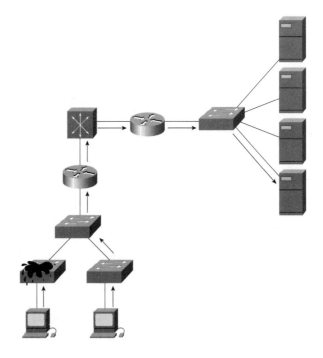

Another single point of failure is the distribution switch. The barebone design assumes that only one distribution switch is needed, and that it provides connection between the users and the servers. If this switch fails, as shown in Figure 11–6, then none of the users can reach the servers or the Internet. Basically, the network becomes nonoperational.

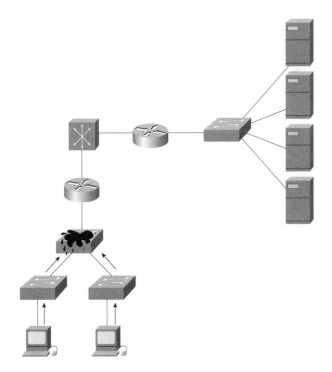

Figure 11–6
Distribution switch failure.

The same situation results if the building block router fails. Again, our blueprint shows only one router that connects users to the Internet and—via the core switch—to the servers. Should the router fail, users have no way to reach the servers or the Internet.

Some network connectivity exists if the server block router fails, as shown in Figure 11–7. Users lose connection to the servers but can still gain access to the Internet. Any traffic that goes straight out to the Internet instead of going to a server first, such as Web browsing, can still pass through the network. Most likely, however, e-mail stops while the server block router is down because e-mail traffic resides on an e-mail server in most cases. The e-mail server cannot send or receive any e-mail traffic from the users or the Internet if the server block router fails.

Figure 11–7
The server block router
fails.

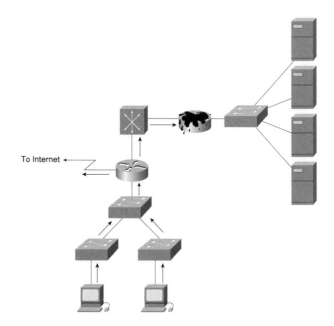

The same situation arises if the core switch or the server block switch fails. Internet connectivity is still available, but the servers are unreachable.

Should one of the servers fail, users can access the other servers and some network operation can still occur.

Because most of the traffic in this network is cross-campus traffic, many failures can occur that disrupt network operation and impact network performance. In the case of this barebone network, the network designer has made the assumption that network downtime does not adversely impact users' productivity. As the network changes and users begin to use it more, higher levels of redundancy need to be added into the network.

DESIGNING MOBILITY

The barebone network design assumes that there is minimal user mobility on the campus. If the network is running only IPX or AppleTalk, then user mobility is not an issue. If the network is running IP, however, the issue of static addressing, as discussed in Chapter 9, "Designing for Change and Growth," may come into effect. Issues include users' needing to re-address their workstations with a new IP address and a new IP default gateway address when they move.

When the building block consists of a single broadcast domain (a single IP subnet), users can move around their assigned building block and still maintain the same IP address and IP default gateway. Figure 11–8 displays this situation.

Because there is only a single subnet in the building block, the distribution switch has a single connection to the router. Therefore, the IP default gateway for all of the users in the building block is the same. In Figure 11–8, it is 150.150.1.1. Wherever the users move, they will still use 150.150.1.1 as the IP default gateway. A user can continue to use the same IP address as well, which is shown as 150.150.1.120 in Figure 11–8.

If there are two broadcast domains in the building block (two IP subnets), users may have to re-address their workstations when they move. Figure 11–9 shows this situation.

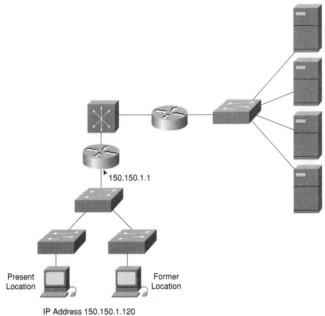

Figure 11–8
A user moves within the
same subnet.

If there are two subnets in a building block, the distribution switch has two connections to the router, with each connection supporting a subnet. If users move from one subnet to another, they cannot keep the same IP address and IP default gateway. In Figure 11–9, the user needs to change the IP default gateway from 150.150.1.1 to 150.150.2.1 and needs to obtain a new IP address that is part of the 150.150.2.0 subnet (in this case, 150.150.2.200).

The users probably don't know that they need to re-address their workstations until they try to connect to the network and don't succeed. As users begin to move around more often, static IP addressing becomes less scalable. If users do not move around, or if there is only a single subnet, then static IP addressing is a scalable solution.

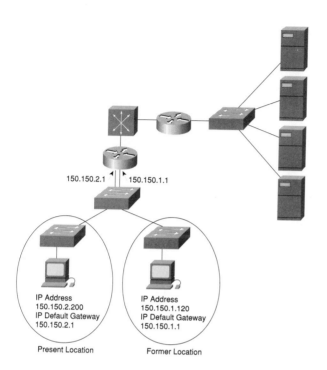

Figure 11–9
A user moves to a different subnet.

150.150.2.1   150.150.1.1

IP Address
150.150.2.200
IP Default Gateway
150.150.2.1

IP Address
150.150.1.120
IP Default Gateway
150.150.1.1

Present Location

Former Location

DESIGNING SECURITY

In the barebone network design, security is minimal. Everyone uses the enterprise servers, so there is no need to employ a filtering mechanism for users. If the network administrator is not worried about outsiders gaining access to the network devices, a network logon security program does not need to be installed.

For administrative purposes, a user name/password login to the servers should be employed. Using this login allows the servers to dictate what directories the user can access. For example, John Smith is a user, but he should not be able to become a superuser and thus access all of the directories on the server.

Keep in mind that minimal security makes it fairly easy for outsiders to gain access to the enterprise servers. Only one user name/password needs to be known to get into the servers because a network logon does not exist. And it's even easier to gain access to the network devices. Without security, outsiders can change configurations and direct the data to go to their own workstations first instead of going to the intended device.

It is important for the network designer to understand the potential security breaches in this network and to feel comfortable with the level of security that resides on the servers and the network devices.

OTHER NETWORK SERVICES

The barebone network typically does not have high network use. Only basic applications, such as word processing applications, database tools, and utilities are run. We purposely have not included items discussed in previous chapters, such as multimedia, traffic priorities, and VLAN implementation, because these network services are not required.

Multimedia applications are not used in a barebone network, and the low level of traffic does not require prioritization at this point. Because the number of users is low, there is no need to implement VLANs. These network services are discussed in the next chapter when we describe the scalable network design.

SMALL BAREBONE NETWORK DESIGN

In very small networks, even the barebone design is overly complex. For networks that have fewer than 50–100 users, a more simplified network design may suffice. All of the characteristics of the barebone design still apply, but the number of network devices and how they are organized changes. Figure 11–10 shows an example of a very small barebone network.

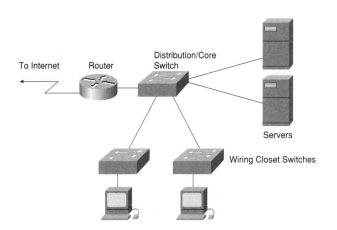

Figure 11–10
Small barebone network design.

In this design, the building block is all that is needed. A unique core switch is not used, and the enterprise servers, which are moved down into the building block, connect to the distribution switch. There is only one broadcast domain (one IP subnet), so all of the users can access the servers. The distribution switch acts as the core switch in this design. The router is used to connect to the Internet, not to separate broadcast domains.

As this network grows, it will migrate to look like the barebone network, with a separate core block and server block.

SUMMARY

The barebone blueprint provides a viable design for small and owner/operator businesses because it's simple to implement and easy to use. Managing the network is straightforward because there are not many network devices. If a network device is misbehaving, it is easy to discover which one it is so that you can correct the problem. Using a network management software package allows the network administrator to manage the network devices for problems, as well as to monitor traffic use during peak times, slow times, and so forth. If the company is growing slowly, then this design will meet bandwidth needs now and in the future. If the need for more network services arises, such as multimedia or higher security, then those services can be added into the existing equipment, thereby keeping cost down and making it optional whether to obtain new equipment.

If your network meets the criteria for a barebone design, keep in mind the following as you plan and implement it:

- Server blocks in a barebone network may be able to connect directly to the core block, saving the cost of some switches and routers.

- Be aware of any single points of failure that can cripple the network and determine whether you need to increase redundancy to avoid them.

- Although security needs are probably minimal, consider whether there is a danger of outsiders gaining access to network devices. If so, a network logon security program is probably a good idea.

- An even simpler design than the barebone design may suffice for very small networks. Such a network may require just a building block and no other foundation units.

This chapter covers the following topics:

- Design requirements and characteristics

- Scalable blueprint

- Traffic patterns

- Designing redundancy

- Addressing multimedia

- Designing security

- Designing mobility

- Building VLANs

- Setting traffic priorities

CHAPTER 12

Design Two—A Scalable Network

The scalable design presents a blueprint for designers who have a dynamic network—one that has a solid base, yet needs to be flexible enough to accommodate moderate growth and change. It is appropriate for networks in which unexpected network downtime adversely impacts the business and users' performance, and for a campus LAN that is expected to grow or change at a moderate rate over the next five years.

DESIGN REQUIREMENTS AND CHARACTERISTICS

The scalable blueprint assumes that the campus LAN has the following design requirements and characteristics:

- Medium to large network size (from 300 up to 15,000 nodes)

- Centralized and distributed servers

- Some bandwidth-intensive applications, including multimedia

- Internet/wide-area connectivity

- Redundancy needed in network

- Downtime will impact users' performance

- Minimum traffic priority needed

- Security needed on the network

- Moderate growth rate

- Mobility occurs

- VLANs can be implemented

Your network does not need to have all of these design characteristics to fit into the scalable blueprint. The list is meant as a guideline to help network designers determine whether this is the correct blueprint to use as a base.

SCALABLE BLUEPRINT

As we established in Chapter 10, "Understanding the Structural Foundation of Network Design," the campus network can be separated into network foundations to make constructing the blueprint easier. The fundamental campus elements for the scalable design are shown in Figure 12–1 and are described in the sections that follow.

Building Block

In the scalable network, there often is more than one building block, either because of the number of users or because there is more than one physical building on the campus. Each building block uses Layer 2 switches in the wiring closet to connect users. The number of wiring closet switches used depends on the number of users that are in the building block. The wiring closet merges into two distribution switches for Layer 2 connectivity. The distributed servers connect directly to the distribution switch. The distribution switches are attached to two routers for Layer 3 functionality.

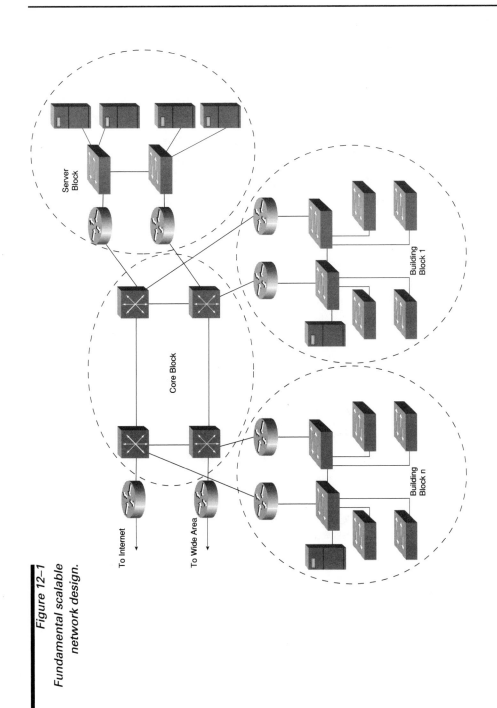

Figure 12–1
Fundamental scalable network design.

Core Block

The core block for a scalable network consists of at least two high-speed Layer 2 switches. Figure 12–1 shows the design with four switches, so we can more readily point out the core block redundancy options. Fast Ethernet, Gigabit Ethernet, and ATM are viable high-speed technologies in the core. FDDI is not recommended because shared FDDI does not typically have enough bandwidth to support the traffic in the scalable network design, and switched FDDI does not allow an easy migration path for higher-speed technologies as they develop in the future.

Server Block

The server block for a scalable network contains the enterprise servers, which typically are located in the data center. The servers connect to Layer 2 switches, which then connect to two routers. The number of switches needed in any given scalable network is dependent on the number of enterprise servers it supports. Two routers are used for redundancy, which we will discuss in later sections of this chapter. No more than two routers are needed in the server block because each switch connects to a unique interface on the same router. The distributed servers are not located in the server block; they reside in the same building block as the users they support.

Connection to the Internet

The scalable network design includes connections to the Internet and the wide area via routers. Most likely, there are remote offices that connect to the campus across the wide area, and several connections to the Internet are also desired.

The routers that connect to the wide area and Internet are dedicated routers that attach to the core. By dedicated routers, we mean that the routers are not part of a building block with users; instead, they are specifically used for the traffic coming in from and going out to the wide area and Internet. The purpose of this setup is to help keep WAN and Internet traffic separate from the campus traffic. Routers that support WAN and Internet connections also need to run different network services (and possibly different routing protocols) than the campus routers do. It makes better design sense, therefore, to use separate devices to handle the two distinct network areas.

TRAFFIC PATTERNS

The scalable network design usually has several broadcast domains. Because the number of users can range from a few hundred to several thousand, it's hard to predict how many are required. However, since this design is scalable and meant to be used as a blueprint, we can start with one building block, core block, and server block and then use a copy-and-paste method to represent additional blocks as needed.

Broadcast Domains in the Server Block

Figure 12–2 shows the scalable design with a single building block, core block, and server block. The server block broadcast domain is circled.

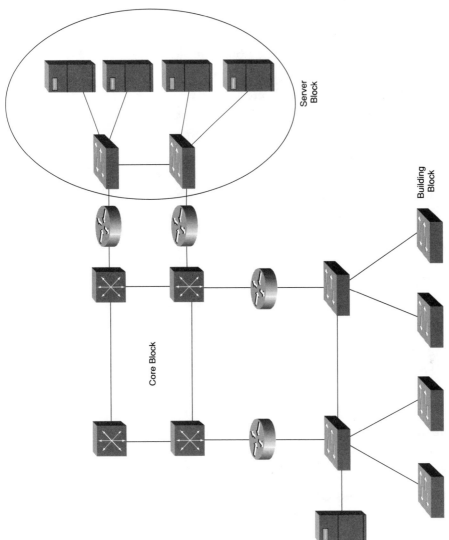

Figure 12-2
Server block broadcast
domain.

The server block contains one broadcast domain. Because our example network contains a limited number of enterprise servers, a single subnet or broadcast domain is sufficient. The domain includes the Layer 2 switches to which the servers are attached.

Many medium-to-large networks have anywhere from 20 to 300 enterprise servers, and may benefit by having two broadcast domains or subnets in the server block. Keep in mind that having all the enterprise servers in a single subnet allows the possibility for a single point of failure, which can bring down the entire server block. Creating additional broadcast domains in the server block provides some protection: If one broadcast domain fails, only some applications become inaccessible, while those on the other domains still function. Ultimately, the network designer must decide how many servers should reside on the same subnet.

Broadcast Domains in the Core Block

The core block typically supports one or two broadcast domains, depending on how you want to structure the router connections.

If you want a single broadcast domain in the core, each router has a single connection to the core block, as shown in Figure 12–3. Each router sends all the data over the single link to the core block, and all router connections are part of the same core broadcast domain.

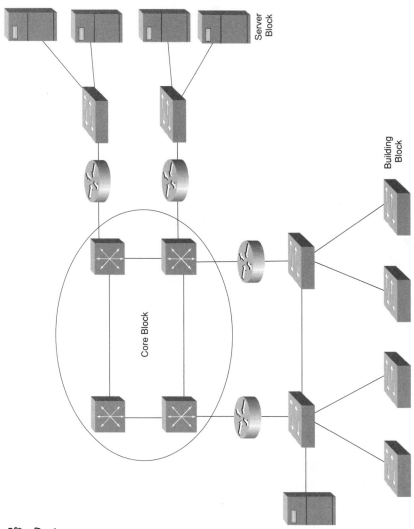

Figure 12–3
Single broadcast domain
in the core block.

If you want to set up *parallelism* (also known as *data load sharing*), as described in Chapter 6, "Network Reliability and Resiliency," the connections need to be different. In this case, each router has two connections to the core block, and there are two subnets that connect into the core. Each subnet is a different broadcast domain. Figure 12–4 shows this situation. To use both links of a router to send traffic across the core, each link must be on a different subnet (broadcast domain).

Notice in Figure 12–4 that the two broadcast domains overlap. To provide data load sharing, each core switch supports both broadcast domains and must be able to pass traffic on both subnets. Each connection from the routers supports a single broadcast domain (subnet).

Broadcast Domains in the Building Block

Each building block usually has more than one broadcast domain, which can be structured in a variety of ways. We'll begin by assuming that there are 800 users in the building block and define the broadcast domains as indicated by the circled areas in Figure 12–5.

A building on this campus has four floors and there are 200 users per floor. Each floor of 200 users can represent a single broadcast domain, thereby making four broadcast domains in this building block. (Keep in mind that this is only one example. There are several ways that the broadcast domains can be broken up in the building block, depending on the actual layout of your buildings and network connections in your network.

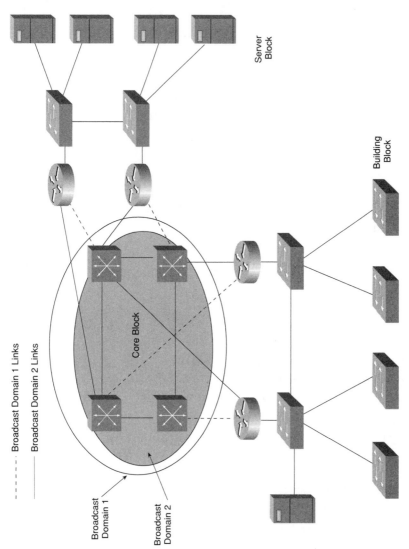

Figure 12–4
Two broadcast domains
in the core block.

Broadcast Domain 1 Links
Broadcast Domain 2 Links

Broadcast Domain 1

Broadcast Domain 2

Core Block

Server Block

Building Block

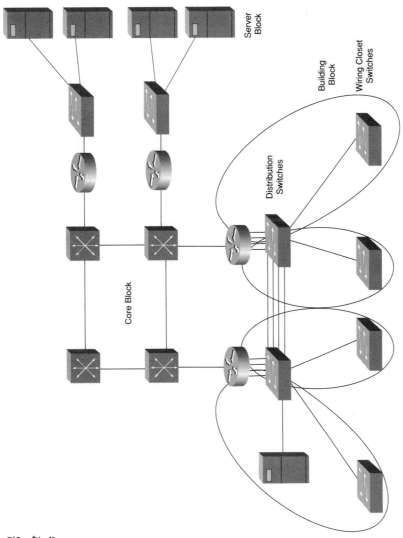

Figure 12-5
Building block broadcast
domains

The four subnets connect to the distribution switches, creating four physical connections to each of the routers, one connection for each subnet, and possibly four connections between the distribution switches, depending on the vendor's implementation. (As an option, you can use VLANs to reduce the number of physical connections from the distribution switches to the routers and between the distribution switches; this option is described later in this chapter.) Both distribution switches support all four broadcast domains, as do the core switches.

The distributed servers can connect to either the distribution switch or a wiring closet switch, depending on the users it supports. For example, if the distributed server is supporting a single subnet of users, and one wiring closet switch supports that subnet, then it makes sense to connect the distributed server to the wiring closet switch.

If, however, several wiring closet switches support the subnet, then it may make more sense to connect the distributed server to the distribution switch. This type of connection is ideal in this situation because the distribution switch is the common point of connection for the broadcast domain.

Another situation arises if the distributed server is supporting multiple subnets or VLANs. In this case, the distributed server should connect to the distribution switch so that each subnet or VLAN can have equal access to it, as shown in Figure 12–5.

If distributed servers are used effectively, there are dedicated distributed servers in each subnet and the local traffic is spread across the building block. As we discussed in Chapter 2, "Server Placement," distributed servers create less traffic across the routers and core, resulting in efficient network performance.

No matter which way you set up your broadcast domains, the traffic patterns in the scalable design are a mix of local and cross-campus traffic. The more distributed servers there are in the building block, the more local traffic there will be on the network. The traffic going to and from the enterprise servers, as well as to and from the Internet, will still be classified as cross-campus.

DESIGNING REDUNDANCY

The scalable design assumes that all portions of the network need to operate correctly during business hours. If a portion of the network goes down, the company loses important functions and user productivity suffers. For this design, we also make the following assumptions:

- The network requires operation for at least two shifts.

- Enterprise servers need to be up 24 hours a day.

- Network downtime needs to be scheduled on the weekends.

Given these parameters, redundancy should begin at the hardware level, especially for critical devices such as the enterprise servers. In addition, some form of network link and data path redundancy, as well as software redundancy, assure resiliency and limit network downtime.

Building Block Redundancy

At the building block level, there are two ways to achieve link and data path redundancy. The first redundancy scheme, as shown in Figure 12–6, consists of redundant links that connect each wiring closet switch to both of the distribution switches. This scheme uses the Spanning Tree Protocol, which is typically "on" by default on the switches.

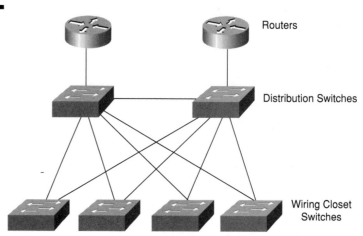

Routers

Distribution Switches

Wiring Closet Switches

You have several options for the use of these wiring closet links. The first method uses one distribution switch as the primary switch and the other distribution switch as the backup switch (*hot standby*) for all the traffic. The backup switch isn't used until a link to the primary switch fails or until the primary switch itself fails. In Figure 12–7, Link 1 carries the traffic and Link 2 stays in standby mode. Distribution Switch A forwards all the traffic and Distribution Switch B is in standby mode.

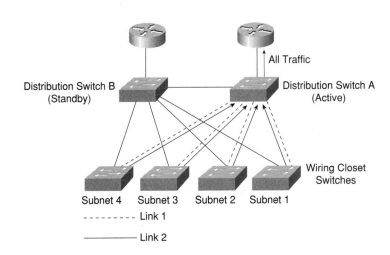

Figure 12–7
*Primary (active) switch and
backup (standby) switch.*

The alternative method is to divide the traffic up so that some traffic goes across to one distribution switch and some traffic goes to the other distribution switch. Traffic in Subnets 1 and 2 can go to one distribution switch, and traffic in Subnets 3 and 4 can go to the other distribution switch.

In Figure 12–8, Subnets 1 and 2 traffic go across Link 1 to Distribution Switch A, and Subnet 3 and 4 traffic go across Link 2 to Distribution Switch B. Both distribution switches forward traffic.

The distribution switch that forwards Subnets 1 and 2 traffic can be the backup switch for the wiring closet traffic in Subnets 3 and 4, and vice versa. This method allows both distribution switches to forward traffic instead of one staying idle.

The connection between the two distribution switches is used in case of router failure. If one of the routers fails, then the traffic will cross over to the other distribution switch and go through the operating router.

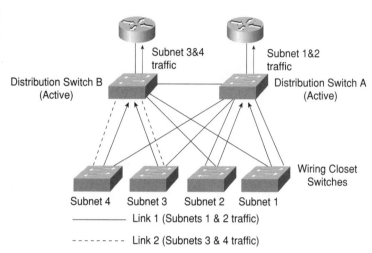

Figure 12–8
Both distribution switches active.

For added insurance against network downtime, you can run the Hot Standby Routing Protocol (HSRP) on the routers. Recall from Chapter 6 that HSRP helps to maintain network operation by having two routers share the same virtual IP and MAC addresses. If the active HSRP router or the link to the active HSRP router fails, the backup HSRP router becomes active. The protocol prevents endstations that have an IP default gateway configured (either statically or via DHCP) from needing to be reconfigured in the event of a failure.

The second building block redundancy scheme, shown in Figure 12–9, also places redundancy at the distribution switch. There is no built-in redundancy from the wiring closets themselves, however.

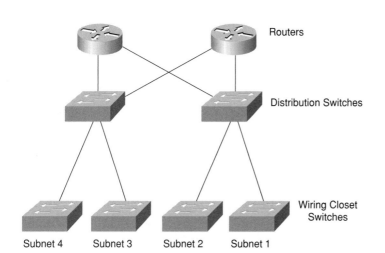

Figure 12–9
Redundancy at the
distribution switch.

Redundancy at the distribution switches is implemented by
setting up redundant links between the distribution switches
and routers, and allowing all of these links to carry traffic. As
shown in Figure 12–10, Distribution Switch A supports Subnets 1 and 2, and connects to both Routers A and B. Distribution Switch B supports Subnets 3 and 4, and also connects
to both Routers A and B.

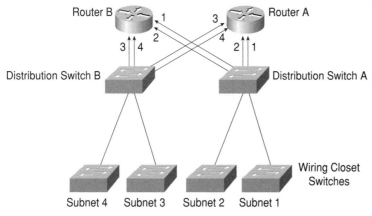

Figure 12–10
Distribution switches
forwarding traffic.

Implicit in this scheme is the network designer's decision that it is acceptable for multiple wiring closets and subnets to lose connectivity in the event of a distribution switch failure.

For added insurance in this design situation, HSRP can also be used at the routers to avoid having to reconfigure the IP default gateway of endstations in case of router failure.

The redundancy method illustrated in Figure 12–10 does not work if there is only one subnet (broadcast domain) in the building block. In this case, all the distribution switches support the same singular subnet. And since the routers cannot have the same subnet on two different interfaces, the distribution switches cannot connect to both routers.

Core Block Redundancy

Redundancy in the core consists of having more than one core switch and placing the connections so that the building block routers connect to different core switches, as shown in Figure 12–11.

Figure 12–11
Core redundancy.

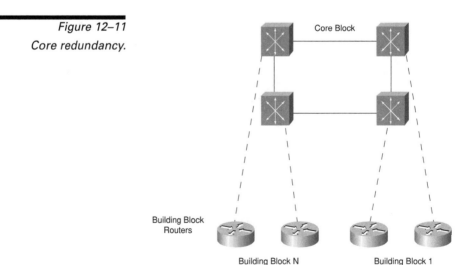

Each building block router is connected to a different core switch, so that if one core switch fails, communication across the core can still occur for subnets connected to the functioning core switches. Figure 12–11 shows single connections from each router to the core. If each router has two connections to the core switches (two broadcast domains in the core), you should make each router connection go to a different core switch, as shown in Figure 12–12.

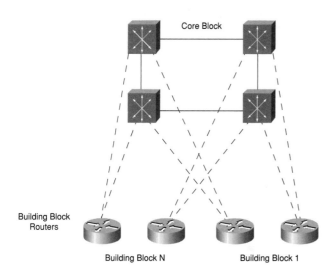

Core Block

Building Block Routers

Building Block N   Building Block 1

Figure 12–12
Core redundancy with two broadcast domains.

Server Block Redundancy

Redundancy in the server block is similar to redundancy in the building block. If there is only a single subnet, then the switches connect to each other and each switch connects to one of the routers, as shown in Figure 12–13.

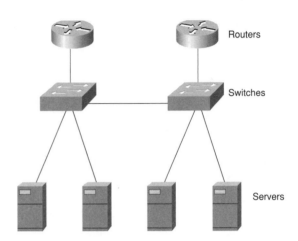

Figure 12–13
Server block redundancy with one subnet.

Or, if there are two subnets in the server block, then each switch supports one subnet. The switches then connect to both routers, as shown in Figure 12–14.

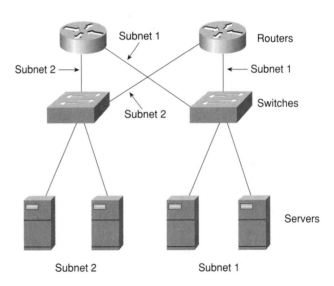

Figure 12–14
Server block redundancy with two subnets.

Redundancy throughout the network foundation—the building block, core block, and server block—should keep the network operating with minimal downtime. An important step in designing redundancy is to assume the failure of a specific device or devices in the network, and then evaluate how efficient the network redundancy implementation is in allowing the network to continue operating normally. In the next section, we explore a variety of failure scenarios and describe the potential impact they can have on network operation.

Potential Points of Network Failure

Before we show failures on the network, we'll show the traffic pattern in a healthy network environment, which is illustrated in Figure 12–15.

Figure 12–15 shows two building blocks, one with wiring closet switch redundancy (Building Block 1) and one with distribution switch redundancy (Building Block 2). Building Block 1 is using both switches to forward traffic.

The example network also has two server blocks, one with a single broadcast domain (Server Block 1) and one with two broadcast domains (Server Block 2). Most networks have a single server block; two are shown in this example so that we can compare and contrast the redundancy opportunities discussed so far. The core is shown using a single broadcast domain (single router connections to the core) for simplicity in this illustration.

Now let's see how failures affect the data path of the network. Figure 12–16 shows a wiring closet switch failure.

In Building Blocks 1 and 2, the users who are connected to the failed wiring closet switch lose connectivity to the network. If any distributed servers are connected to the failed wiring closet switch, the users also lose connectivity to those distributed servers.

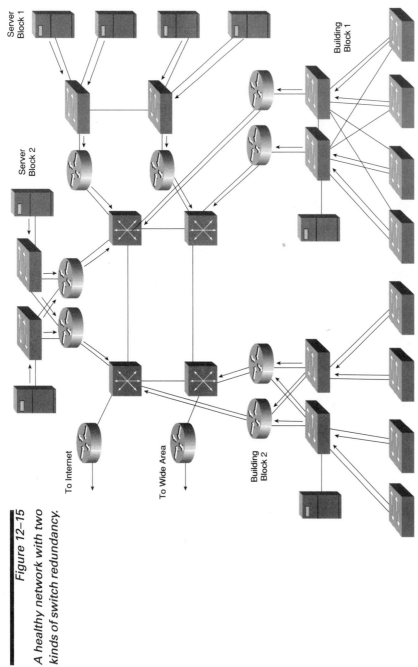

Figure 12–15
A healthy network with two kinds of switch redundancy.

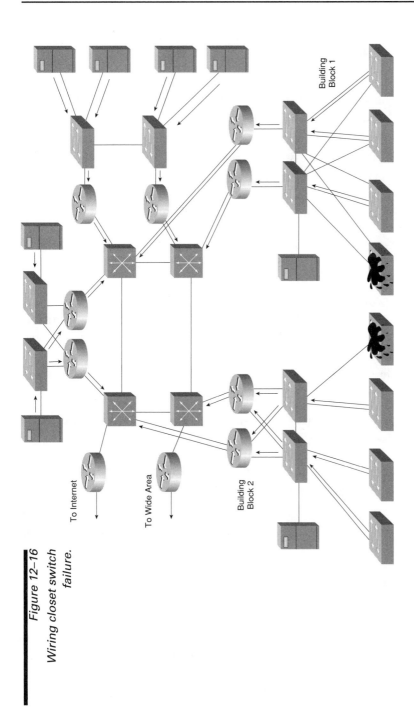

Figure 12–16
Wiring closet switch failure.

Figure 12–17 shows a distribution switch failure and a switch failure in the server block.

In Building Block 1, none of the users lose connectivity to the network. Spanning Tree redirects the traffic from Distribution Switch B to Distribution Switch A. Users do, however, lose connection to the distributed server in Building Block 1 because the server is directly connected to the failed Distribution Switch B. Users also lose access to the enterprise servers connected to the failed distribution switches in Server Blocks 1 and 2.

In Building Block 2, the users connected to failed Distribution Switch C lose connectivity to the network and all resources. Notice that the wiring closet switches do not connect to both distribution switches, so Spanning Tree cannot redirect the traffic. Users connected to the operating distribution switch maintain connectivity and can also access the distributed server. All users, however, lose access to the enterprise servers that are connected to the failed distribution switches in Server Blocks 1 and 2.

Figure 12–18 shows a router failure; in this situation, none of the users lose connectivity to the network.

For Building Block 1, Distribution Switch A detects the failed link to Router A and redirects the traffic over Distribution Switch B to Router B. In Building Block 2, Distribution Switch C detects Router C's failure and sends the traffic directly to Router D.

The distribution switches in the server blocks behave in the same manner; the failed link to the router is detected and the traffic is redirected. All of the enterprise servers and distributed servers remain operational. Because this network also has HSRP, it automatically brings up the HSRP standby router so that users do not have to reconfigure their stations with a new IP default gateway address.

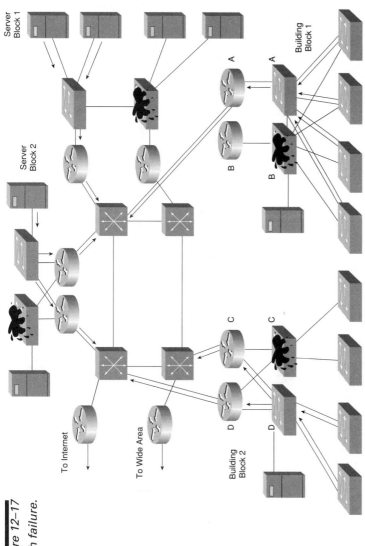

Figure 12-17
Distribution switch failure.

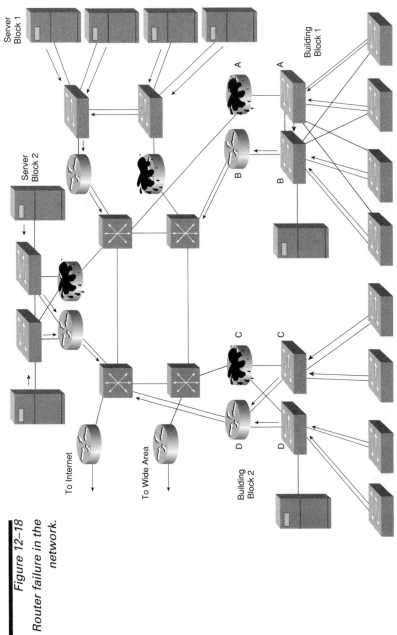

Figure 12–18
Router failure in the network.

We next need to see the impact of a core switch failure. Figure 12–19 shows a single core switch failure and Figure 12–20 shows two core switches failing. Both figures show a single broadcast domain in the core. Once we explore this scenario, we'll show these same failures using two broadcast domains in the core.

As Figure 12–19 shows, there is no loss of connectivity due to one core switch failing—a data path exists through an operating core switch. The traffic within Building Block 1 is redirected through Router A to reach the operating core switch instead of going through Router B. The traffic in Building Block 2 does not need to be redirected, and travels as it normally does in a healthy network.

When two core switches fail, as shown in Figure 12–20, some connections are lost. In this example, Building Block 1 has not lost connectivity to the campus because the traffic can be rerouted. It has, however, lost connection to the WAN and Internet.

The illustration also shows that Building Block 2 has lost connectivity through the core. Building Block 2 cannot gain access to the enterprise servers because Router D is connected to the failed core switch. Although Router C can connect to an operating core switch, the core switch can send traffic to the WAN only; no traffic can be sent through the campus because failed core switches surround the operating core switch.

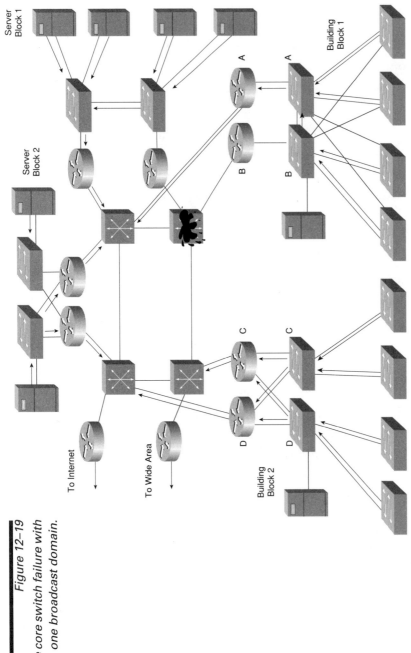

Figure 12-19
One core switch failure with one broadcast domain.

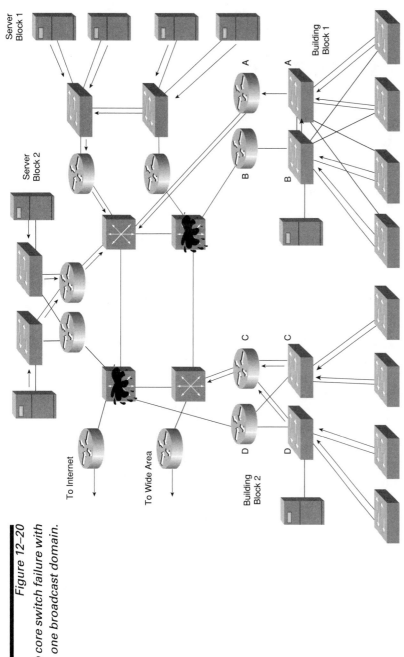

Figure 12–20
Two core switch failure with
one broadcast domain.

The impact on the network can be different if a core switch or combination of switches other than the ones indicated in Figure 12–19 and Figure 12–20 fails. As you've probably noticed, building blocks may or may not lose connectivity to the campus network, depending on which core switch fails. Here again, a solid scalable design identifies which part of the campus core should be protected from failure as much as possible. Then it sets in motion a scheme to ensure that critical core operations have sufficient backup redundancy to allow important campus functions to remain operational should a core switch failure occur.

The previous examples assumed one broadcast domain for the core. We'll now look at the same core switch failures, but allow multiple router connections (two broadcast domains). For simplicity's sake, we will only look at Building Block 2, which previously lost connection to the enterprise servers due to a failure in the core (refer to Figure 12–20). Figure 12–21 shows the new design that has two broadcast domains in the core.

As you can see, having multiple connections to the core switches from the routers allows Building Block 2 users to reach the enterprise servers. This is possible because traffic goes through Router C to the operating core switch, then on to the enterprise servers.

As a final note, we'll expand this discussion and look at multiple failures in the network—a worst-case scenario. Figure 12–22 combines all the failures that we have just described and illustrated in Figure 12–16 through 12–21.

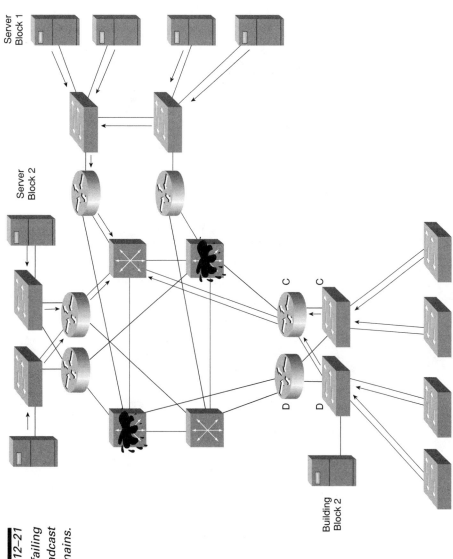

Figure 12–21
Two core switches failing
with two broadcast
domains.

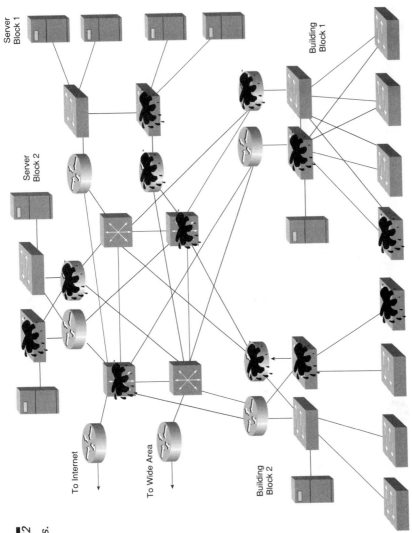

Figure 12–22
Multiple device failures.

In this worst-case scenario, all of the users in Building Blocks 1 and 2 lose connectivity to the core, and therefore cannot access the server block. A limited number of users in Building Block 2 can access the WAN, but no connections to campus resources exist. Although a lot of redundancy exists in this network design (duplicate links, Spanning Tree, HSRP for the routers, and so forth), you can see that it's not foolproof.

It is important for the network designer to determine which network failures the network can tolerate without losing critical user or server connectivity. Essentially, the design must be based on an understanding of how many failures the network can withstand before becoming inoperable and should also include as much protection as possible for important business operations.

ADDRESSING MULTIMEDIA

The scalable design assumes that multimedia applications are allowed on the network. As described in Chapter 4, "Factoring in Multimedia Traffic," these applications are a mix of text, images, sounds, and motion traveling over the network. Because of their diversity and potential for high bandwidth use, special functions must be implemented on the devices to allow multimedia applications to work effectively across the campus.

The most important multimedia consideration is the traffic characteristics. Most likely, multimedia is being sent as multicast traffic so that several users can take advantage of the application (such as video conferencing, distance learning, or real-time imaging). In this case, IGMP must be set up on the multimedia server, the routers, and on the receiving endstations. In addition, the routers need a multicast routing protocol (such as MOSPF, DVMRP, PIM dense-mode, or PIM sparse-mode) to move multimedia traffic between the servers and endstations.

The exception to these requirements is when multimedia is sent as unicast traffic (such as a two-way video conferencing application, or some shared whiteboard applications). In this case, IGMP may still be needed on the devices, but a specific multicast routing protocol is not necessary on the routers. The multimedia traffic in this situation is handled like any other unicast traffic on the network (e-mail, file transfers, or Web browsing)—it goes to the single endstation that it is meant for.

In our scalable design, we provide two multimedia network scenarios; both of them are based on multicast traffic because this traffic requires multicast routing on the network. The first scenario uses DVMRP, which can be replaced with PIM dense-mode (remember from Chapter 4 that DVMRP and PIM dense-mode behave similarly in the network). Our second scenario for multimedia design uses PIM sparse-mode.

No matter which routing protocol you use, keep in mind that multicast traffic is a point-to-multipoint operation and that it has a tendency to flood packets onto the network. The goal in multimedia network design is to use as little bandwidth as possible in terms of multicast flooding. The fewer devices that are flooded by multicast packets, the higher the network performance, resulting in more efficient multimedia application transfer. The scenarios we present try to limit this inherent flooding characteristic.

The first step in designing for multimedia is to determine where the multimedia servers are placed in the network. In most cases, the multimedia servers should reside in the server block and act as enterprise servers. Usually, more than one specific group uses any given multimedia application, so distributed multimedia servers do not make sense. However, if there are multimedia applications that only a specific group use, then putting those applications on the appropriate distributed server is effective.

Once the multimedia server is in place, we next need to configure DVMRP on the appropriate network devices. This first network scenario is illustrated in Figure 12–23, and shows that all the routers in the campus need to have DVMRP configured on them. If the routers in the server block are not configured, the multimedia applications go nowhere. If the routers in the building block are not configured, they cannot forward the multicast traffic to the requesting endstations.

The path that the multicast traffic takes after DVMRP is configured is also shown in Figure 12–23. Several requesting endstations in Building Block 2 send their IGMP Joins to the multimedia server and the multimedia server responds by sending out the multicast traffic. DVMRP floods the traffic everywhere. The router in the server block sends the multicast traffic into the core and the core sends it out all of its ports.

When the routers in the building blocks receive the multicast traffic, they send the traffic out to the distribution switches. The distribution switches in turn flood the traffic to all of the wiring closet switches and the traffic eventually reaches all of the endstations.

As shown in Figure 12–23, when the routers in Building Block 1 learn that there are no receivers for this application, they prune the traffic. Also recall that DVMRP continually checks for new members, thereby forcing the router to routinely flood the traffic in case a station has joined the group, and then prunes back when none are found.

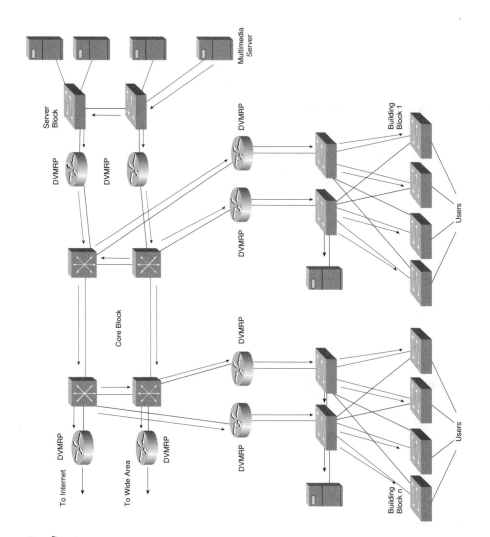

Figure 12–23
DVMRP configuration and multimedia traffic pattern.

Because there are endstations that want the application in Building Block 2, the routers there will continue to flood the multicast traffic. If there is no filtering or dynamic multicast registration configured on the switches, then the switches continue to send the multicast packets to all of the endstations. With some form of multicast registration enabled, the switch sends the multicast traffic only to the endstations that use the application.

This scenario shows one way of supporting multicast applications in the scalable network. DVMRP/PIM dense-mode works best when many users on the campus use the same multimedia application (such as a company-wide meeting broadcast over the network) because the routers do not need to prune the multicast traffic in many places.

The next scenario for multimedia design uses PIM sparse-mode as the routing protocol to reduce multimedia flooding on the network. With PIM sparse-mode, we set up a Rendezvous point so that all IGMP registrations go to the Rendezvous point, and all the initial video streams also go to the Rendezvous point instead of flooding throughout the network. Figure 12–24 shows a designated Rendezvous point router on the network.

Our design shows a Rendezvous point on the building block router. Placed on this router instead of the server block router, PIM sparse-mode instructs the server block routers to send out the multimedia multicast traffic as unicasts to the Rendezvous point. This prevents multicast flooding in the core block. The core switches simply forward the unicast packets to the Rendezvous point router.

Figure 12–25 shows the initial data paths for two endstations that join the same multimedia group using PIM sparse-mode.

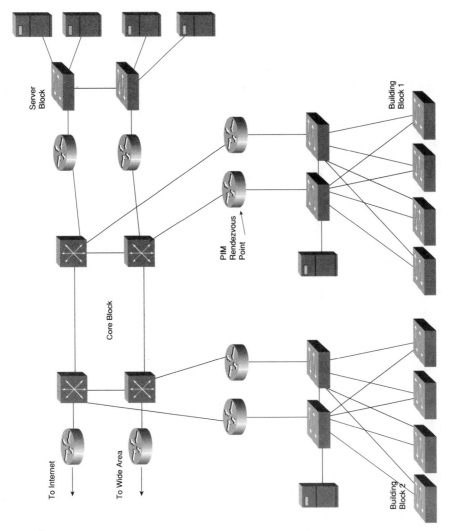

Figure 12–24
Rendezvous point router
in the scalable network.

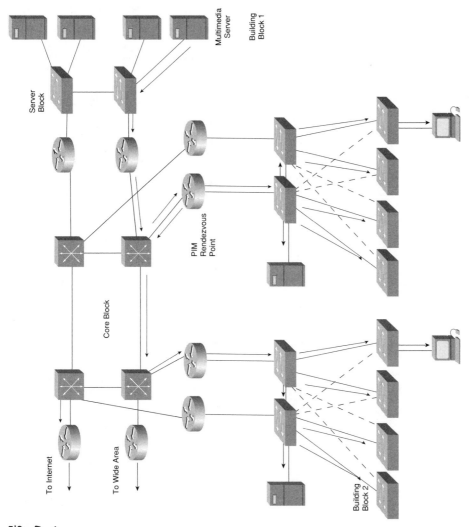

Figure 12–25
Initial multicast data path
using PIM sparse-mode.

After the endstations send their IGMP Joins to the multimedia server, the multimedia server sends the multicast traffic out to the network. The router in the server block knows that the traffic needs to go to the Rendezvous point first, so it sends the traffic, in the form of a unicast, to the Rendezvous point router. The Rendezvous point router then sends the traffic out the interfaces that support the two requesting endstations. For Building Block 1, the multimedia traffic reaches the endstation through the distribution and wiring closet switches. These switches flood the multicast packet to all endstations if there is no filtering or multicast registration set up, similar to the DVMRP design.

The Rendezvous point router also sends the traffic via the core to the router in Building Block 2 because an endstation in that building block joins the same multimedia application. In turn, the router sends the multicast traffic to the endstation through the distribution and wiring closet switches, as is done in Building Block 1.

After this initial path successfully forwards the data, PIM sparse-mode optimizes the data path, as shown in Figure 12–26.

The router in the server block now sends the multimedia traffic directly to the router in Building Block 2 to reach the endstation in Building Block 2, instead of going through the Rendezvous point router in Building Block 1. The path from the video server to the endstation in Building Block 1 is already optimized, so it does not change.

PIM sparse-mode works best when there are a small number of users on the campus using the same multimedia application (such as a video conference with the executive officers), because it does not routinely flood the network with multicast traffic.

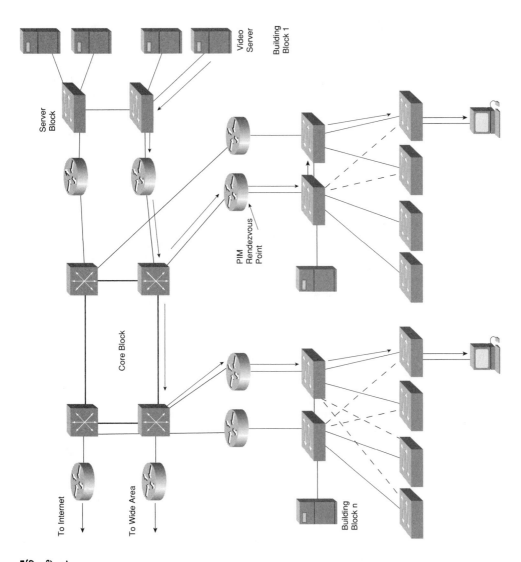

Figure 12–26
PIM sparse-mode
optimized data path.

DESIGNING SECURITY

The scalable design contains several levels of network security to prevent unauthorized access. First, the network is configured with user authentication. A network logon is required that contains a valid username and password to gain access to the campus. Second, each server is configured with user login security, also in the form of a username/password, so that only known users who enter valid passwords are allowed access to the servers.

The scalable design further augments network protection by placing security on the network infrastructure. Configuring access lists on the routers does this. As we discussed in Chapter 8, "Addressing Security Issues," implementing access lists on the routers allows the network itself to become another gate that users must pass through before connecting to servers. Figure 12–27 shows where we have placed access lists on the network.

The routers in the server block use the access lists to prevent unauthorized users from gaining access to the enterprise servers. Access lists on the routers in the building blocks allow only specific users to access the distributed servers. To prevent outside users from freely accessing devices on the network, access lists are also placed on the routers that connect the Internet and WAN to the campus.

Collectively, the security measures described for this blueprint provide an adequate amount of protection. As an additional measure of security, route authentication can be configured on the routers so that only valid paths are used within the network. Route authentication can ensure that other devices are not successful if they try to impersonate the default gateway in order to grab data from the network. And if some of the employees are working with classified or sensitive data, consider using one of the encryption methods described in Chapter 8.

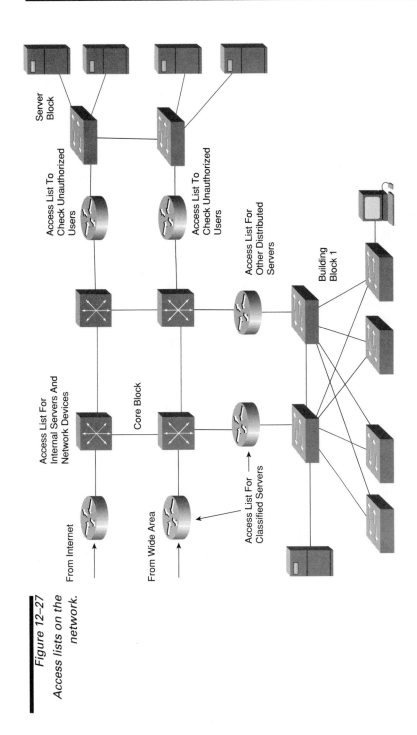

Figure 12-27
Access lists on the
network.

DESIGNING MOBILITY

To accommodate user growth and mobility, the scalable design uses a dynamic IP addressing scheme. DHCP software (described in Chapter 9, "Designing for Change and Growth") is configured on a server that allocates IP addresses to clients, and the endstations support DHCP client software. Certain routers are configured to forward IP broadcast packets as unicast packets so that the DHCP server can receive them, as shown in Figure 12–28. The relevant routers are labeled as IP/BootP helpers in the figure.

The routers in the building blocks need to be able to understand and forward DHCP messages. The routers in the server block do not need to understand the messages because they are unicasts directed to the DHCP server by the time that these routers see them. Because remote users log onto the campus via the WAN router, it has the IP/BootP helper configured on it as well.

The building block routers direct the DHCP Discover and Request messages to the DNS/DHCP server in the form of a unicast, thereby keeping broadcast traffic to a minimum.

Each time users log onto the network, they may or may not get a new IP address (depending on the lease time set in the DHCP server). When users move to another floor or building, they automatically get a new IP address and a new IP default gateway address. Once DHCP is configured on the clients, there should be no need for static addressing on the endstations.

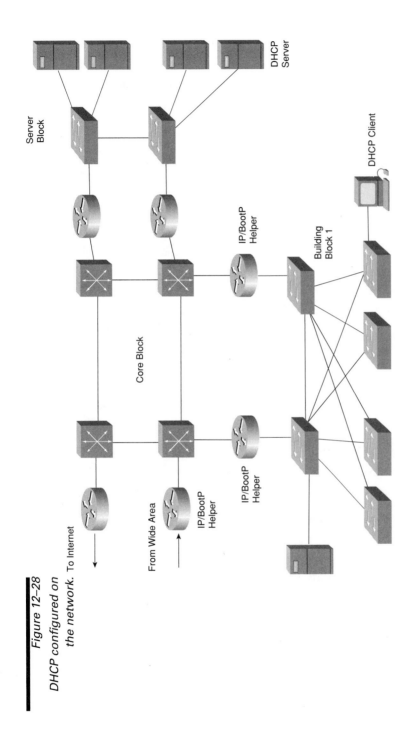

Figure 12–28
DHCP configured on
the network.

Enabling DHCP on the clients, routers, and server is a straightforward task. The more difficult task is to allocate a sufficient number of addresses for each subnet on the DHCP server. Most of this work can be accomplished while setting up the DHCP server for the first time. Allocating more addresses and subnets can be done on the DHCP server as the need arises, such as when a new building is added to the campus or a single broadcast domain is split into two separate broadcast domains.

By implementing DHCP in the scalable network design, user mobility and growth is easier to manage for the network administrator, and the arduous task of assigning and reassigning static addresses is eliminated.

BUILDING VLANs

In the scalable network design, VLANs are used for broadcast domain control rather than high user flexibility. This means that there are no VLANs that span the network; instead, the VLANs will stay local to the distribution switch. Depending on the size of the broadcast domain, the VLANs may span a couple of wiring closets or stay within a single wiring closet.

Our blueprint, illustrated in Figure 12–29, shows there are four VLANs in the building block, which represent the four broadcast domains or subnets we have been using throughout the scalable design discussion

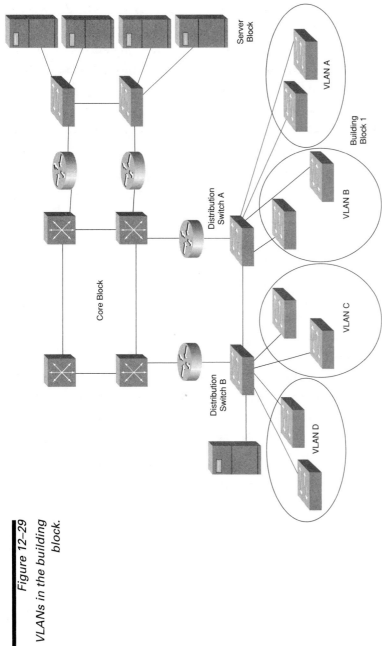

Figure 12–29
VLANs in the building block.

In this example, the VLANs span two switches, which, although they may or may not be in the same wiring closet, are on the same floor. Switches in the same VLAN have their primary links going to the same distribution switch. Figure 12–29 shows that the primary links for VLANs A and B go to Distribution Switch A, and the primary links for VLANs C and D go to Distribution Switch B.

If a user on VLAN A moves to another switch that only supports VLAN C or D, the user then becomes part of VLAN C or D and cannot remain part of VLAN A.

The distributed server can support a single VLAN or multiple VLANs, depending on who needs to access it. VLAN technology does allow a server to belong to multiple VLANs with a single physical connection to the switch.

As we discussed earlier in this chapter, the distribution switch needs to have a separate physical link to the router for each subnet the switch supports. Implementing VLANs takes away this requirement. The distribution switch needs only a single physical link to the router or a link to each router (depending on the redundancy method chosen), and it can support all the VLANs over that single link.

The core of the network needs to support only one or two VLANs. The core typically does not have so many connections that it needs two VLANs to support all of them. (The practical limit for the number of connections one VLAN can accommodate is roughly 250, the maximum size of a Class C IP subnet.) If you stay within the guidelines of safe network design, there won't be more than 40 connections in the subnet (or VLAN) to the core block.

The total number of connections is only one constraint on the number of VLANs that the core needs to support. Another constraint is the connections per router. If each router has only one connection to the core switches, then only one VLAN is necessary in the core block. However, if the network designer wants each router in the building blocks to have two connections to the core block for the sake of redundancy, as shown in Figure 12–30, then one connection supports the first VLAN (VLAN 10), and the second connection supports the other VLAN (VLAN 20).

Only a single VLAN is necessary for the server block, unless two VLANs are desired for redundancy, as with the core block. The server block VLAN implementation looks similar to the building block implementation. Figure 12–31 shows one VLAN in the server block, and Figure 12–32 shows two VLANs in the server block.

Because VLANs emulate a physical connection, it is important to describe what may happen to the traffic flow in the VLANs when a network device fails. We'll begin with the VLAN paths for wiring closet switch redundancy in the building block, which is shown in Figure 12–33.

We can see that the links between the distribution switches and the routers support all four VLANs. Even though Distribution Switch A only has users on VLANs A and B, and Distribution Switch B only has users on VLANs C and D, both switches support VLANs A to D for redundancy.

Now let's suppose that Router A fails, as shown in Figure 12–34. Distribution Switch A sends the VLAN traffic over to Distribution Switch B. Distribution Switch B then forwards the traffic up to Router B.

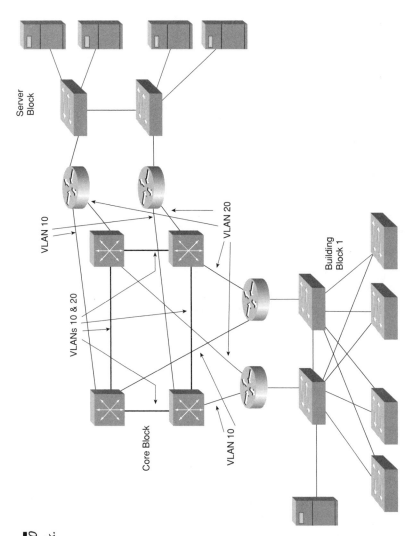

Figure 12–30
VLANs in the core block.

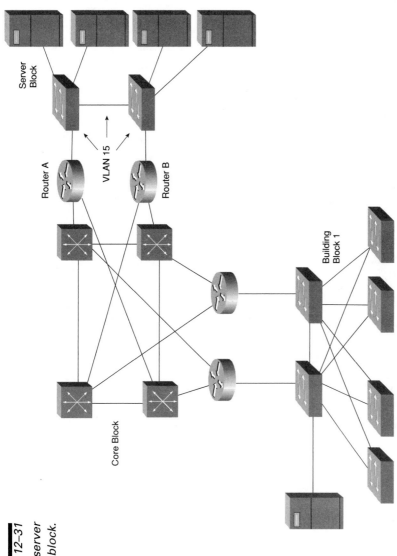

Figure 12–31
Single VLAN in the server block.

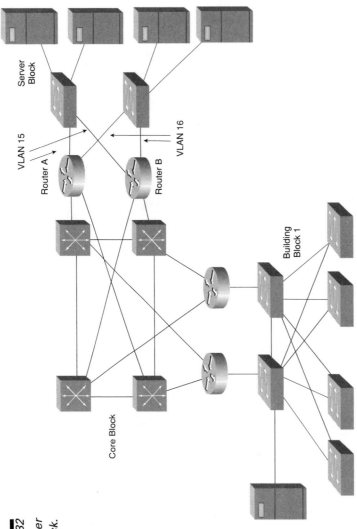

Figure 12–32
Two VLANs in the server block.

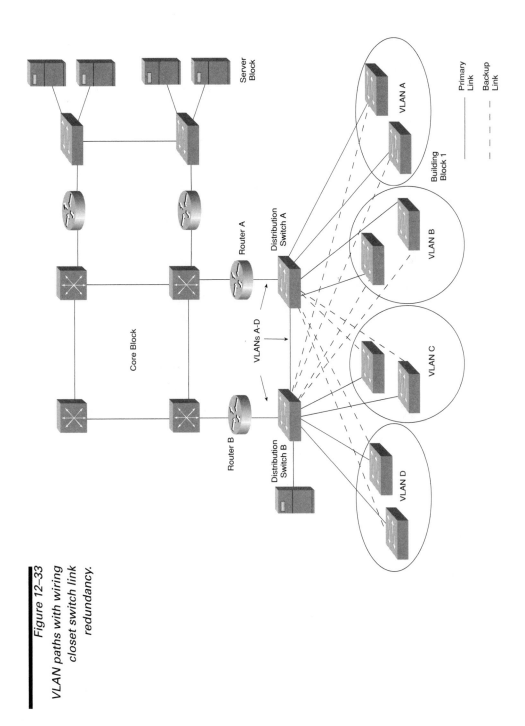

Figure 12–33
VLAN paths with wiring
closet switch link
redundancy.

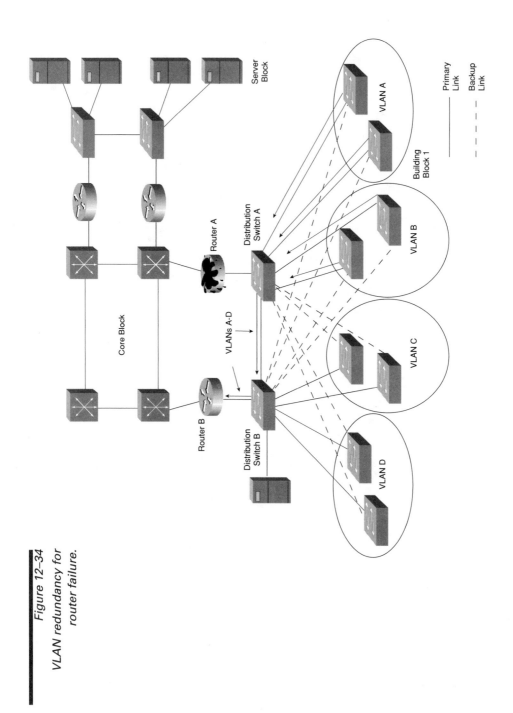

Figure 12–34
VLAN redundancy for router failure.

If Distribution Switch A fails, the wiring closet switches can send their traffic to Distribution Switch B instead, as shown in Figure 12–35.

Now let's look at the same two situations, but use redundancy at the distribution switch. Figure 12–36 shows the VLAN paths for distribution switch redundancy.

Each distribution switch connects to both routers instead of only one. Distribution Switch A has VLANs A and B going to both Routers A and B. Distribution Switch B likewise has VLANs C and D going to both Routers A and B. This allows the traffic on all VLANs to be spread across both routers (load sharing).

If Router A fails, all the traffic from both Distribution Switches A and B goes to Router B because they can no longer send traffic through Router A.

If Distribution Switch A fails, VLANs A and B lose connectivity to the rest of the network because there is no wiring closet switch redundancy. VLANs A and B cannot reach Distribution Switch B.

If Router A fails in the server block, all of the server block traffic goes through the switches to Router B, whether there is one or two VLANs, because it can no longer use Router A.

As a wrap-up to this VLAN section, Figure 12–37 shows the scalable network design with VLANs implemented throughout the network.

By using VLANs for broadcast domain control instead of user flexibility (allowing the same VLAN to reside throughout the network), traffic management becomes easier, and traffic patterns are more stable and predictable across the campus.

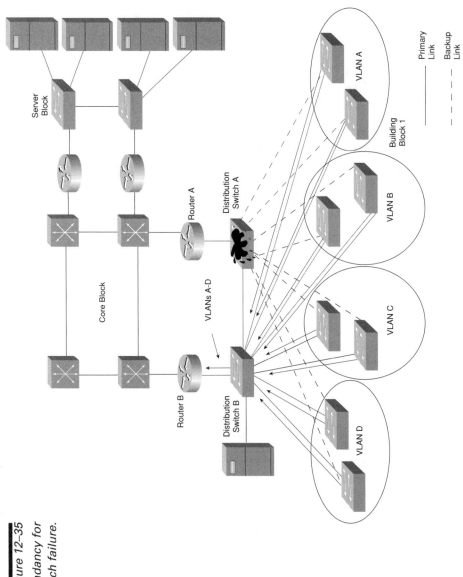

Figure 12–35
VLAN redundancy for distribution switch failure.

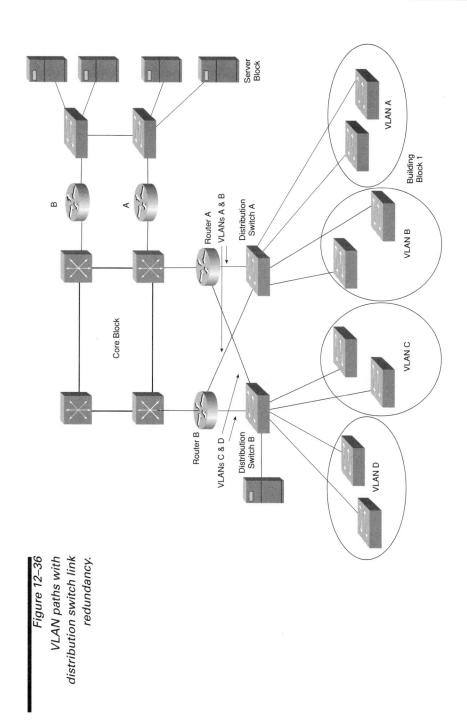

Figure 12-36

VLAN paths with
distribution switch link
redundancy.

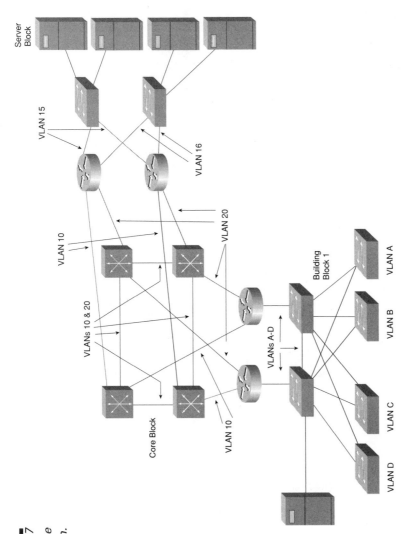

Figure 12-37
VLANs throughout the
scalable network design.

SETTING TRAFFIC PRIORITIES

As we discussed in Chapter 7, "Setting Traffic Priorities," the need for traffic prioritization in the campus today is low. When applications such as voice and real-time video become more frequently used, traffic-prioritization methods will guarantee higher performance for these applications. The scalable network design can easily support traffic prioritization via a simple configuration of the routers when the need for it arises.

If you need to prioritize traffic today, RSVP is one way to accomplish this in a scalable network. As you may recall, the RSVP protocol, which operates in tandem with a routing protocol and a queuing mechanism, supports campus applications. Figure 12–38 shows where RSVP fits into the campus network to enhance application performance.

Because RSVP is a Layer 3 function for network devices, all routers in the network support it. It is important for the building block routers to use RSVP so that they can send the request for bandwidth from the endstations through the network to the servers that support the specific application.

It's also important for the server block routers to run RSVP so that they know which data coming from the servers should receive dedicated bandwidth. The routers connecting to the WAN should support RSVP because remote users have very limited available bandwidth.

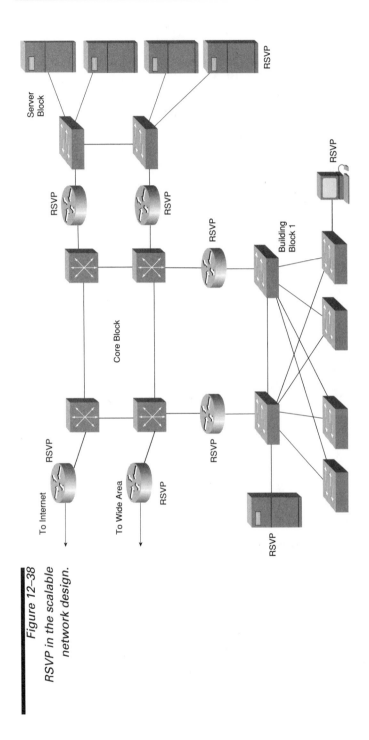

Figure 12–38
RSVP in the scalable
network design.

Some applications that run on the endstations support RSVP and some do not. For example, a multimedia application may support RSVP at the server, but not at the client side. And voice running over the network probably does not support RSVP because the telephone system does not have the capability to set up or respond to RSVP requirements. In these situations, the routers must set up the RSVP request to guarantee bandwidth for these applications.

Typically, the routers also run one of the queuing methods discussed in Chapter 7. The queuing method can be run along with RSVP or any other traffic-prioritization technique that is used in the network.

The scalable network design is set up so that traffic-prioritization methods can be added easily when the need arises, without much modification to the network.

SUMMARY

This chapter's discussion of scalable network design has considered network characteristics and design criteria individually: redundancy, multimedia support, security, mobility, VLANs, and traffic prioritization. To conclude, Figure 12–39 shows all of these characteristics combined into a complete, scalable network design.

All of the networking components play an important part in creating a stable, high-performance network. As you might expect, managing this network can be a complicated task. Network-monitoring tools, network-management packages, and an understanding of the network's capabilities help to support this network efficiently. Knowing the traffic baselines in the network provides a solid foundation when troubleshooting or planning for future growth.

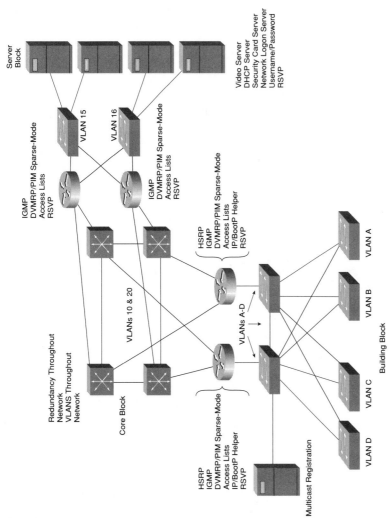

Figure 12-39
Complete scalable network design.

If your network meets the criteria for a scalable design, keep in mind the following as you plan and implement it:

- It may be wise to divide the server block and core block into more than one broadcast domain to avoid a single point of failure. Each building block probably has more than one broadcast domain.

- An important step in planning redundancy is to analyze how the redundancy methods succeed or fail to keep portions of the network operational, assuming the failure of a specific network device.

- The scalable network needs to support multimedia applications, so it should be configured with DVMRP, PIM dense-mode, or PIM sparse-mode, depending on the number of users of such applications.

- At a minimum, scalable network security includes network logon, server login, and access lists on the routers. If additional security is needed, route authentication and encryption methods can be used.

- Mobility is a design criterion of the scalable network, so a dynamic IP addressing scheme is needed, such as DHCP.

- VLANs in the scalable network are implemented largely for broadcast domain control rather than for user flexibility.

This chapter covers the following topics:

- A complex network blueprint

- Traffic patterns

- Designing redundancy

- Addressing multimedia

- Designing security

- Designing mobility

- Implementing VLANs

- Setting traffic priorities

CHAPTER 13

Design Three—A Complex Network

The complex design is in most ways an expansion of the scalable design described in Chapter 12, "Design Two–A Scalable Network." The complex design presents a blueprint for designers who have a demanding network: One that supports a lot of bandwidth-intensive applications, has high network utilization, and offers high user flexibility and room for network growth. This blueprint is appropriate for busy networks that must always be stable and in which unexpected network downtime severely reduces user productivity and business profitability.

The complex design does not necessarily support more users than the scalable design does. In both designs, the number of users is less relevant than the kinds of services provided and the quality of performance demanded. The important difference between the scalable and complex designs is that the complex design offers higher network services, such as extended redundancy for network stability, added encryption for increased network security, and more complex VLAN implementation for higher user flexibility.

The complex blueprint assumes that the campus LAN has the following design requirements and characteristics:

- Medium-to-large network size (from 300 up to 15,000 nodes)

- Centralized and distributed servers

- Bandwidth-intensive applications, including multi-media

- Frequent use of critical applications

- Internet/wide area connectivity

- High reliability/redundancy throughout the network

- Downtime severely compromises user performance

- Security is crucial throughout network

- Moderate growth rate

- Mobility occurs

- VLANs can be implemented

Your network does not need to have all of the listed design characteristics to fit into the complex blueprint. The list is meant as a guideline to help network designers determine whether this is the correct blueprint to use as a base.

A COMPLEX NETWORK BLUEPRINT

As discussed in Chapter 10, "Understanding the Structural Foundation of Network Design," the campus network can be separated into network foundations: the building block, core block, and server block. The network foundations for the complex campus design, similar to those of the scalable campus design, areshown in Figure 13–1.

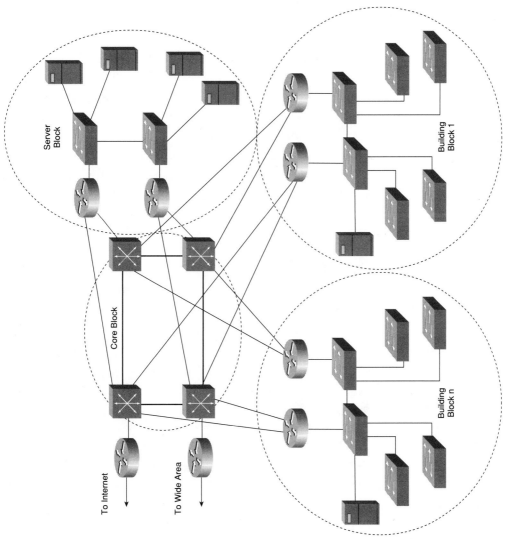

Figure 13–1
Network foundations of
the complex network
design.

Building Block

In the complex design, there is usually more than one building block, either because of the high number of users or because there is more than one building on the campus. Each building block uses Layer 2 switches in the wiring closet to connect users. The wiring closet switches merge into two distribution switches for Layer 2 connectivity. The distributed servers connect directly to the distribution switch. The distribution switches are attached to two routers for Layer 3 functionality. The routers connect to the core block.

Core Block

The core block for a complex network consists of at least two high-speed Layer 2 switches. Figure 13–1 shows the design with four switches so that we can more readily point out the core block redundancy options. Fast Ethernet, Gigabit Ethernet, or ATM are viable high-speed technologies in the core for the complex design.

Server Block

The server block for a complex network contains the enterprise servers, which are located in the data center. The servers connect to Layer 2 switches, which then connect to two routers. The number of switches needed in any given complex network is dependent on the number of enterprise servers that the network supports. In Figure 13–1, two routers are used for redundancy, which we will discuss in later sections of this chapter. No more than two routers are needed in the server block because each switch connects to a unique interface on the same router. The distributed servers are not located in the server block, but instead reside in the same building block as the users they support.

Connection to the Internet

The complex network design includes connections to the Internet and the wide area via routers. Most likely, remote offices, telecommuters, and mobile users need to connect to the campus across the wide area, and several connections to the Internet are needed.

The routers that connect to the wide area and Internet are dedicated routers that attach to the core. They are dedicated in the sense that they have a specific, restricted purpose: they handle traffic coming in and out of the wide area and Internet, and are not part of a building block with users. The purpose of this setup is to help keep WAN and Internet traffic separate from the campus traffic. Routers that support WAN and Internet connections need to run different network services (and possibly different routing protocols) than the campus routers. It makes better network design sense, therefore, to use separate devices to handle the two distinct network areas.

TRAFFIC PATTERNS

The complex network design usually has several broadcast domains. The following sections show possible broadcast domains in the complex blueprint for a server block, a core block, and a single building block. You can extrapolate from these models to calculate the broadcast domains in additional building blocks or server blocks on your campus, as needed.

BROADCAST DOMAINS IN THE SERVER BLOCK

Figure 13–2 shows the complex blueprint—with a single building block, core block, and server block—with the server block broadcast domains highlighted.

Many complex networks have anywhere from 20 to 300 enterprise servers, and therefore require at least two broadcast domains or subnets in the server block. Keep in mind that having all the enterprise servers in a single subnet allows the possibility of a single point of failure, which can bring down the entire server block. Because the complex network cannot afford any part of the server block to be inaccessible, it uses a minimum of two subnets. Later in this chapter, we show in more detail how two subnets in the server block provide added redundancy.

Broadcast Domains in the Core Block

The core block supports two broadcast domains to handle the traffic load of a complex network, as shown in Figure 13–3.

The complex network supports a lot of bandwidth-intensive applications and runs at a high utilization rate. As a result, there must be data load sharing on the routers connecting the building block and server block to the core to support this traffic. With two broadcast domains (subnets) in the core block, each building and server block router has two connections to the core block, allowing both connections to forward traffic.

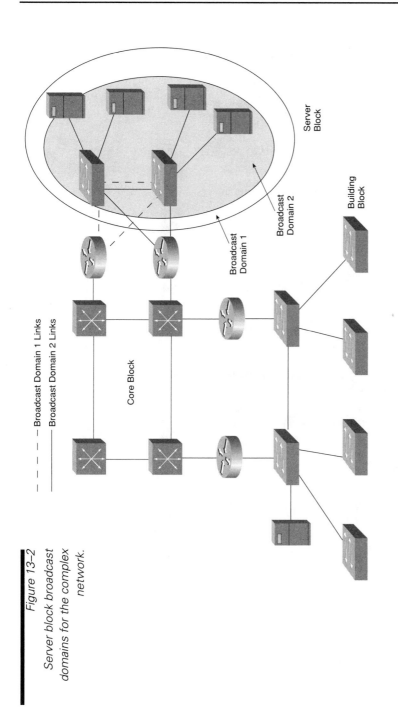

Figure 13–2
Server block broadcast
domains for the complex
network.

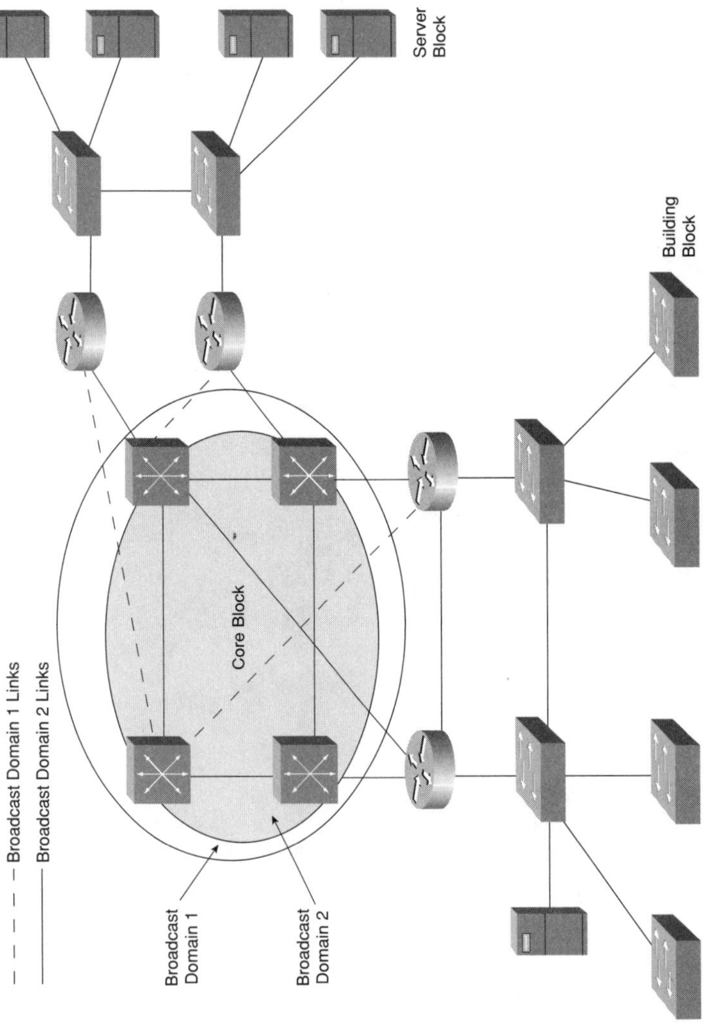

Figure 13-3

Core block broadcast
domains in the complex
design.

Server
Block

Building
Block

Core Block

Broadcast
Domain 1

Broadcast
Domain 2

– – – – Broadcast Domain 1 Links
———— Broadcast Domain 2 Links

Broadcast Domains in the Building Block

Each building block in the complex design usually has more than one broadcast domain. The same scenario works here as in the scalable design—four broadcast domains in the building block, as shown in Figure 13–4. (Remember that there are several ways to organize broadcast domains in the building blocks, and they vary, depending on the actual layout of your buildings and their network connections.)

The distribution switches and the two routers support all four broadcast domains. Each wiring closet switch supports one broadcast domain (unless VLANs are implemented, as discussed later in this chapter).

The distributed servers in the building block can connect to either the distribution switch or to a wiring closet switch, depending on the users they support. For example, if the distributed server supports a single subnet of users who connect to one wiring closet switch, it makes sense to connect the distributed server to that wiring closet switch.

On the other hand, if the distributed server supports users who connect to several wiring closet switches, the distributed server should connect to the distribution switch. This type of connection is optimal because the distribution switch is the common point of connection for all the users in the broadcast domain.

The same is true if the distributed server supports multiple subnets—again, because the distribution switch is the common point of connection and can allow each subnet to have equal access to the server. This type of setup is shown in Figure 13–4.

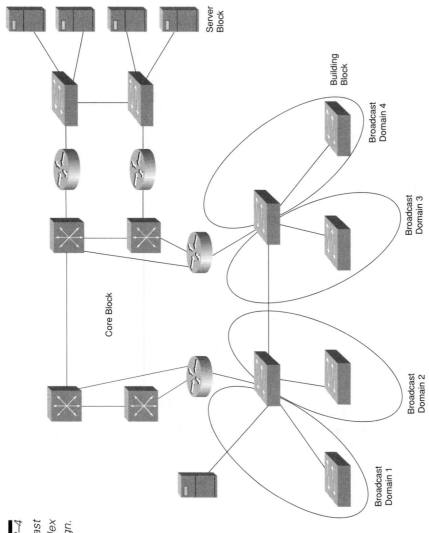

Figure 13–4
Building block broadcast domains in the complex design.

If distributed servers are used effectively, there are dedicated distributed servers in each subnet and the local traffic is spread across the building block. As we discussed in Chapter 2, "Server Placement," distributed servers create less traffic across the routers and core, resulting in efficient network performance.

No matter how you set up your broadcast domains, the traffic patterns in the complex design consist of both local and cross-campus traffic. The more distributed servers you have in the building block, the more local traffic is on the network. The traffic going to and from the enterprise servers, as well as to and from the wide area or Internet, comprises the cross-campus traffic.

DESIGNING REDUNDANCY

The complex design places a higher priority on network operation than on the cost to implement redundancy. If the network goes down, the company may lose a lot of money while the network is not operational. Stock-trading companies, for example, can't afford any downtime during trading hours. Other companies that are at 100-percent production capacity every hour of every day also cannot withstand long periods of network failure.

The blueprint for the scalable design provides redundancy throughout the network, but there are still circumstances under which it can go down and users can lose connectivity. The complex design implements a greater level of redundancy and reduces the possibility of network failure.

The first area of redundancy is component redundancy within the network devices. Spare power supplies, fans, and processors provide the first level of protection against failure.

In addition, some form of network link and data path redundancy, as well as software redundancy, assures resiliency and limits network downtime. This level of redundancy is included in the building block, core block, and server block for the complex design.

Building Block Redundancy

At the building block level, we discussed two options of redundancy for the scalable design: wiring closet switch redundancy and distribution switch redundancy. (These two options are shown in Figure 12–6 and Figure 12–9, respectively.) The complex design combines these two options to provide a higher level of protection, as illustrated in Figure 13–5.

Figure 13–5

Complex design building block redundancy.

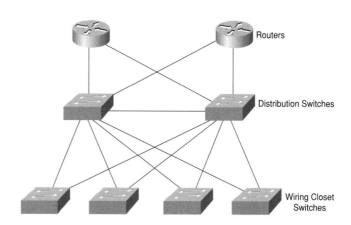

As you can see, there are redundant links from the wiring closet switches to the distribution switches (wiring closet switch redundancy), and also connections from each distribution switch to both routers (distribution switch redundancy). This combination provides the highest level of device failure protection and link failure protection.

Traffic can travel a variety of ways in the building blocks by using these redundancy schemes. For brevity, we will cover just one, illustrated in Figure 13–6.

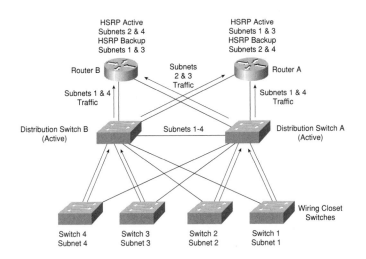

Figure 13–6
Traffic pattern with building block redundancy.

Each wiring closet switch represents a subnet. Wiring Closet Switches 1 and 2 forward their traffic to Distribution Switch A, and use Distribution Switch B as a backup. Wiring Closet Switches 3 and 4 forward their traffic to Distribution Switch B, and use Distribution Switch A as a backup. The connection between distribution switches supports all four subnets.

Distribution Switch A sends traffic from Subnets 1 and 4 to Router A, and sends traffic from Subnets 2 and 3 to Router B. Distribution Switch B sends traffic from Subnets 1 and 4 to Router B, and sends traffic from Subnets 2 and 3 to Router A.

In a healthy network (one with no failures), both routers forward traffic. Distribution Switch A sends only traffic from Subnets 1 and 2 (it is the backup switch for Subnets 3 and 4). By sending traffic from Subnet 1 to Router A and traffic from Subnet 2 to Router B, both of these links are active. Likewise,

Distribution Switch B sends only traffic from Subnets 3 and 4 (it is the backup switch for Subnets 1 and 2). It sends traffic from Subnet 3 to Router A and traffic from Subnet 4 to Router B.

The connection between Distribution Switch A and Distribution Switch B is used if a link from a distribution switch to one of the routers fails or if the router itself fails. We'll show this failure scenario later on in the chapter.

HSRP is also used on the routers to prevent the user from losing connectivity. Router A is the active HSRP router for Subnets 1 and 3, and Router B is the active HSRP router for Subnets 2 and 4. If either the active HSRP router or the link to the active HSRP router fails, the backup HSRP router becomes active.

To further protect the user from loss of connectivity, NIC card redundancy is used at the workstations in the building block. The workstations have two NIC cards installed, each of which connects to different wiring closet switch, as shown in Figure 13–7.

One NIC forwards data and the other NIC is used for backup. Providing this type of redundancy for the workstation is a simple matter of supplying two RJ-45 jacks at the workstation area so those users can connect both NIC cards to the network. Once connected, NIC redundancy protects the user from losing connectivity in case of a wiring closet switch failure.

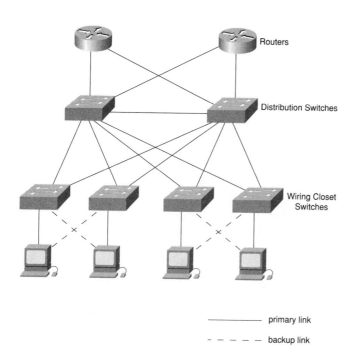

Figure 13–7

Workstation NIC redundancy.

Core Block Redundancy

In setting up the scalable design, we use a partial mesh for redundancy in the core; that is, each core switch is connected to some but not all of the other core switches. Core block redundancy in the complex design, however, utilizes a full mesh of connections; that is, each core switch connects to all the other core switches. Figure 13–8 compares the partial and full mesh designs.

Figure 13–8

Core block redundancy: comparison of scalable design and complex design.

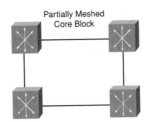

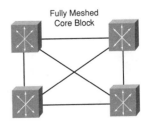

By using the full mesh in the complex design, multiple data paths can be utilized in case of failure. In this example, each core switch has three available data paths to forward the traffic, as opposed to the two data paths offered by the scalable design.

The complex design also has two connections from each building block router to the core block, as shown in Figure 13–9.

Figure 13–9

Connection from building blocks to complex core block.

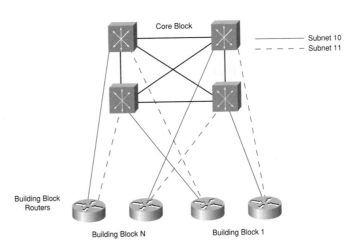

The building block routers connect to different core switches to provide multiple paths into the core block. For the two routers in each building block in Figure 13–12, there are connections to four core switches. Each router connects both Subnets 10 and 11 to the core block. The routers can forward traffic on both links.

Server Block Redundancy

Server block redundancy in the complex design includes placing NIC redundancy on the servers. This redundancy allows the enterprise servers to connect to both distribution switches, as shown in Figure 13–10.

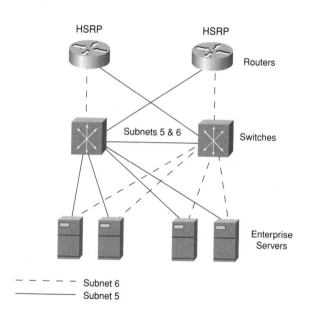

Figure 13–10
Server NIC redundancy.

Each NIC card in the server belongs to a different subnet (in our example, one for Subnet 5 and one for Subnet 6). Both NIC cards can be used in tandem to send traffic in a healthy network. In case of a switch failure, the failure is detected and only one NIC card handles the traffic.

The two distribution switches connect to each other to provide an extra path out to the network. Each switch connects to both routers to provide additional paths to the network and support for data load sharing between the routers in the server block. The routers are utilizing HSRP.

When we put it all together, redundancy in the complex design provides protection for all components and data paths throughout the network: the building blocks, core block, and server block, as shown in Figure 13–11.

The network is prepared for failures and can stay operational when these failures occur. The next section examines how the complex redundancy design behaves when network failures do happen.

Potential Points of Network Failure

Before showing failures on the network, we'll show the traffic pattern in a healthy network environment, which is illustrated in Figure 13–12.

The workstations in the building block have NIC redundancy, and there is both wiring closet switch redundancy and distribution switch redundancy. The distribution switches send traffic to both routers. The core switches are fully meshed, and the building block routers have two connections each to the core block. The server block uses connections from both switches to both routers and the servers have multiple NIC cards. Additionally, Spanning Tree is configured on the network for the switches, and HSRP is configured on the routers.

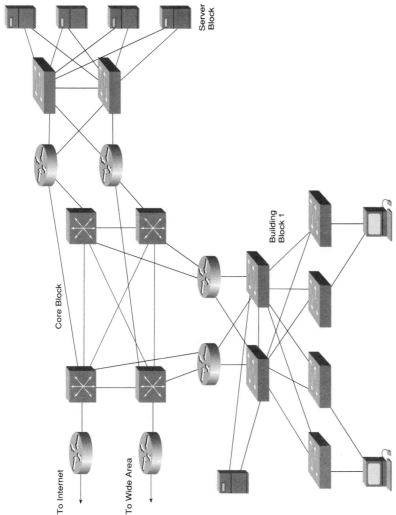

Figure 13–11
Complex design with
redundancy.

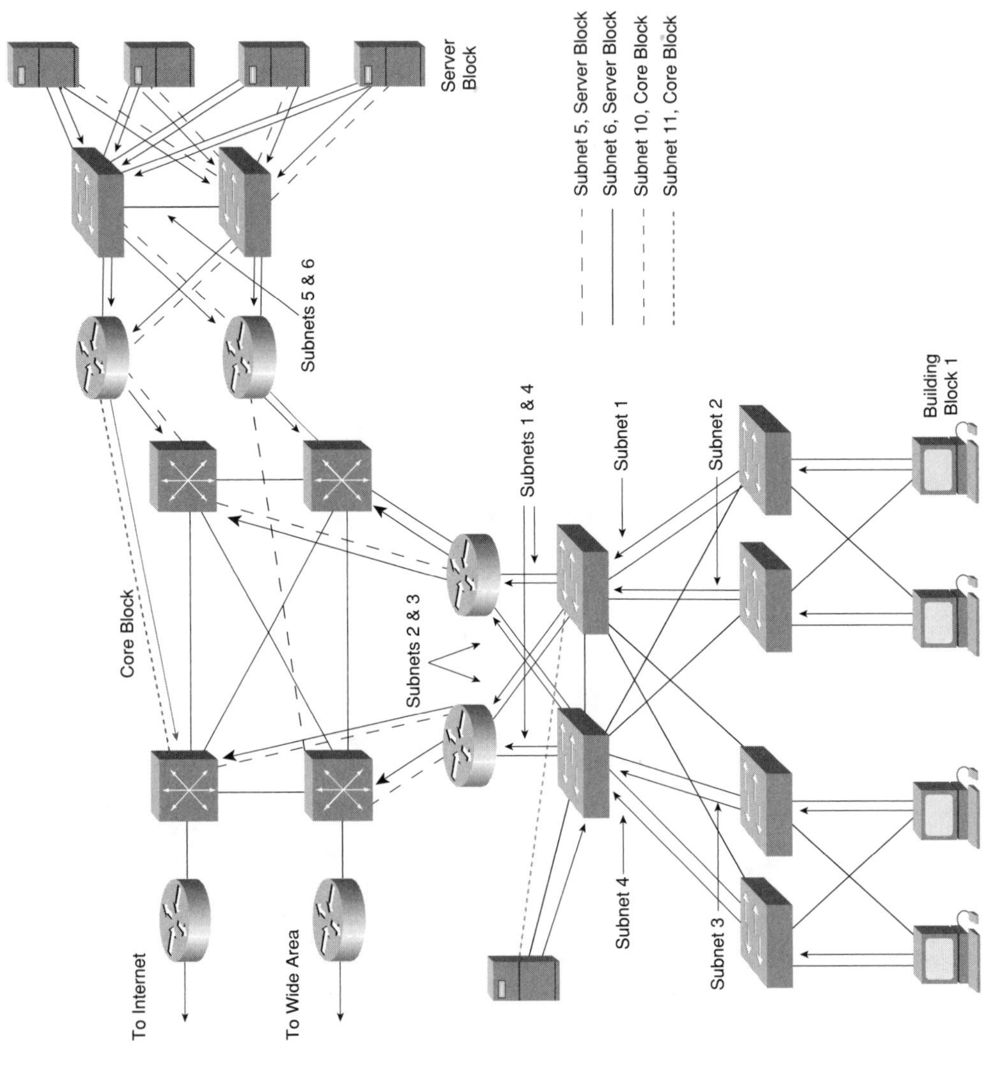

Figure 13–12
Healthy complex network design.

Let's take a look at the way failures affect the network and user connectivity. First, consider a wiring closet switch failure and a server switch failure, as shown in Figure 13–13.

Because the workstations in the complex design have dual NIC cards installed, the users still have access to the network and there is no loss of connectivity with failure of a wiring closet switch. The failed switch in the server block does not cause loss of connectivity for any of the enterprise servers because they also have dual NIC cards.

Even with both a wiring closet and a server switch failure, the network is still completely operational due to the redundancy methods used.

Now, suppose that there is a distribution switch failure in the building block, as shown inFigure 13–14.

None of the users has lost connectivity in the building block. Spanning Tree has redirected the traffic to go from the wiring closet switches to Distribution Switch A instead of Distribution Switch B. Distribution Switch A forwards the traffic to both Routers A and B. Because the distributed server has dual NICs, it connects to Distribution Switch A and the users can still access it.

Figure 13–15 shows a router failure in both the building block and the server block.

Distribution Switches A and B detect the lost connections to Router A. Distribution Switch A sends the traffic for Subnet 1 over to Distribution Switch B, and Distribution Switch B sends it to Router B. Distribution Switch A sends the traffic for Subnet 2 directly to Router B without going through Distribution Switch B.

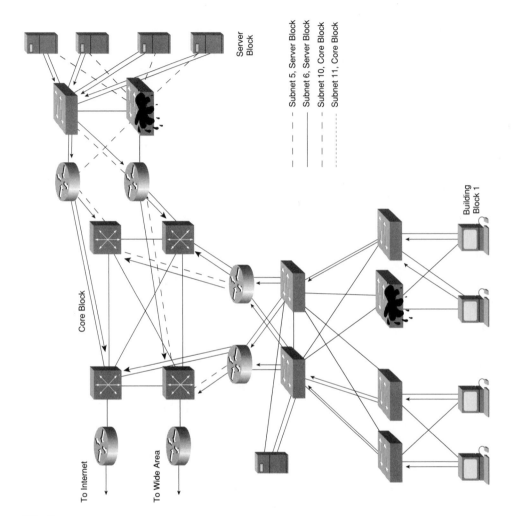

Figure 13–13
Two switch failures in the
complex design.

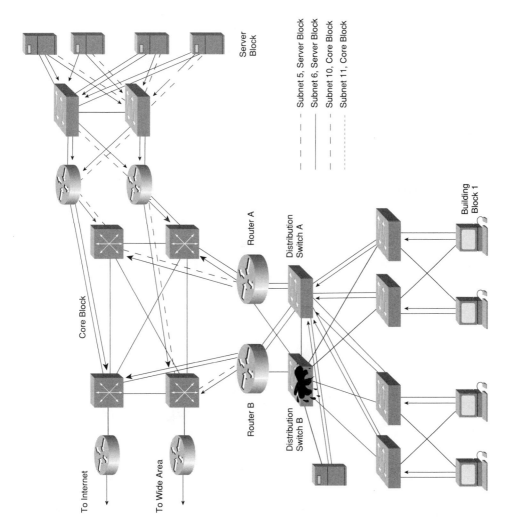

Figure 13–14
Distribution switch failure in the complex design.

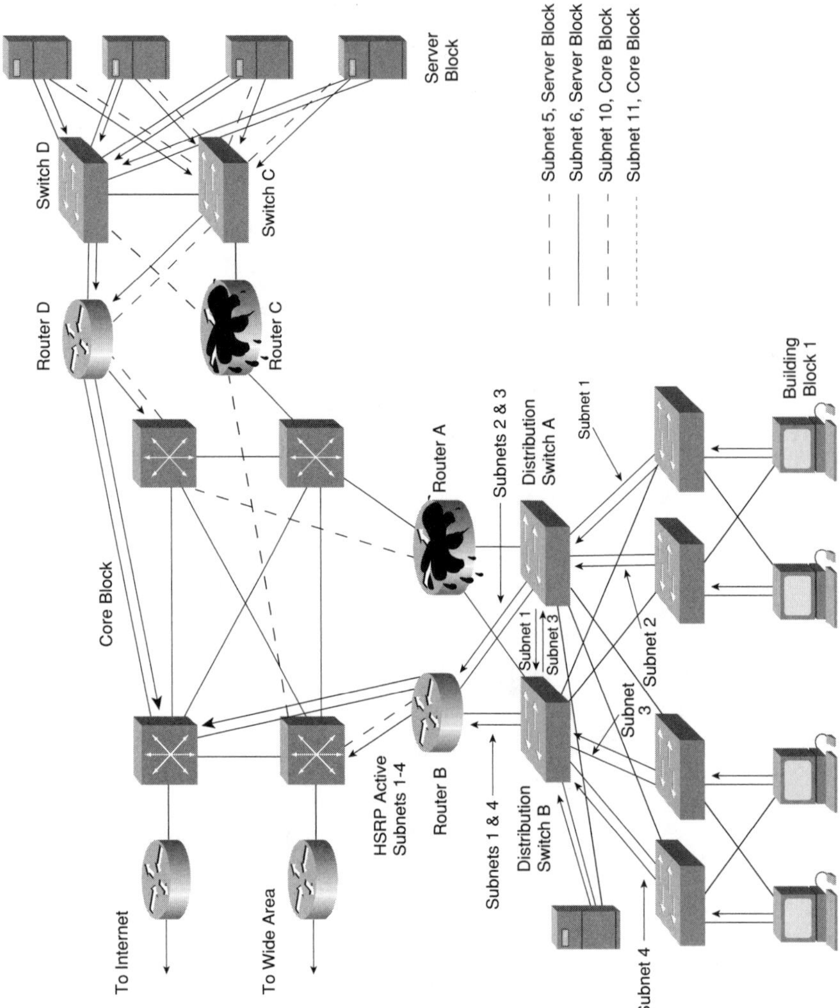

Switch D

Switch C

Server Block

Router D

Router C

Core Block

Router A

Subnets 2 & 3

Distribution Switch A

Subnet 1

Building Block 1

Subnet 1

Subnet 2

To Internet

To Wide Area

HSRP Active Subnets 1-4

Router B

Subnet 1

Subnet 3

Subnet 2

Subnet 3

Subnets 1 & 4

Distribution Switch B

Subnet 4

Subnet 3

Subnet 4

Subnet 5, Server Block

Subnet 6, Server Block

Subnet 10, Core Block

Subnet 11, Core Block

Figure 13–15
Router failure in the complex design.

Likewise, Distribution Switch B sends the traffic for Subnet 3 over to Distribution Switch A, and Distribution Switch A sends the traffic to Router B. Distribution Switch B forwards the traffic on Subnet 4 directly to Router B, as it usually does.

HSRP automatically brings up the HSRP standby router (Router B), so the users do not have to reconfigure their stations with a new IP default gateway address. There is no loss of connectivity in the building block.

In the server block, Switch C detects the lost connection to Router C and sends traffic from Subnet 5 to Router D. Switch D continues to send traffic from Subnet 6 to Router D. All of the enterprise servers remain operational.

Let's examine a situation in which both a distribution switch and a router fail, as shown in Figure 13–16.

In this scenario, Distribution Switch A can only forward traffic on Subnets 2 and 3 to Router B. The users who are connected to Subnets 1 and 4 would lose connectivity to the network if they didn't have NIC redundancy. With NIC redundancy, however, all users maintain connectivity.

Each workstation has connection to two subnets via the wiring closet switches. The users that connect to Subnet 1 can also connect to Subnet 2. Users that connect to Subnet 3 can also connect to Subnet 4. Because Subnets 1 and 4 cannot remain operational through the network, all the workstations on those subnets send traffic through their backup NICs that are on either Subnet 2 or 3.

Therefore, all the users become part of Subnets 2 and 3. Although Distribution Switch A can only forward traffic from Subnets 2 and 3, the users stay connected to the network because of the NIC redundancy.

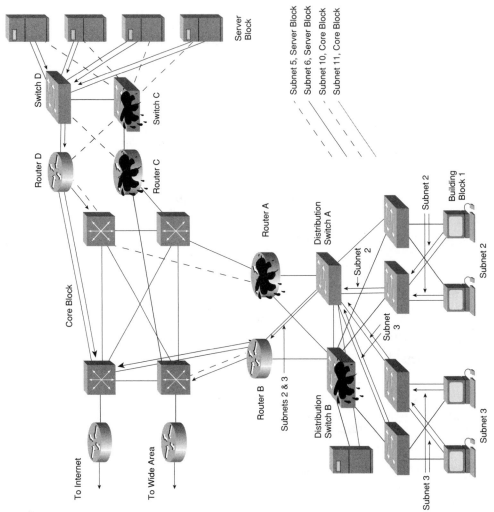

Figure 13–16
Complex design switch and
router failures.

In the server block, the enterprise servers are actively connected to both Subnets 5 and 6. When the path to Subnet 5 fails, the servers send all the traffic on Subnet 6 and maintain network operation.

Now, take a look at what happens to the network with multiple core switch failures, as shown in Figure 13–17.

For this scenario, we track only what happens when the users in the Building Block try to reach the enterprise servers in the server block.

The multiple connections from Routers A and B and the full mesh connections of the core switches ensure network connections through the core. The building block switches behave as if they were in a healthy network and are not aware that there are network failures.

Router A sends all of its traffic into the core on Subnet 10 to Core Switch D. Router B sends all of its traffic into the core block on Subnet 10 to Core Switch B. Core Switch B forwards the traffic to Core Switch D and Core Switch D forwards the traffic to Router D. The traffic that needs to reach the enterprise servers can do so. Core Switch B also forwards the traffic directly to Router C, which then sends the traffic to the enterprise servers.

We conclude this discussion by looking at multiple failures in the network, a worst-case scenario. For purposes of comparison, Figure 13–18 shows multiple failures in the scalable design; Figure 13–19 shows these same failures in the complex design, with devices and subnets labeled.

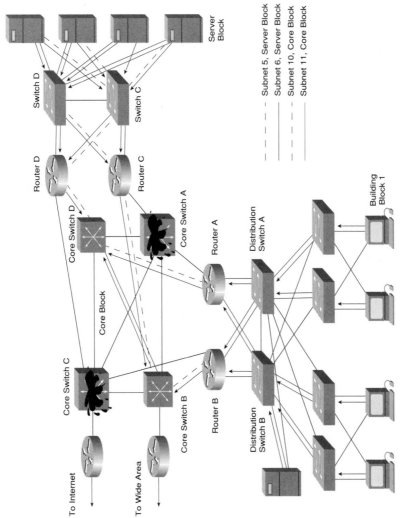

Figure 13-17
Core switches failing in the
complex design.

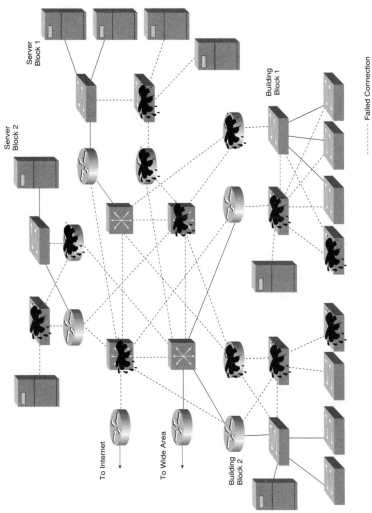

Server
Block 1

Building
Block 1

Failed Connection

Server
Block 2

To Internet

To Wide Area

Building
Block 2

Figure 13–18
Multiple device failures in the
scalable design.

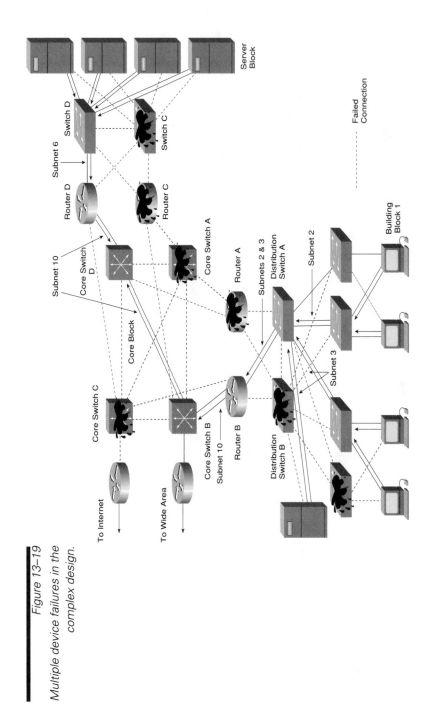

A quick review shows that all the users lose connectivity to the campus network, as well as to the wide area and Internet, in the scalable design. In the complex design, however, all the users maintain connectivity to the campus network and the wide area. Although a direct connection to the Internet is blocked, users can still reach the Internet if the Internet router has a connection to either Core Switch B or Core Switch D, or if there is more than one Internet router on the campus (which is very common).

The added redundancy features of the complex design help to maintain the fault tolerance in this worst-case scenario. Workstation NIC card redundancy allows the workstations to get around the failed wiring closet switch and connect onto the operating Subnets 2 and 3. Spanning Tree in the Building Block enables the wiring closet switches to send traffic to Distribution Switch A. Distribution Switch A sends traffic to Router B on Subnets 2 and 3.

The redundant connection from Router B to the core enables Router B to send all the traffic to Core Switch B on Subnet 10. The full mesh in the core block provides a path for Core Switch B to send the data to operating Core Switch D and on to Router D in the server block on Subnet 10. Finally, the enterprise servers with NIC redundancy maintain connectivity to the network through Switch D and Router D on Subnet 6.

The redundancy in the complex design provides for the highest fault tolerance and is the best choice for networks that must always have campus network operation.

ADDRESSING MULTIMEDIA

The complex design assumes that several multimedia applications regularly run on the network. These applications are usually a combination of multicast and unicast multimedia traffic.

For the scalable design, we showed two valid scenarios for handling multicast traffic: one using DVMRP and one using PIM sparse-mode. Because the complex network supports a lot of bandwidth-intensive applications and runs at a high network-utilization rate, we use PIM sparse-mode for the multicast routing protocol here. PIM sparse-mode does not flood as much multicast traffic as does DVMRP. However, DVMRP may work successfully in the complex design. Refer to the "Addressing Multimedia" section in Chapter 12, "Design Two—A Scalable Network," to examine the DVMRP design.

The goal in designing for multimedia is to use as little bandwidth as possible in terms of multicast flooding. The fewer devices that are flooded by multicast packets, the higher the network performance, resulting in more efficient multimedia application support. With this in mind, take a look at how the complex design supports multiple multimedia applications.

Figure 13–20 shows the complex design with the multimedia requirements. Two multimedia servers are sending multicast traffic and one is sending unicast traffic.

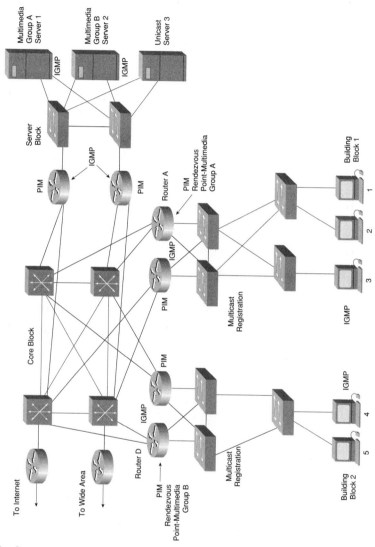

Figure 13–20
Complex design with multimedia.

The indicated servers, routers, and workstations in Figure 13–20 have IGMP running, and the indicated routers have PIM sparse-mode configured to support the multicast traffic. All of the switches are set up with multicast address registration to reduce the multicast flooding on the network. (As you recall from Chapter 4, "Factoring in Multimedia Traffic" the switch can be configured to send multimedia out only on those ports that are members of a multimedia group.)

Router A is the Rendezvous point for the multicast traffic (Multimedia Group A) coming from Server 1 and Router D is the Rendezvous point for the multicast traffic (Multimedia Group B) coming from Server 2. By placing the Rendezvous points on the building block routers, the core block is not flooded by multicasts because the multimedia servers send the multimedia traffic as unicast traffic to the Rendezvous points. A Rendezvous point is not needed for the unicast traffic coming from Server 3.

Let's examine the traffic flow after the hosts have sent their IGMP Joins to the multimedia servers and the servers start sending the traffic. Figure 13–21 shows the path that the traffic takes from the multimedia servers.

Workstations 1 and 4 are members of Multimedia Group A. The multimedia traffic goes from Server 1 through the core block to Router A, the Rendezvous point for Multimedia Group A, as unicast traffic. Router A then sends the multimedia traffic to Workstations 1 and 4.

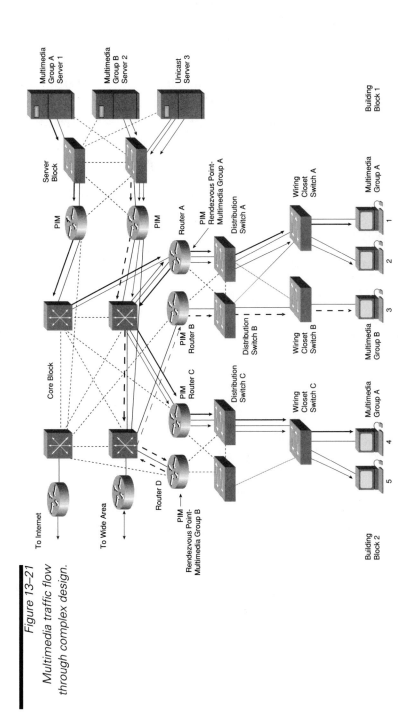

Figure 13–21
Multimedia traffic flow
through complex design.

To reach Workstation 1, Router A sends the multimedia traffic as multicasts to Distribution Switch A because Router A does not know who the exact recipient is. Distribution Switch A forwards it to Wiring Closet Switch A. Wiring Closet Switch A sends the traffic to Workstation 1. Because all the switches support multicast registration, the multicast traffic is not flooded out all of the switches' ports.

To reach Workstation 4, Router A sends the multimedia traffic directly to Router C through the core block. Because Router A knows that the multimedia traffic is going to Router C, this traffic is still sent as unicast traffic, not multicast traffic. When Router C receives the traffic, Router C forwards it to Distribution Switch C as multicast traffic, as Router A did. Distribution Switch C forwards the multicast traffic to Wiring Closet Switch C, which sends it to Workstation 4.

Workstation 3 is a member of Multimedia Group B. Server 2 first sends the multimedia traffic to Router D, the Rendezvous point for Multimedia Group B. Router D then sends the traffic to Workstation 3.

To reach Workstation 3, Router D sends the traffic directly to Router B through the core. Because Router D knows that the multimedia traffic is going to Router B, this traffic is still sent as unicast traffic, not multicast traffic. When Router B receives the traffic, Router B forwards it to Distribution Switch B as multicast traffic because the router does not know who the exact recipients are. Distribution Switch B forwards the multicast traffic to Wiring Closet Switch B, which sends it to Workstation 3.

Workstations 2 and 5 are using the multimedia application that resides on Server 3, which is a unicast application. Server 3 sends the application as unicast traffic directly to Workstation 2 (it uses Workstation 2's address as the destination address). The server also sends the application, again as unicast traffic, directly to Workstation 5 (it uses Workstation 5's address as the destination address).

For Workstations 2 and 5, PIM sparse-mode is not used. Instead, the network treats this traffic as any other unicast traffic. The traffic goes through Router A in Building Block 1 to Workstation 2, and the traffic goes through Router C in Building Block 2 to Workstation 5.

As you may recall from Chapter 4, PIM sparse-mode optimizes the data path once the path has been established. Figure 13–22 shows the optimized traffic patterns.

The path from Server 1 to Workstation 1 does not change because it already is the most optimized path between the two devices. The paths from Server 3 to Workstations 2 and 5 do not need to be optimized because, as stated earlier, these stations are receiving unicast traffic and don't use PIM sparse-mode.

The path from Server 2 to Workstation 3 and the path from Server 1 to Workstation 4, however, are optimized. To reach Workstation 3, the multicast traffic no longer needs to go through the Rendezvous point for Multimedia Group B (Router D). The router in the server block now sends the multicast traffic directly to Router A, which then forwards it over to Workstation 3.

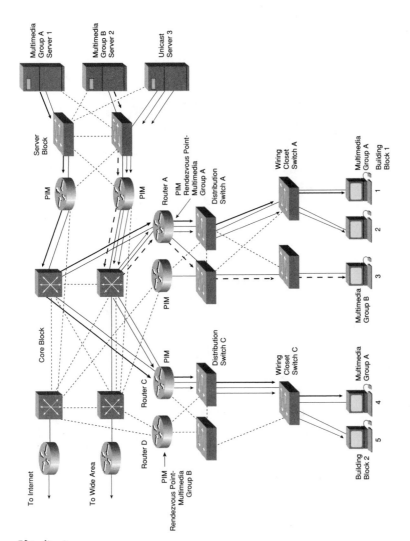

Figure 13–22
Optimized multimedia traffic
patterns in complex design.

To reach Workstation 4, the traffic no longer goes through the Rendezvous Point for Multimedia Group A (Router A). The router in the server block now sends the multicast traffic directly to Router C, which then forwards it over to Workstation 4.

When supporting multiple multimedia applications on the network, pay close attention to where the Rendezvous points are placed in the network. To prevent a traffic bottleneck at the Rendezvous point, be sure that your design implements more than one Rendezvous point to support the multimedia applications, instead of using a single Rendezvous point to handle all of the traffic.

DESIGNING SECURITY

The complex design utilizes several security mechanisms, as illustrated in Figure 13–23. It supports network logon as its base level of security for the network. It also has server login for user authorization. For an additional level of security, the routers support access lists to protect the servers from unauthorized users, and route authentication to prevent other devices from acting as default gateways. All of these mechanisms were also used in the scalable design.

The complex network goes beyond the scalable network's security design in several ways. First, it uses login on the network infrastructure (routers and switches) for additional authorization security. Only designated individuals can log in to routers and switches to change their configurations.

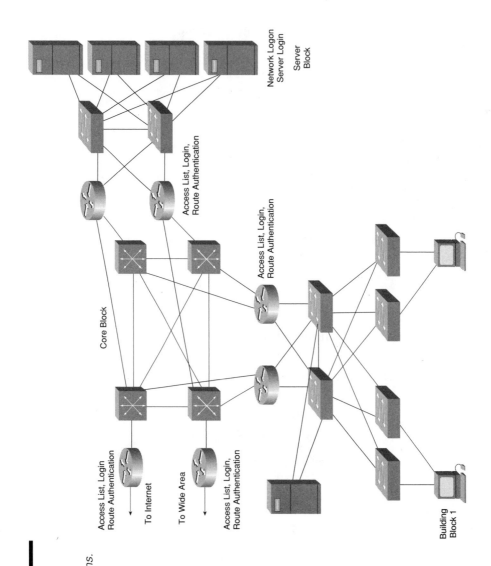

Figure 13–23
Complex design with
authentication and
authorization mechanisms.

The complex design also adds encryption to provide data integrity on the network. As we discussed in Chapter 8, "Addressing Security Issues," there are two places where encryption can take place: at the routers, and between the workstation and server.

Encryption on the routers should be placed on all of the routers in the network: the building block routers, server block routers, and the wide area routers. This provides the highest data integrity for the network infrastructure.

However, as we also discussed in Chapter 8, encryption on the router provides only partial data integrity on the campus network.

The reason becomes clear when you look at the traffic pattern. In all three network blueprints, routers separate the building blocks and server block from the core block. When data is sent from a workstation to a server, or vice versa, the traffic crosses two routers. With encryption at the router, the traffic is only encrypted when going across the core block, as shown in Figure 13–24.

If the data is grabbed by another user in the building block before it reaches the router, the data is readable. Even more critical, unauthorized users in the server block can read the data after it passes through the router. Because most network traffic goes to the enterprise servers, the server block is a likely spot for a security breach and information theft. This situation is unacceptable for highly sensitive data.

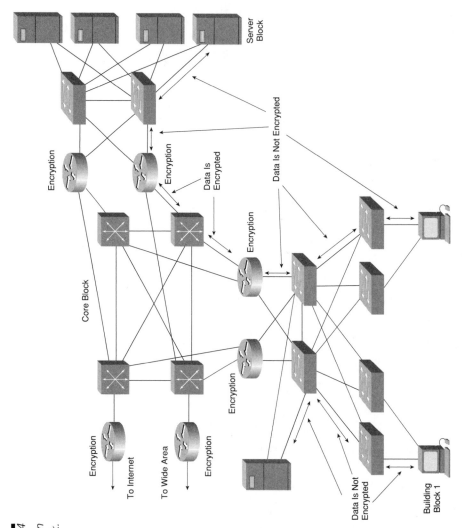

Figure 13–24
Router-encrypted traffic on the complex network.

If your network carries extremely sensitive data, workstation and server encryption should be implemented along with the router encryption, as shown in Figure 13–25. In this way, complete data integrity can be achieved throughout the network.

The level of encryption used at the workstation should be based on the level of confidentiality required for the document to be sent across the network. If the document requires complete confidentiality, then hash functions, and asymmetric and symmetric encryption can all be used for data integrity. These encryption methods work together to secure the sender's and receiver's identity (hash functions and asymmetric encryption), and to guarantee integrity of both the document (symmetric encryption) and the data path that it is being forwarded on (asymmetric encryption). If the document does not require this much confidentiality, then fewer encryption methods can be used.

You should place encryption on those workstations that need complete data integrity, but you probably do not need to place it on all the workstations in the network. Encryption does slow down the performance of workstations and some network devices, so it should only be used where it is needed.

Designing Mobility

To accommodate user growth and mobility, the complex design uses a dynamic IP addressing scheme. DHCP software (described in Chapter 9, "Designing for Change and Growth") is configured on a server that allocates IP addresses to clients, and the endstations support DHCP client software. Certain routers are configured to forward IP broadcast packets as unicast packets so that the DHCP server can receive them, as shown in Figure 13–26. The relevant routers are labeled as IP/BootP helpers in the figure.

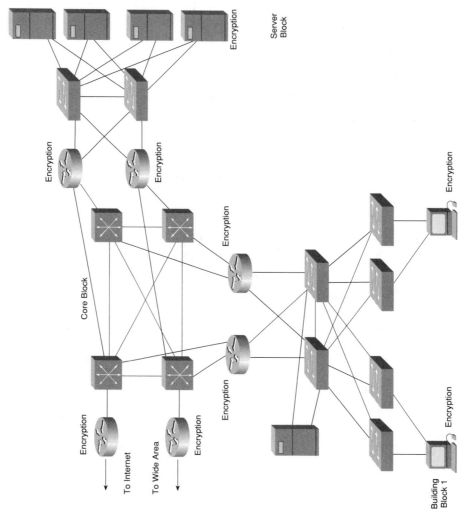

Figure 13–25
Workstation and router
encryption on the complex
network.

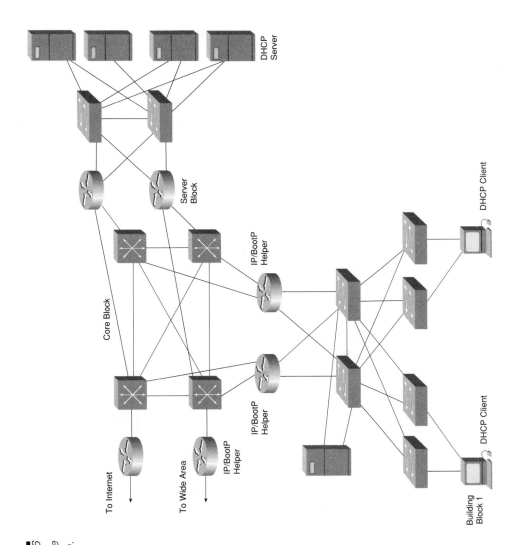

Figure 13–26
DHCP support in the complex design.

The building block routers transform the DHCP broadcasts into unicast frames and forward them through the network to the DHCP server. The routers in the server block do not need to understand DHCP broadcasts because by the time these routers see the DHCP Discover and Request frames, the frames are unicasts directed to the DHCP server. The routers in the server block simply send these unicasts to the DHCP server.

Because remote users log onto the campus via the WAN router, it has the IP/BootP helper configured on it as well.

The building block routers direct the DHCP Discover and Request messages to the DNS/DHCP server in the form of a unicast, thereby keeping broadcast traffic to a minimum.

Each time that users log onto the network, they may or may not get a new IP address (depending on the lease time set in the DHCP server). When users move to another floor or building, they automatically get new IP and IP default gateway addresses. Once DHCP is configured on the clients, there should be no need for static addressing on the endstations.

Enabling DHCP on the stations, routers, and DHCP server is a straightforward task. The more difficult task is to allocate the correct amount of addresses for each subnet on the DHCP server. The more complex the subnetting scheme, the more difficult this allocation becomes. For example, if one subnet supports 200 users, the next subnet supports only 100 users, and so on (so that each subnet on the network does not support the same number of users), then allocating the addresses for each subnet on the DHCP server becomes a formidable task. If you set up your subnetting scheme so that each subnet supports the same number of users, then allocating addresses becomes easier, and DHCP remains scalable as the network grows.

Implementing DHCP in the complex network design makes user mobility and growth easier to manage for the network administrator by eliminating the arduous task of assigning and re-assigning static addresses.

IMPLEMENTING VLANS

VLANs can be implemented in several ways in the complex network. For tight broadcast domain control, we recommend using the VLAN method described in the scalable network design. However, if supporting user flexibility is more important than maintaining tight broadcast control in the complex design, two other implementations are available: VLANs within the building block and user-level VLANs.

VLANs within the Building Block

VLANs within the building block is an extension of VLANs at the distribution switch, which we described in the scalable design and show here in Figure 13–27. Note that each VLAN in the scalable design connects to just one distribution switch. In contrast, for the complex design, each VLAN can extend across both distribution switches, instead of being limited to just one, as shown in Figure 13–28.

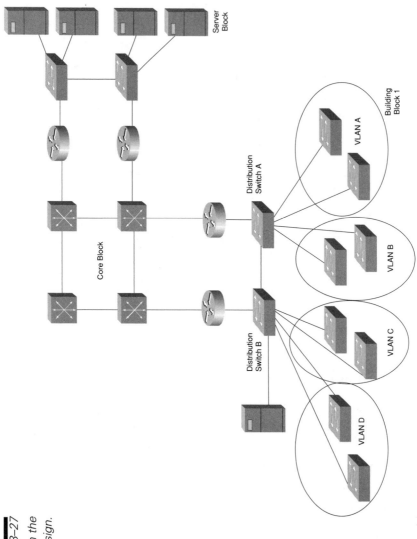

Figure 13–27
Building block VLANs in the scalable design.

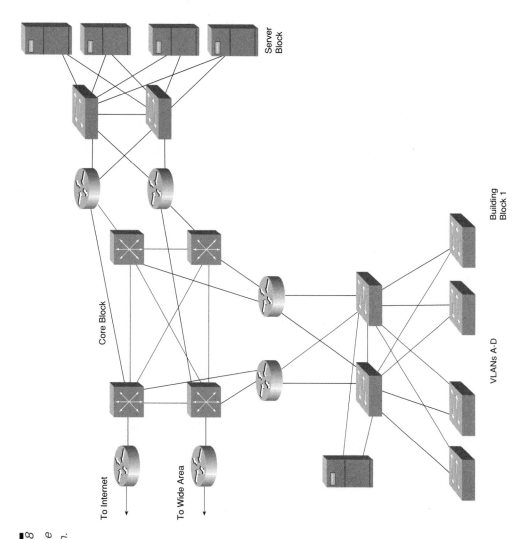

Figure 13–28
Building block VLANs in the complex design.

In both designs, there are four broadcast domains in the building block; therefore, there are four VLANs. In the scalable design, each wiring closet switch supports only one VLAN. The distribution switches support all four VLANs only when a router failure occurs. (The link between the distribution switches then carries all VLAN traffic.) In the complex design, all of the wiring closet switches and distribution switches support all four VLANs.

In the complex design, each wiring closet switch needs to forward traffic on all four VLANs, whereas the scalable design shows that each wiring closet switch only needs to forward traffic for a single VLAN. The complex design thus provides a bit more user flexibility, but it also creates worse traffic patterns because the broadcast traffic for all four VLANs crosses both distribution switches, as well as all the wiring closet switches.

The complex design provides user flexibility in the following manner: If users on VLAN A move to another switch within the same building block, they remain part of VLAN A and do not need to join another VLAN. It does not matter which distribution switch they connect to because both distribution switches support all the VLANs in the building block. If users move to another building block, however, they must join a different VLAN because the VLANs do not span multiple building blocks.

To support the users in the VLAN, the links to the routers load balance the VLAN traffic, as shown in Figure 13–29.

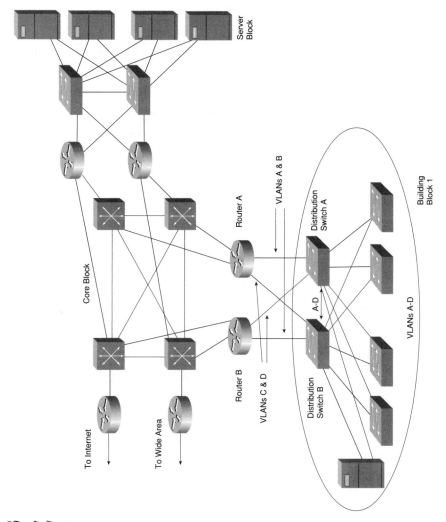

Figure 13–29
Load balancing on the complex design's VLAN router connections.

The figure shows that Distribution Switch A sends traffic from VLANs A and B to Router A, and traffic from VLANs C and D to Router B. Likewise, Distribution Switch B sends traffic from VLANs A and B to Router B, and traffic from VLANs C and D to Router A. All of the connections from the distribution switches to the routers are actively forwarding traffic. The link between the distribution switches supports all four VLANs for intra-VLAN traffic, as well as redundancy.

As with the scalable design, the distributed server in the building block can support either a single VLAN, or all four VLANs. The distributed server should connect to the distribution switch, however, because the VLANs span multiple wiring closets and the distribution switch is the common point of connection for the VLANs.

All intra-VLAN traffic (traffic within the same VLAN) cross the link connecting the two distribution switches, as shown in Figure 13–30.

This link is no longer reserved just for redundancy, as in the scalable design. Instead, this link forwards intra-VLAN traffic, such as traffic to the distributed server.

All inter-VLAN traffic (traffic between VLANs) must be routed through the router, as shown in Figure 13–31.

Even though Station A and Station B reside on the same wiring closet switch, the traffic from Station A must travel to Router A and be routed to Station B's VLAN. To reach Station C, Station A's traffic is forwarded to either Router A; or sent across to Distribution Switch B and forwarded to Router B, and then sent over to Station C. Compared to the VLANs in the scalable design, this VLAN implementation makes managing traffic patterns more complicated, but it does offer higher levels of user flexibility.

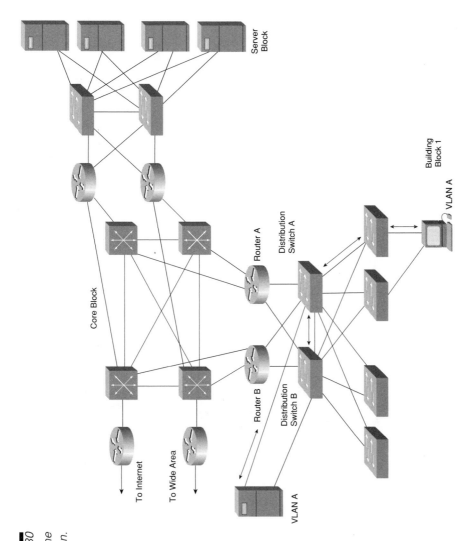

Figure 13-30
Intra-VLAN traffic in the building block VLAN design.

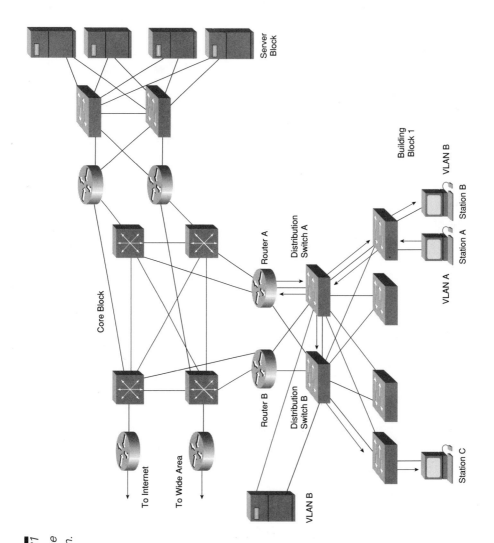

Figure 13–31

Inter-VLAN traffic in the building block VLAN design.

User-level VLANs

The second way that VLANs can be implemented in the complex design is with user-level VLANs, also known as cross-campus VLANs. Figure 13–32 shows this method.

As you can see, the same VLAN can reside in two different building blocks. In this situation, the wiring closet switches need to support a variety of VLANs. One wiring closet switch can support VLANs A, B, C, and E; and another wiring closet switch can support VLANs C, E, G, and H. The distribution switches need to support all the VLANs that are on the wiring closet switches.

This VLAN method is very difficult to implement due to the location of the routers. Intra-VLAN traffic cannot cross the routers and stay in the same broadcast domain. An alternative network design can help this VLAN implementation, however, as shown in Figure 13–33.

In this alternative design, the routers are placed off of the distribution switches and do not connect to the core block switches. The routers are not in the path of the intra-VLAN traffic, but are still responsible for inter-VLAN routing. In this scenario, the routers are no longer used to maintain broadcast domain separation between the building block and core block for all the VLANs.

Let's take a look at three traffic situations for the alternative design: intra-VLAN traffic, broadcast traffic, and inter-VLAN traffic. Figure 13–34 shows intra-VLAN traffic in this new design.

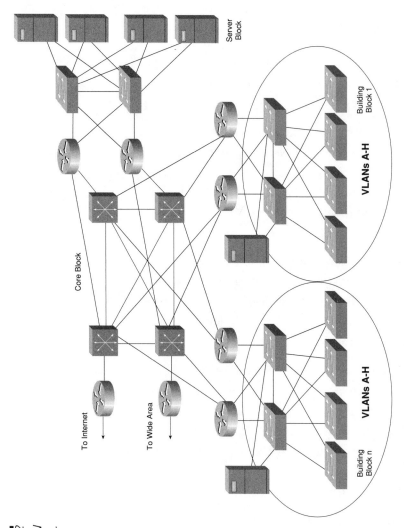

Figure 13–32
User-level VLAN
implementation.

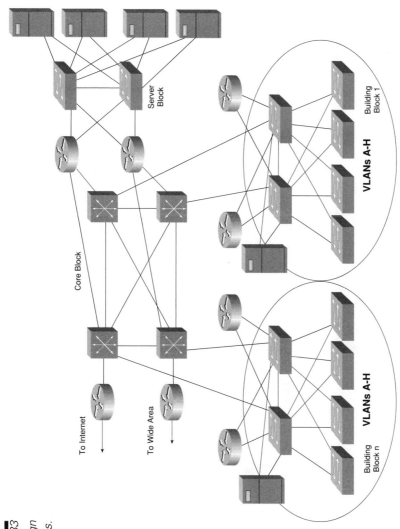

Figure 13–33
Alternative complex design
to support user-level VLANs.

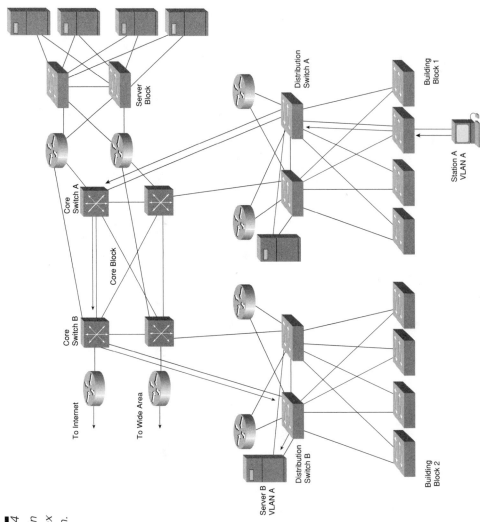

Figure 13–34
Intra-VLAN traffic in
user-level VLAN complex
design.

Unicast traffic is sent from Station A to Server B in VLAN A. As we can see, the traffic originates in Building Block 1, and goes through Distribution Switch A to Core Switch A without going through a router. Core Switch A sends the traffic to Core Switch B. Core Switch B sends the traffic over to Building Block 2 through Distribution Switch B, again without going through a router. The traffic then reaches Server B.

What happens if the traffic is broadcast traffic? Figure 13–35 shows broadcast traffic behavior in VLAN A.

Because the routers do not separate the broadcast domain between Building Block 1 and the core block, the broadcast traffic propagates throughout the core block and into Building Block 2. The routers in the server block stop the broadcast traffic from entering the server block. If there are a lot of broadcasts, however, then a lot of valuable bandwidth is used up in both the core block and the building blocks.

Finally, consider inter-VLAN traffic in this new design, which is illustrated in Figure 13–36.

The traffic going from any station within VLAN A to any station within any other VLAN must pass through a router. If the traffic originates in Building Block 1 on Station A, then either Router A or B routes the traffic. The appropriate router sends the traffic either across the core block to Station B in Building Block 2 or sends data to Distribution Switch B and over to Station C.

Another issue you should be aware of is that a user-level VLAN design prevents the intra-VLAN traffic from being able to take advantage of some of the network security we've discussed, such as network layer encryption or access lists. Any traffic that does not pass through a router does not go through these security gates.

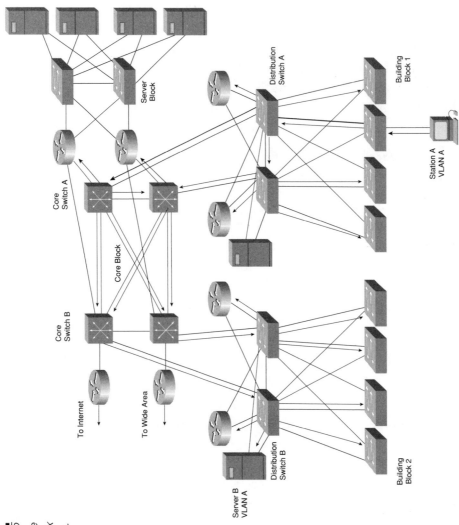

Figure 13–35
Broadcast traffic in the
user-level VLAN complex
design.

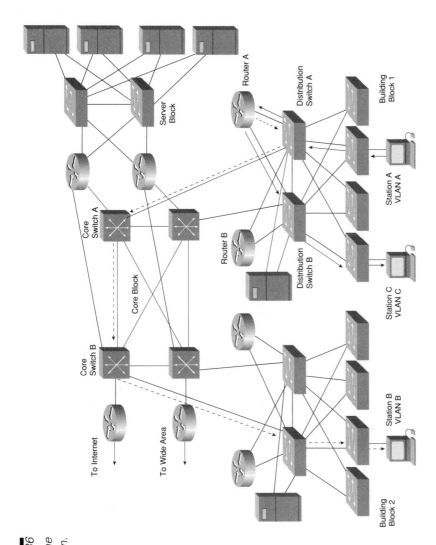

Figure 13–36
Inter-VLAN traffic in the complex design.

A user-level VLAN can, however, be appropriate for critical or time-sensitive applications, and be structured to provide some traffic pattern stability. In this case, the design allows one VLAN to exist everywhere on the network and restricts the other VLANs to exist only within a single building block. We show this scenario in Figure 13–37.

VLAN A is the only VLAN that spans the building blocks. The users in this VLAN are sharing a specific time-critical application. The other users on the network do not use this application and all other VLANs are restricted within the building block. Therefore, most of the traffic is predictable in this design except for some of the traffic in VLAN A. It also makes sense to place the critical application on a distributed server that resides in VLAN A, rather than place it on an enterprise server.

Core Block and Server Block VLANs

The way in which the core block supports VLANs depends on the VLAN implementation used in the building blocks. If each VLAN is restricted within a single building block, then the core block needs to support only two VLANs, as shown in Figure 13–38.

Because there are two router connections from each building block router to the core block, there needs to be two core block VLANs, rather than one. In our example, one router connection supports VLAN 10 and one router connection supports VLAN 20. Both links can forward traffic simultaneously.

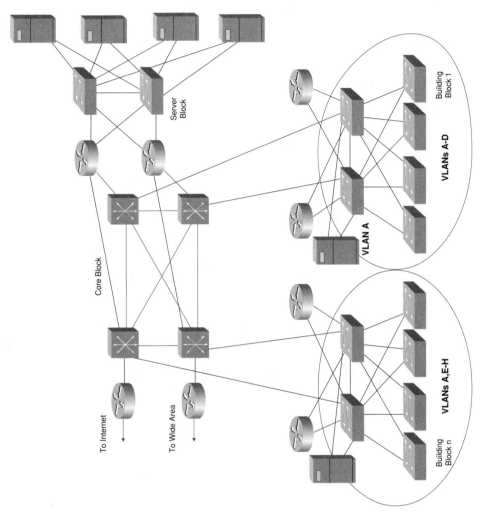

Figure 13-37
User-level VLAN for a specific application.

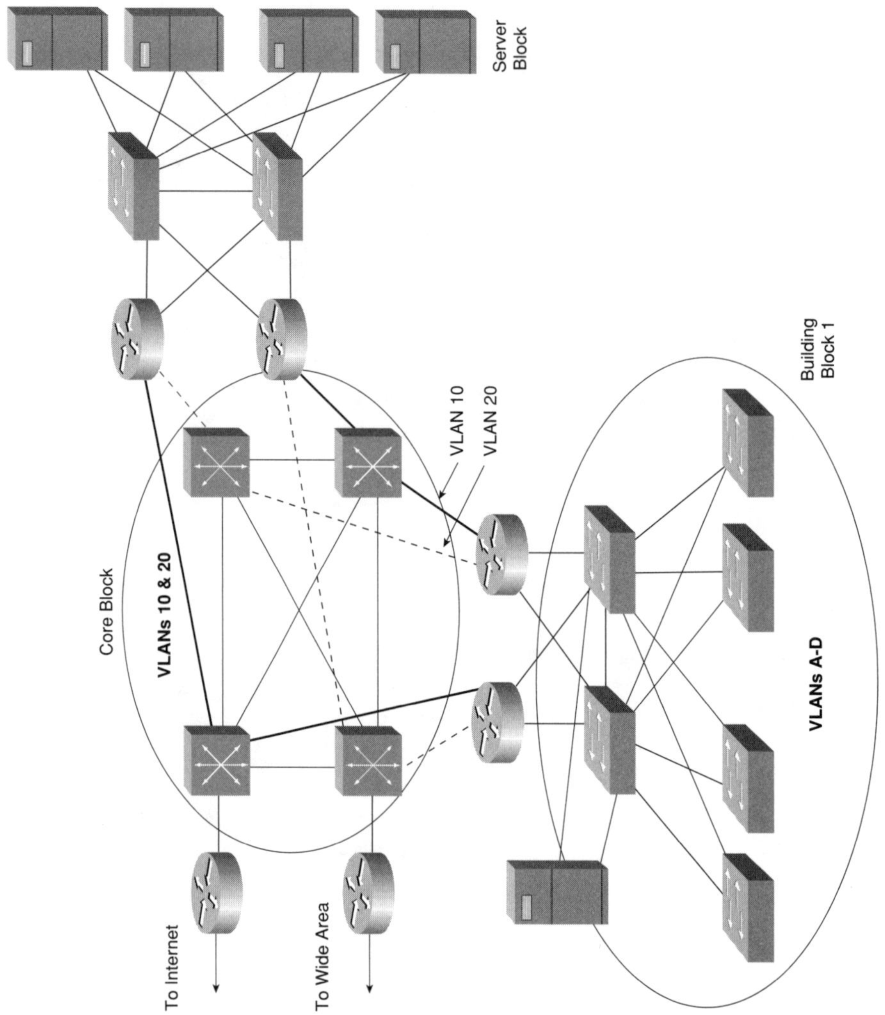

Figure 13–38
Two VLANs in the complex
design core block.

If a VLAN can span building blocks (user-level VLANs), then the core block supports more than two VLANs. For example, if there are 10 VLANs throughout the building blocks, then the core block needs to support all 10 VLANs, as shown in Figure 13–39.

When user-level VLANs are used, the building block routers do not connect to the core switches, as explained earlier. They do, however, support all VLANs. Additionally, the links connecting the distribution switches to the core switches, as well as the links between the core switches, must support all the VLANs.

In the complex design, the server block needs to support only two VLANs. As discussed earlier, the server block supports two subnets because there are multiple NIC cards in the enterprise servers, and each NIC card supports a subnet. Each subnet relates to a VLAN. The connections between the switches and routers each support a VLAN, as shown in Figure 13–40.

Failure Scenarios for VLANs

As we did in the scalable design, we'll explore a few failure scenarios for VLANs in the complex design, starting with router failure. Figure 13–41 shows VLANs spanning the building block, and Figure 13–42 shows user-level VLANs. In both figures, Router A in the building block and Router C in the server block failed.

Both figures show that in the building block, Distribution Switch A sends the traffic to Router B because it detects that Router A is down. In Figure 13–41, traffic for VLANs 1-2 is sent through Distribution Switch B, and then Distribution Switch B sends it to Router B. Distribution Switch A continues to send traffic for VLANs 3-4 directly to Router B because this is the normal traffic flow for these VLANs.

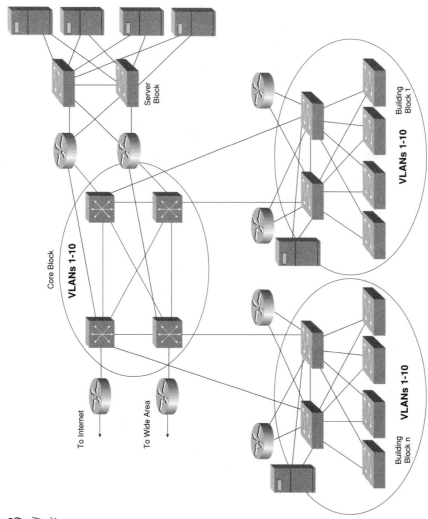

Figure 13–39
Core block supporting all
VLANs in the complex
design.

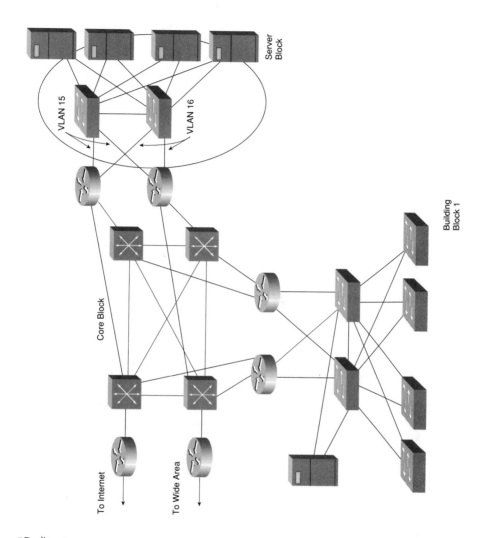

Figure 13–40
VLANs in the server block of the complex design.

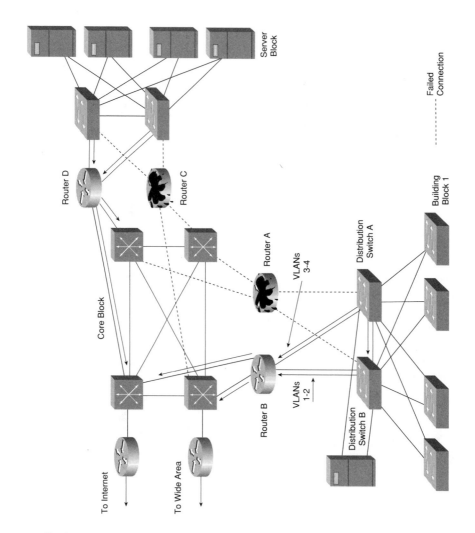

Figure 13–41
Building block VLAN
redundancy for router failure
in the complex design.

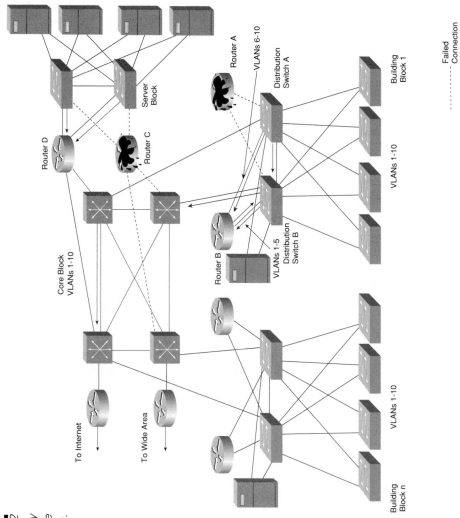

Figure 13–42
User-level VLAN redundancy for router failure in the complex design.

In Figure 13–42, Distribution Switch A sends traffic for VLANs 1-5 through Distribution Switch B, and then Distribution Switch B sends it to Router B. Distribution Switch A continues to send traffic for VLANs 6-10 directly to Router B because this is the normal traffic flow for those VLANs.

Both figures show that Router B sends all the traffic from the building block to the core block. In the server block, the switches forward all the traffic to Router D.

Now, suppose that Distribution Switch A fails. The wiring closet switches send the traffic to Distribution Switch B, regardless of which VLAN implementation is used. Figure 13–43 shows the building block VLANs, and Figure 13–44 shows the user-level VLANs with the distribution switch failure.

As a wrap-up to this VLAN section, Figure 13–45 shows the complete VLAN design for the complex network. The VLANs corresponding to each connection are labeled by number and letter. The illustration depicts this design using building block VLANs, which can be replaced with user-level VLANs.

Although building block VLANs or user-level VLANs provide user flexibility throughout the network, keep in mind that these methods maintain less traffic pattern stability when compared with VLANs used for broadcast domain control. If traffic pattern stability becomes an issue, consider the VLAN strategy explained in the scalable network design.

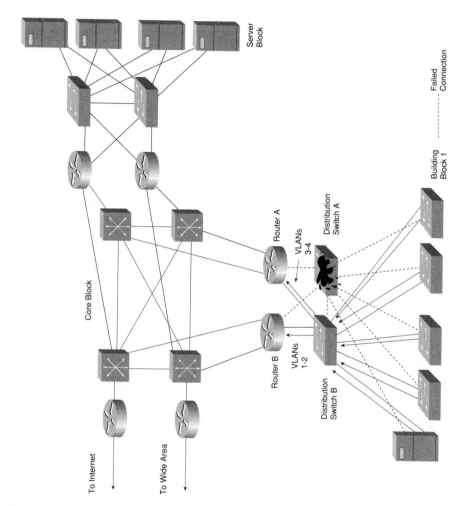

Figure 13-43
Building block VLAN
redundancy for distribution
switch failure in the complex
design.

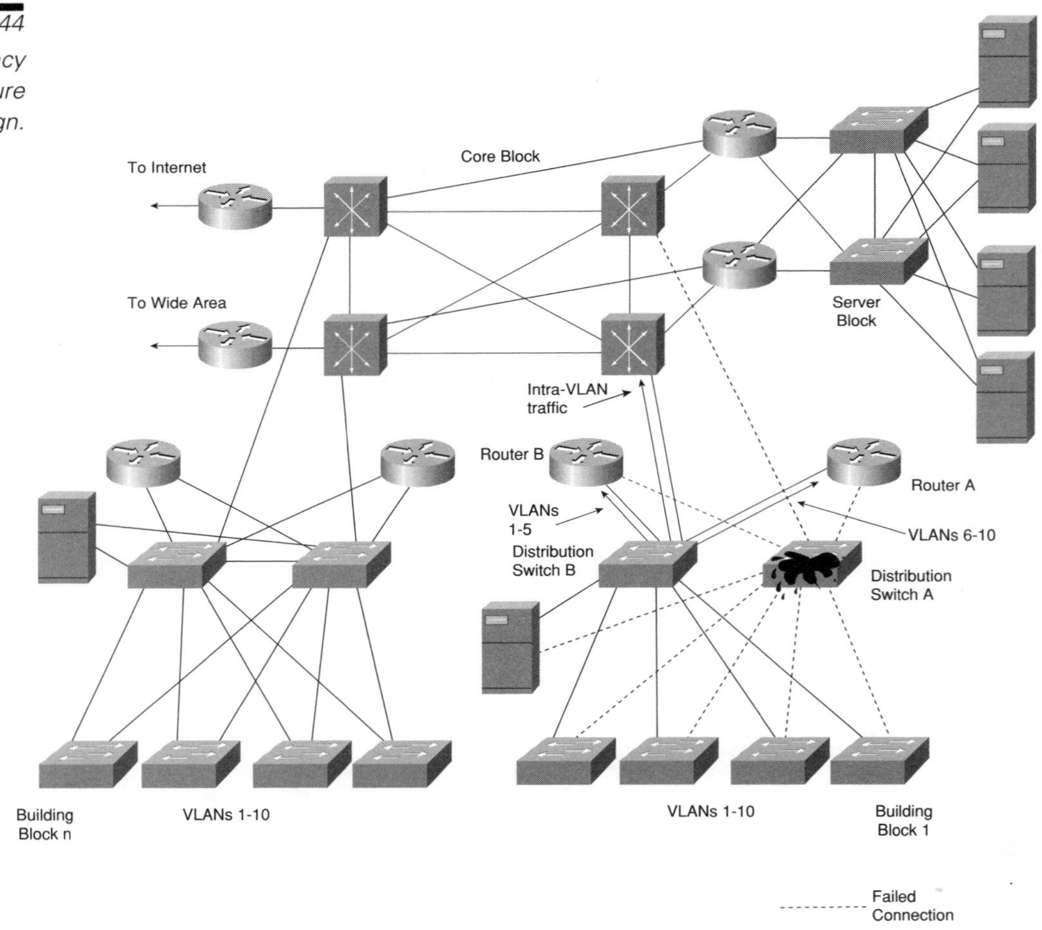

Figure 13-44
User-level VLAN redundancy
for distribution switch failure
in the complex design.

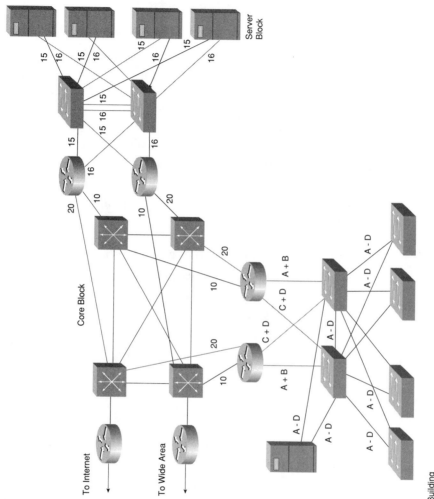

Figure 13–45
VLANs throughout the
complex network design.

SETTING TRAFFIC PRIORITIES

Just as with the scalable design, the need for traffic prioritization in the complex network design is low. When applications such as voice and real-time video become more frequently used, traffic prioritization methods will guarantee higher performance for these applications.

The complex network design can easily support traffic prioritization when the need for it arises. As an example, we will show how an application shared by a group of users can be supported with traffic-prioritization techniques.

A group of five users are using an application that is very delay-sensitive. The network may be able to support the application's delay requirements without using traffic prioritization, but the users don't want to risk it. Instead, they want their workstations, as well as the network infrastructure, to prioritize this application above others on the network. Figure 13–46 shows the complex network design supporting this application with traffic prioritization.

First, the users' workstations must have enough bandwidth to handle the application. In Figure 13–46, each of these stations has a 100-Mbps connection to the wiring closet switch. Also, a 100-Mbps connection exists between the wiring closet switches and the distribution switches, and between the distribution switches and the building block routers. The 100-Mbps connections can be either Fast Ethernet or ATM running at 155Mbps.

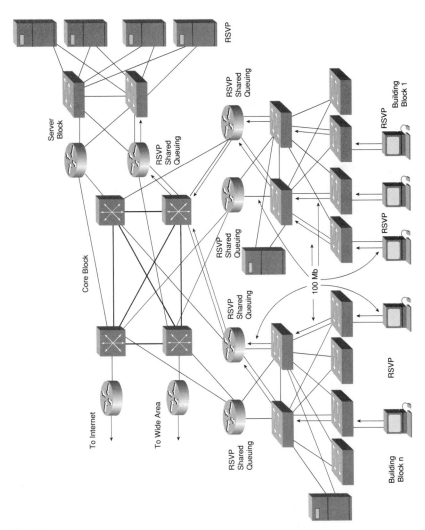

Figure 13–46
Traffic prioritization in the complex design.

Next, the routers support shared queuing and RSVP. As you may recall from Chapter 7, "Setting Traffic Priorities," shared queuing allows both the prioritized application and low bandwidth traffic to pass through the router at the same time.

The application that the group wants to run requires 3MB of bandwidth. RSVP will guarantee the 3MB of bandwidth that this application requires from the network. As you can see in Figure 13–46, the building block routers and the server block routers are running RSVP and supporting the 3MB of bandwidth across the network.

The workstations are also running RSVP. The application supports RSVP, so it sends the request out onto the network to reserve 3MB of bandwidth while it is running. The enterprise server that is running the application supports RSVP as well. As the RSVP requests come in, the server reserves 3MB of bandwidth for this application.

With the complex design, as more applications on the network require dedicated bandwidth or a minimum delay guarantee, traffic prioritization can be easily implemented to support these additional needs.

SUMMARY

The complex network design supports all of the components of design that we've discussed in this book: traffic patterns, redundancy, multimedia, security, mobility, VLANs, and traffic prioritization. To tie it all together, the complete picture of the complex network blueprint is shown in Figure 13–47.

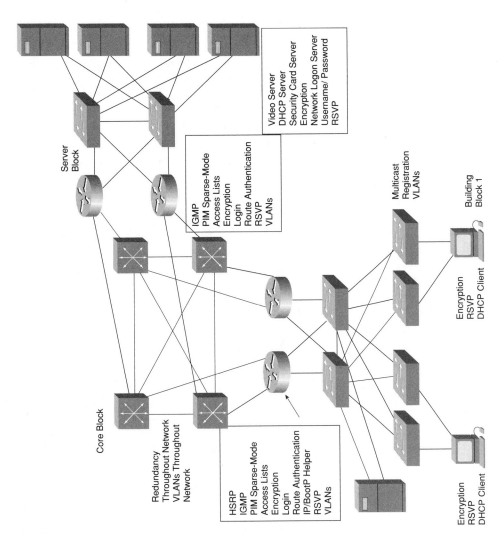

Video Server
DHCP Server
Security Card Server
Encryption
Network Logon Server
Username/Password
RSVP

Server
Block

IGMP
PIM Sparse-Mode
Access Lists
Encryption
Login
Route Authentication
RSVP
VLANs

Multicast
Registration
VLANs

Building
Block 1

Encryption
RSVP
DHCP Client

Core Block

Redundancy
Throughout Network
VLANs Throughout
Network

HSRP
IGMP
PIM Sparse-Mode
Access Lists
Encryption
Login
Route Authentication
IP/BootP Helper
RSVP
VLANs

Encryption
RSVP
DHCP Client

Figure 13–47
Complete complex design
blueprint.

This network involves a lot of network services that are necessary in order to create a robust, high-performance network. As with the scalable design, managing this network can be extremely complicated. Network-monitoring tools, network-management packages, and an understanding of the network's capabilities help to support this network efficiently. Knowing the traffic baselines in the network provides a solid foundation when troubleshooting or planning for future growth.

It is also important for the network support staff to gain expertise in the areas of the network that they support. For example, one network support person should be responsible only for the security on the network. This person then becomes an expert on security, but not necessarily an expert on multimedia support. Managing the network after it is implemented is just as important as the initial network design.

If your network meets the criteria for a complex design, keep in mind the following as you plan and implement it:

- To avoid a single point of failure, dividing the server block and core block into more than one broadcast domain is wise. Each building block also usually has more than one broadcast domain.

- In the building block, using wiring closet switch redundancy, distribution switch redundancy, and NIC redundancy at workstations can maximize redundancy.

- In the core block, a full mesh offers the maximum redundancy: Each core switch connects to every other core switch.

- In the server block, NIC redundancy at the servers and distribution-switch redundancy are advisable.

- The presence of multicast traffic requires choosing the appropriate multicast routing protocol for your particular complex network.

- All of the security methods discussed in Chapter 8, "Addressing Security Issues," probably need to be implemented—including encryption on the routers, servers, and some or all of the workstations.

- A dynamic IP addressing scheme such as DHCP is needed to accommodate user mobility.

- User-level VLANs or building block VLANs that span multiple wiring closet switches and distribution switches can facilitate user flexibility (but with some loss of traffic pattern stability).

- As with the scalable network, conducting a failure analysis is a critical design step for the complex network. Analyze what could happen in broadcast domains, VLANs, and the overall network if a device or devices fail.

This chapter covers the following topics:

- Voice-over-data

- Internet-influenced changes

- Technology and device evolution

- Network management

CHAPTER 14

Preparing for the Future

As indicated throughout this book, the campus LAN continues to evolve. In this chapter, we describe some of what's in store for the future of the campus network.

VOICE-OVER-DATA

One change on the horizon that will impact the campus is voice traffic going over the data network. Moving voice traffic from the telephony network onto the data network is just beginning to occur, and will exponentially increase in both the short and long term. This will happen mostly across the WAN, in an effort to reduce the high cost of long distance telephone connections. But, just as Web-based applications and multimedia have moved from the WAN to the LAN, voice-over-data will be adopted and integrated into the campus network as well. It will be a logical transition for two primary reasons: the campus is the headquarters for the data network, housing the enterprise servers and network backbone; and the campus is also the center location for the voice network, containing the company's main PBX and extensive voice applications.

INTERNET-INFLUENCED CHANGES

We've already examined how the enormous adoption and use of the Internet and World Wide Web have changed the way companies operate. The Web contains highly interactive applications that deliver information more quickly, cheaply, and easily than at any other time in the computer industry. The delivery of Web-based applications has empowered the consumer through the commercial Internet, and at the same time, driven a revolutionary approach to the re-engineering of internal business processes.

The next goal is to automate the many processes required by the new electronic commerce. For example, when a customer purchases a product through the Internet or Web, that purchase creates actions, and activates changes and updates dynamically. These actions include creating the purchase order, setting up billing and shipping to the customer, and updating the inventory, all of which occur automatically. Once this process is in place, the next goal is to tie the company's vendors into the inventory databases, allowing them to instantaneously track the status of supplies they need to ship to the company. All of these plans require changes and upgrades to the network, as well as new applications and support for the new applications.

TECHNOLOGY AND DEVICE EVOLUTION

The direction for campus LAN transport technologies continues to be toward offering higher speed and capacity. Gigabit Ethernet is the newest high-bandwidth transport technology; and ATM, a recent high-bandwidth transport, continues to be fine-tuned. More changes are possible, and these changes again stem from developments on the Internet. For example, there is an experimental computer network called vBNS—the very high-speed backbone network service. Launched in 1995, vBNS connects research institutions over fiber-optic cable at speeds of 622 million bits-per-second (bps). The goal is to increase the speed to 2.4 billion bps within two years.

Although vBNS is an Internet technology and not available to everyone (the National Science Foundation awards institutional grants to connect to the network), its success inevitably will filter down to the campus network.

As can be expected, equipment manufacturers will pursue ways to make their products faster, smarter, and capable of offering more bandwidth. We described the recent emergence of Layer 3 switches, which integrate Layer 2 switching capability with Layer 3 router functionality. The next step for Layer 3 switches is to offer all the Layer 3 network services at a higher performance rate than that which a router can provide today.

NETWORK MANAGEMENT

Network management will continue to play an important role in the future just as it does today. As applications increase and become linked with other applications, tracking and monitoring them on the network will become more important and more challenging. For example, when companies integrate business functions, as we described in the automated business scenario, it will be done on an application basis. The application used to create a purchase order will be linked to the application that sets up the billing, which will be linked to the application that updates the inventory data base, and so forth. As this evolution happens, it will be increasingly important for network managers to have up-to-date network management tools that will monitor the speed and response times of these new applications.

SUMMARY

These future trends naturally lead toward more and more complex data networks. Designing a robust campus LAN may become tricky at times, but not impossible. If a new trend catches you by surprise, you should be able to meet the new challenge head-on if your network foundation is solid. The same steps presented throughout this book should be used for the future: understand traffic patterns on the network, factor in the essential elements for the network, and design the network to provide optimal performance and scalability as it grows and changes.

APPENDIX A

Technical References

The sources described on the following pages give you more information about the technical material we provide in this book. For your information, we list the following relevant documents:

- RFC reports

- Internet drafts

- ATM Forum standards

- IEEE specifications

- Additional reading

WHERE TO GET INFORMATION

In January 1993, the InterNIC was established as a collaborative project between AT&T, General Atomics, and Network Solutions, Inc. Two major categories of services were identified as having significant value: services provided by the Info Scout, and second-level support to campus network information center (NIC) organizations. In 1995, Network Solutions, Inc. requested and was granted the opportunity to continue offering these services, which are now known as InterNIC Support Services and Net Scout Services.

The InterNIC continues to participate in Internet forums and collaborate with the research and education community to promote Internet services, explore new tools and technologies, and contribute to the rapidly growing Internet community. Information regarding RFCs, Internet-drafts, working documents, and other technical material can be obtained electronically by contacting InterNIC at:

Email: **admin@ds.internic.net**

World Wide Web: **http//www.internic.net**

RFC REPORTS

The most comprehensive collection of network information is a series of reports, each of which is called a Request for Comment (RFC). Each RFC has a title and an RFC number: for example, *Internet Protocol*, RFC-791.

This body of work, previously managed by Government Systems, Inc., is now the responsibility of the Internet Engineering Task Force (IETF). IETF is the protocol engineering, development, and standardization arm of the Internet Architecture Board, a technical advisory group of the Internet Society. The IETF is a large, open international community of network designers, operators, vendors, and researchers concerned with the evolution of the Internet protocol architecture and the smooth operation of the Internet.

The InterNIC maintains an archive that contains IETF's RFC documents. The RFCs are all listed in an index titled *rfc-index*. The index is not definitive, because titles do not always indicate the contents. To obtain one or more RFCs, contact InterNIC at the address previously listed, or view the RFC index directly via their Web site:

http://www.internic.net/ds/rfc-index.html

Table A–1 lists the RFCs referenced in this book.

Table A–1   *RFC titles and numbers*

Title	RFC Number
Address Resolution Protocol (ARP)	RFC 826
Data Encryption Standard (3DES)	RFC 1851
Distance Vector Multicast Routing Protocol (DVMRP)	RFC 1075, See also: draft-ietf-idmr-dvmrp-v3-05.txt
Dynamic Host Configuration Protocol (DHCP)	RFC 2131
Host Extensions for IP Multicasting	RFC 1112
Internet Group Management Protocol (IGMP)	RFC 1112
Internet Protocol (IP)	RFC 791
Message Digest 4 Algorithm (MD4)	RFC 1320
Message Digest 5 Algorithm (MD5)	RFC 1321
Multicast OSPF (MOSPF)	RFC 1584
Open Shortest Path First (OSPF)	RFC 2178
PIM Sparse-mode	RFC 2117
Proxy ARP	RFC 1027
Resource Reservation Protocol (RSVP)	RFC 2205
Routing Information Protocol (RIP)	RFC 1058
Routing Information Protocol (RIP) Version 2	RFC 1723

INTERNET-DRAFTS

Internet-Drafts are working documents of the Internet Engineering Task Force (IETF), its areas, and its working groups. Note that other groups may also distribute working documents as Internet-Drafts.

Internet-Drafts are draft documents that are valid for a maximum of six months; they may be updated, replaced, or made obsolete by other documents at any time.

The InterNIC maintains an archive that contains Internet-Draft documents. The documents are all listed in an index, titled *internet-drafts*. The index is not definitive because titles do not always indicate the contents. To obtain one or more Internet-Drafts, contact InterNIC at the address previously listed, or view the Internet-Drafts directly via their Web site:

http://www.internic.net/internet-drafts

Table A–2 lists the Internet-Drafts referenced in this book.

Table A–2 *Internet-Draft titles and numbers*

Internet-Draft Title	Reference
Hot Standby Routing Protocol (HSRP)	draft-li-hsrp-00.txt
Internet Group Management Protocol (IGMP) Version 2	draft-ietf-idmr-igmp-v2-08.txt
Next Hop Routing Protocol (NHRP)	draft-ietf-ion-nhrp-appl-02.txt
Open Shortest Path First (OSPF) Version 2	draft-ietf-ospf-ver2-00.txt
Protocol Independent Multicast (PIM) dense-mode	draft-ietf-idmr-pim-dm-05.txt

ATM FORUM STANDARDS

The ATM Forum is an international, nonprofit organization that was formed to accelerate the use of ATM (Asynchronous Transfer Mode) products and services through a convergence of interoperability specifications.

ATM Forum-approved specifications are available via their Web site:

http://www.atmforum.com/atmforum/specs

Table A–3 lists the ATM standards referenced in this book.

Table A–3   *ATM standards titles and number*

ATM Standard Title	Reference
ATM UNI Signalling Specification Vers 4.0	af-sig-0061.00
LAN Emulation (LANE) 1.0	af-lane-0021.000
LAN Emulation (LANE) 2.0 LUNI Interface	af-lane-0084.000
LAN Emulation (LANE) 2.0 LNNI Interface	*work in progress*
MPOA 1.0	af-mpoa-0087.000

IEEE SPECIFICATIONS

The Institute of Electrical and Electronics Engineers (IEEE) is a professional society that was founded in 1884 by a handful of practitioners of the new electrical engineering discipline. Today, IEEE is comprised of more than 320,000 members in 147 countries. Members of IEEE focus on advancing the theory and practice of electrical electronics, computer engineering, and computer science.

The IEEE Standards is a program that develops and disseminates voluntary, consensus-based industry standards involving current electro-technology.

IEEE approved specifications are available via their Web site:

http://www.standards.ieee.org

Table A–4 lists the IEEE standards referenced in this book.

Table A–4 *IEEE specification titles and numbers*

IEEE Specification Title	Description
IEEE 802.1q	A work in progress to address VLAN interoperability
IEEE 802.1d	Spanning Tree Protocol

ADDITIONAL READING

The following industry-related documents and publications may be of interest:

Ford, Merilee, et al. *Internetworking Technologies Handbook*, Cisco Press, 1997.

"Data Encryption Standard" (FIPS-46) U.S. National Bureau of Standards, Federal Information Processing Standard (FIPS) Publication 46, January 1977.

"Secure Hash Standard" (FIPS-180-1) National Institute of Standards and Technology, U.S. Department of Commerce, April 1995.

"The Digital Signature Standard," *Communication of the ACM*, Vol. 35, July 1992.

Diffie, W., and Hellman, M., "New Directions in Cryptography," *IEEE Transactions on Information Theory*, Vol. IT-22, No. 6, November 1996.

Glossary

A

ABR—Available Bit Rate. QoS class defined by the ATM Forum for ATM networks. ABR is used for connections that do not require timing relationships between source and destination. ABR provides no guarantees in terms of cell loss or delay; it provides only best-effort service. Traffic sources adjust their transmission rates in response to information they receive describing the status of the network and its capability to successfully deliver data. Compare with **CBR**, **UBR**, and **VBR**.

Access list—List kept by routers to control access to or from the router for a number of services (for example, to prevent packets with a certain IP address from leaving a particular interface on the router).

Acknowledgment—Notification sent from one network device to another to acknowledge that some event (for example, receipt of a message) has occurred. Sometimes abbreviated as ACK. Compare to **NAK**.

Address—Data structure or logical convention used to identify a unique entity, such as a particular process or network device.

Address resolution—Generally, a method for resolving differences between computer-addressing schemes. Address resolution usually specifies a method for mapping network layer (Layer 3) addresses to data link layer (Layer 2) addresses.

Address Resolution Protocol—See **ARP**.

Algorithm—Well-defined rule or process for arriving at a solution to a problem. In networking, algorithms are commonly used to determine the best route for traffic from a particular source to a particular destination.

AppleTalk protocol—Series of communications protocols designed by Apple Computer. Two phases currently exist. Phase 1, the earlier version, supports a single physical network that can have only one network number and be in one zone. Phase 2, the more recent version, supports multiple logical networks on a single physical network and allows networks to be in more than one zone.

Application layer—Layer 7 of the OSI reference model. This layer provides services to application processes (such as electronic mail, file transfer, and terminal emulation) that are outside of the OSI model. The application layer identifies and establishes the availability of intended communication partners (and the resources required to connect with them), synchronizes cooperating applications, and establishes agreement on procedures for error recovery and control of data integrity. See also **Data link layer, Network layer, Physical layer, Presentation layer, Session layer,** and **Transport layer.**

ARP—Address Resolution Protocol. Internet protocol used to map an IP address to a MAC address. Defined in RFC 826.

Asymmetric encryption—Encryption method that uses both public and secret (or private) keys, and that provides data security and sender authentication. Each endstation creates a public/private key pair. When two endstations want to send confidential data to each other, they agree on the encryption algorithm to use, and then they exchange their public keys. Also referred to as *public key encryption*.

ATM—Asynchronous Transfer Mode. International standard for cell relay in which multiple service types (such as voice, video, or data) are conveyed in fixed-length (53-byte) cells. Fixed-length cells allow cell processing to occur in hardware, thereby reducing transit delays. ATM is designed to take advantage of high-speed transmission media such as E3, SONET, and T3.

ATM LANE—See **LANE**.

ATM MPOA—See **MPOA**.

Authentication—Determining the origin of information from an end user or a device such as a host, server, switch, or router.

Authorization—Securing the network by specifying which areas of the network (applications, devices, and so forth) a user is allowed to access.

Autonomous system—Collection of networks under a common administration sharing a common routing strategy. Autonomous systems are subdivided by areas. An autonomous system must be assigned a unique 16-bit number by the IANA. Sometimes abbreviated as AS.

Available Bit Rate—See **ABR**.

B

Backbone—Part of a network that acts as the primary path for traffic that is most often sourced from, and destined for, other subnetworks. Also referred to as *core.*

Backup links—Physical redundant connections between network devices. Also referred to as *network link redundancy.*

Bandwidth—Rated throughput capacity of a given network medium or protocol.

Bandwidth allocation—Process of assigning bandwidth to users and applications served by a network. Involves assigning priority to different flows of traffic based on how critical and delay-sensitive they are. This makes the best use of available bandwidth, and if the network becomes congested, lower-priority traffic can be dropped.

Bandwidth percentage queueing—Allocating a certain percentage of processing bandwidth in the network device to process high-priority traffic and giving the remaining processing bandwidth to the other traffic.

Banyan VINES—See **VINES.**

Baseline—Characterization of the normal traffic flow in the network.

BOOTP—Bootstrap Protocol. Protocol used by a network node to determine the IP address of its Ethernet interfaces in order to affect network booting.

Broadcast—Data packet that is sent to all nodes on a network. Broadcasts are identified by a broadcast address. Compare with **multicast** and **unicast**. See also **broadcast address.**

Broadcast address—Special address reserved for sending a message to all stations. Generally, a broadcast address is a MAC destination address of all ones (ffffff). Compare with **multicast address** and **unicast address**. See also **broadcast**.

Broadcast and Unknown Server (BUS)—See **BUS**.

Broadcast domain—The set of all devices that receives broadcast frames originating from any device within the set. Broadcast domains are typically bounded by routers because routers do not forward broadcast frames.

Broadcast propagation—Network device sends a broadcast frame out all of its ports, resulting in the broadcast frame traveling throughout the network.

Broadcast storm—Undesirable network event in which many broadcasts are sent simultaneously across all network segments. A broadcast storm uses substantial network bandwidth and typically causes network time-outs.

Building block—Network domain that consists of the switching and routing devices required to connect users to the network, and which provides distributed network services and network intelligence.

BUS—Broadcast and Unknown Server. Multicast server used in ELANs that floods traffic addressed to an unknown destination and forwards multicast and broadcast traffic to the appropriate clients. See also **ELAN**.

C

CBR—Constant Bit Rate. QoS class defined by the ATM Forum for ATM networks. CBR is used for connections that depend on precise clocking to ensure undistorted delivery. Compare with **ABR, UBR,** and **VBR.**

Cell delay—In ATM, specifies the amount of time that can elapse between when the cell is sent and when it is received.

Cell loss—The acceptable number of cells that can be dropped due to congestion.

Centralized server—Server that supports either all or a majority of network users. Also referred to as *enterprise server.*

Class of Service—See **COS.**

Client—Node or software program (front-end device) that requests services from a server.

Client/server—Term used to describe distributed computing (processing) network systems in which transaction responsibilities are divided into two parts: client (front end) and server (back end). Both terms (client and server) can be applied to software programs or actual computing devices.

Collapsed backbone—Nondistributed backbone in which all network segments are interconnected by way of an internetworking device. A collapsed backbone might be a virtual network segment existing in a device such as a hub, a router, or a switch.

Component redundancy—Computer, router, switch, or other computer system that contains two or more of each of the most important subsystems, such as two disk drives, two CPUs, or two power supplies. Also referred to as *redundant system*.

Concentrator—1. Generally, a term used to describe a device that serves as the center of a star-topology network. 2. Hardware or software device that contains multiple independent yet connected modules of network and internetwork equipment. Hubs can be active (where they repeat signals sent through them) or passive (where they do not repeat, but merely split, signals sent through them). 3. In Ethernet and IEEE 802.3, an Ethernet multiport repeater. Also referred to as a *hub*.

Congestion—Traffic in excess of network capacity.

Constant Bit Rate—See **CBR**.

Core—See **Backbone**.

Core block—Network domain responsible for transferring cross-campus traffic as quickly as possible without doing any processor-intensive operations (Layer 3 functionality).

COS—Class of Service. Indication of the way an upper-layer protocol requires that a lower-layer protocol treat its messages.

Cross-campus traffic—Traffic that crosses the backbone of the network, travels through a router, or both.

D

Data link layer—Layer 2 of the OSI reference model. This layer provides reliable transit of data across a physical link. The data link layer is concerned with physical addressing, network topology, line discipline, error notification, ordered delivery of frames, and flow control. The IEEE has divided this layer into two sublayers: the MAC sublayer and the LLC sublayer. Sometimes simply called *link layer*. Roughly corresponds to the data link control layer of the SNA model. See also **Application layer, Network layer, Physical layer, Presentation layer, Session layer,** and **Transport layer.**

Data load sharing—See **Load sharing.**

Data path loops—More than one data path between two endpoints through switches that are actively forwarding data.

Data path redundancy—Software protocols that determine the way data travels over these network links. Data path redundancy determines how to send data across the multiple network links.

Data storage backup—Process of making a copy of the data that resides on a server.

Data stream—All data transmitted through a communications line in a single read or write operation.

DECnet—Group of communications products (including a protocol suite) developed and supported by Digital Equipment Corporation. DECnet/OSI (also called DECnet Phase V) is the most recent iteration, and supports both OSI protocols and proprietary Digital protocols. Phase IV Prime supports inherent MAC addresses that allow DECnet nodes to coexist with systems running other protocols that have MAC address restrictions.

Decryption—The reverse application of an encryption algorithm to encrypted data, thereby restoring that data to its original, unencrypted state. See also **Encryption**.

Dedicated bandwidth queuing—Allocating a dedicated amount of processing bandwidth on the network device for the prioritized traffic at all times.

Default gateway—IP address on the router that traffic goes to first in order to get to the rest of the network.

Delay—1. Time between the initiation of a transaction by a sender and the first response received by the sender. 2. Time required to move a packet from source to destination over a given path.

Destination address—Address of a network device that is receiving data. See also **Source address**.

Device—See **Node**.

DHCP—Dynamic Host Configuration Protocol. Provides a mechanism for allocating IP addresses dynamically so that addresses can be reused when hosts no longer need them. Defined in RFC 2131.

DHCP Acknowledge—Frame sent by the DHCP server to the DHCP client that allocates the IP address to that client.

DHCP Address Lease Time—Amount of time a DHCP client can keep the IP address allocated by the DHCP server.

DHCP client—Endstation that uses DHCP to obtain an IP address from the DHCP server on the network.

DHCP Discover frame—Broadcast frame sent out from the DHCP client to the network asking for an IP address.

DHCP No Acknowledge (NAK)—Frame sent by the DHCP server to the DHCP client that refuses to allocate the IP address to that client.

DHCP Offer frame—Frame sent by the DHCP server in response to a DHCP Discover frame with an available IP address for the DHCP client.

DHCP Request frame—Broadcast frame sent from the DHCP client asking to use the IP address that was offered in the DHCP Offer frame.

DHCP server—Server that allocates IP addresses to DHCP clients.

Digital signature—String of bits appended to a message (an encrypted hash) that provides authentication and data integrity.

Distance Vector Multicast Routing Protocol—See **DVMRP**.

Distributed server—Server that supports a specific group of users on the network. Also referred to as *local* or *workgroup server*.

Distribution switch—Switch used as a consolidation point for wiring closet switches.

Distribution switch VLANs—VLANs that exist on specific distribution switches. VLANs cannot span the entire network but can span multiple wiring closet switches.

Domain Name System (DNS)—System used in the Internet for translating names of network nodes into addresses.

DVMRP—Distance Vector Multicast Routing Protocol. Multicast routing protocol, largely based on RIP. Packets are forwarded on all outgoing interfaces until pruning and truncation occurs. DVMRP uses IGMP to exchange routing datagrams with its neighbors. Defined in RFC 1075. See also **IGMP.**

Dynamic Host Configuration Protocol (DHCP)—See DHCP.

Dynamic username/password—Security mechanism that incorporates a constantly changing password that can be used only once.

Dynamic VLANs—Endstation VLANs that are automatically configured based on a user profile and typically require a centralized database for profile storage.

E

EIGRP—Enhanced Interior Gateway Routing Protocol. Advanced version of IGRP developed by Cisco. Provides superior convergence properties and operating efficiency, and combines the advantages of link state protocols with those of distance vector protocols. Compare with **IGRP.** See also **OSPF,** and **RIP.**

ELAN—Emulated LAN. ATM network in which an Ethernet or Token Ring LAN is emulated using a client-server model. ELANs are composed of an LEC, an LES, a BUS, and an LECS. Multiple ELANs can exist simultaneously on a single ATM network. ELANs are defined by the LANE specification. See also **BUS, LANE, LEC, LECS,** and **LES.**

Email—Electronic mail. Widely used network application in which text messages are transmitted electronically between end users over various types of networks using various network protocols.

Emulated LAN—See **ELAN**.

Encryption—Application of a specific algorithm to alter the appearance of data, making it incomprehensible to those who are not authorized to see the information. See also **Decryption**.

End router—Router that connects to end user subnets, and is responsible for forwarding the multicast stream to those subnets.

Endstation—See **Node**.

Enterprise server—Server that supports either all or a majority of network users. Also referred to as *centralized server*.

Ethernet—Baseband LAN specification invented by Xerox Corporation and developed jointly by Xerox, Intel, and Digital Equipment Corporation. Ethernet networks use CSMA/CD and run over a variety of cable types at 10 Mbps. Ethernet is similar to the IEEE 802.3 series of standards.

F

Fast Ethernet—Any of a number of 100-Mbps Ethernet specifications. Fast Ethernet offers a speed increase ten times that of the 10BaseT Ethernet specification, while preserving such qualities as frame format, MAC mechanisms, and MTU. Such similarities allow the use of existing 10BaseT applications and network-management tools on Fast Ethernet networks. Based on an extension to the IEEE 802.3 specification. Compare with **Ethernet**.

FDDI—Fiber Distributed Data Interface. LAN standard, defined by ANSI X3T9.5, specifying a 100-Mbps token-passing network using fiber-optic cable, with transmission distances of up to 2 KM. FDDI uses a dual-ring architecture to provide redundancy.

File transfer—Category of popular network applications that allow files to be moved from one network device to another.

Filter—Generally, a process or device that screens network traffic for certain characteristics, such as a source address, destination address, or protocol, and determines whether to forward or discard that traffic based on the established criteria.

Firewall—Router or access server (or several routers or access servers) designated as a buffer between any connected public networks and a private network. A firewall router uses access lists and other methods to ensure the security of the private network.

FIFO—First In, First Out. Method of sending traffic through a device.

Flooding—Traffic-passing technique used by switches and bridges, in which traffic received on an interface is sent out all of the interfaces of that device except the interface on which the information was originally received.

Forwarding—Process of sending a frame toward its ultimate destination by way of an internetworking device.

Frame—Logical grouping of information sent as a data link layer unit over a transmission medium. Often refers to the header and trailer, used for synchronization and error control, which surround the user data contained in the unit.

Full mesh—Term describing a network in which devices are organized in a mesh topology, with each network node having either a physical circuit or a virtual circuit connecting it to every other network node. Provides a great deal of redundancy, but because it can be prohibitively expensive to implement, it is usually reserved for network backbones. See also **Mesh** and **Partial mesh**.

G

Gigabit Ethernet—IEEE 802.3z. Gigabit Ethernet offers a speed increase 100 times that of the 10BaseT Ethernet specification, while preserving such qualities as frame format, MAC mechanisms, and MTU. Based on an extension to the IEEE 802.3 specification. Compare with **Ethernet**.

Group address—See **multicast address**.

H

Hardware address—See **MAC address**.

Hash—Resulting string of bits from a hash function.

Hash function—A mathematical computation that results in a string of bits (digital code); the function is not reversible to produce the original input.

Helper address—Address configured on an interface to which broadcasts received on that interface will be sent.

Hop—Term describing the passage of a data packet between two network nodes (for example, between two routers). See also **Hop count**.

Hop count—Routing metric used to measure the distance between a source and a destination. RIP uses hop count as its sole metric. See also **Hop**.

Host—Computer system on a network. Similar to the term *node*, except that *host* usually implies a computer system; *node* generally applies to any networked system, including access servers and routers. See also **Node**.

Host address—Part of an IP address that designates which node on the subnetwork is being addressed.

Host group—Dynamically determined group of IP hosts identified by a single IP multicast address.

Host name—Name given to an endstation for identification purposes.

Hot backup links—Physical back up links are already in place, ready to activate through Spanning Tree without manual intervention.

Hot Standby Router Protocol—See **HSRP**.

HSRP—Hot Standby Routing Protocol. Provides high network availability and transparent network topology changes. HSRP creates a Hot Standby router group with a lead router that services all packets sent to the Hot Standby address. The lead router is monitored by other routers in the group, and if it fails, one of these standby routers inherits the lead position and the Hot Standby group address.

Hub—1. Generally, a term used to describe a device that serves as the center of a star-topology network. 2. Hardware or software device that contains multiple independent yet connected modules of network and internetwork equipment. Hubs can be active (where they repeat signals sent through them) or passive (where they do not repeat, but merely split, signals sent through them). 3. In Ethernet and IEEE 802.3, an Ethernet multiport repeater, sometimes referred to as a *concentrator*.

I

Identity—Who a user is on the network.

IEEE 802.1q—VLAN standard for VLAN support across frame media. Expected ratification in 1998.

IGMP—Internet Group Management Protocol. Used by IP hosts to report their multicast group memberships to an adjacent multicast router. Defined in RFC 1112. See also **Multicast router.**

IGMP Join—A message sent by the endstation to the multimedia server, asking whether the endstation can become a member of a certain multimedia application.

IGMP Leave—A message sent by the endstation to the multimedia server, asking to be removed from the multimedia application membership.

IGMP Query—Message sent by the multicast router out its interfaces, inquiring whether there are any members of a multimedia group. An IGMP Query is sent for each multimedia group.

IGMP Report—A message sent by an endstation, in response to an IGMP Query to the router, acknowledging membership to the multimedia group.

IGRP—Interior Gateway Routing Protocol. An IGP developed by Cisco to address the problems associated with routing in large, heterogeneous networks. Compare with **Enhanced IGRP**. See also **OSPF** and **RIP**.

Integrity—Keeping data safe as it traverses the network.

Interface—1. Connection between two systems or devices. 2. In routing terminology, a network connection.

Intermediate router—Router that receives a multicast stream and has other routers connected to it that it sends the multicast stream to.

Internet—Term used to refer to the largest global internetwork, connecting tens of thousands of networks worldwide and having a "culture" that focuses on research and standardization based on real-life use. Many leading-edge network technologies come from the Internet community. The Internet evolved in part from ARPANET. At one time called the DARPA Internet.

Internet Group Management Protocol—See **IGMP**.

Inter-VLAN—Data transfers that travel from one VLAN to a different VLAN.

Intra-VLAN—Data transfers that occur within the same VLAN.

IP—Internet Protocol. Network layer protocol in the TCP/IP stack offering a connectionless internetwork service. IP provides features for addressing, type-of-service specification, fragmentation and re-assembly, and security. Defined in RFC 791.

IP address—32-bit address assigned to hosts using TCP/IP. An IP address belongs to one of five classes (A, B, C, D, or E) and is written as four octets separated by periods (dotted decimal format). Each address consists of a network number, an optional subnetwork number, and a host number. The network and subnetwork numbers together are used for routing, while the host number is used to address an individual host within the network or subnetwork. A subnet mask is used to extract network and subnetwork information from the IP address.

IP destination address—IP address of a network device that is receiving data. See also **IP source address, MAC destination address,** and **MAC source address.**

IP multicast—RFC 1112. Routing technique that allows IP traffic to be propagated from one source to a number of destinations or from many sources to many destinations. Rather than sending one packet to each destination, one packet is sent to a multicast group identified by a single IP destination group address.

IP source address—IP address of a network device that is sending data. See also **IP destination address, MAC destination address,** and **MAC source address.**

IPX—Internetwork Packet Exchange. NetWare network layer (Layer 3) protocol used for transferring data from servers to workstations.

IPX SAP—Internetwork Packet Exchange Service Advertisement Protocol. Protocol that provides a means of informing network clients about available network resources and services via routers and servers.

L

LAN—Local-area network. High-speed, low-error data network covering a relatively small geographic area (up to a few thousand meters). LANs connect workstations, peripherals, terminals, and other devices in a single building or other geographically-limited area. LAN standards specify cabling and signaling at the physical and data link layers of the OSI model. Ethernet, FDDI, and Token Ring are widely used LAN technologies.

LANE—LAN Emulation. Technology that allows an ATM network to function as a LAN backbone. The ATM network must provide multicast and broadcast support, address mapping (MAC-to-ATM), SVC management, and a usable packet format. LANE also defines Ethernet and Token Ring ELANs. See also **ELAN**.

LAN Emulation Client—See **LEC**.

LAN Emulation Configuration Server—See **LECS**.

LAN Emulation Server—See **LES**.

LANE Network-to-Network Interface—See **LNNI**.

LANE User-to-Network Interface—See **LUNI**.

Layer 3 switch—Switch that filters and forwards packets based on MAC addresses and network addresses. A subset of **LAN switch**. Also referred to as *multilayer switch*.

LEC—LAN Emulation Client. Entity in an end system that performs data forwarding, address resolution, and other control functions for a single end system within a single ELAN. An LEC also provides a standard LAN service interface to any higher-layer entity that interfaces to the LEC. Each LEC is identified by a unique ATM address, and is associated with one or more MAC addresses reachable through that ATM address. See also **BUS**, **ELAN**, **LECS**, and **LES**.

LECS—LAN Emulation Configuration Server. Entity that assigns individual LANE clients to particular ELANs by directing them to the LES that corresponds to the ELAN. There is logically one LECS per administrative domain, and this serves all ELANs within that domain. See also **BUS**, **ELAN**, **LEC**, and **LES**.

LES—LAN Emulation Server. Entity that implements the control function for a particular ELAN. There is only one logical LES per ELAN, and it is identified by a unique ATM address. See also **BUS**, **ELAN**, **LEC**, and **LECS**.

Link—Network communications channel consisting of a circuit or transmission path and all related equipment between a sender and a receiver.

LNNI—LAN Emulation Network-to-Network Interface. Supports communication between the server components within a single ELAN. Phase 1 LANE protocols do not allow for the standard support of multiple LESs or BUSs within an ELAN. Phase 2 addresses these limitations.

Load sharing—In routing, the capability of a router to distribute traffic over all its network ports that are the same distance from the destination address. Good load-sharing algorithms use both line speed and reliability information. Load sharing increases the utilization of network segments, thus increasing effective network bandwidth.

Local server—See **distributed server.**

Local traffic—Traffic that remains within a small part of the network. This type of traffic does not enter the network backbone or cross a router.

LocalTalk—Apple Computer's proprietary baseband protocol that operates at the data link and physical layers of the OSI reference model. LocalTalk uses CSMA/CD and supports transmissions at speeds of 230.4 Kbps.

Loop—Route in which packets never reach their destination, but simply cycle repeatedly through a constant series of network nodes.

LUNI—LAN Emulation User-to-Network Interface. The ATM Forum standard for LAN emulation on ATM networks. LUNI defines the interface between the LAN Emulation Client (LEC) and the LAN Emulation Server components.

M

MAC—Media Access Control. Lower of the two sublayers of the data link layer defined by the IEEE. The MAC sublayer handles access to shared media, such as whether token passing or contention will be used.

MAC address—Standardized data link layer address that is required for every port or device that connects to a LAN. Other devices in the network use these addresses to locate specific ports in the network, and to create and update routing tables and data structures. MAC addresses are six bytes long and are controlled by the IEEE. Also referred to as a *hardware address*.

A MAC address is 48 bits in length. This is normally represented as 12 sequential hexidecmial values. For example, a router's MAC address might be 0000.0ce5.b7cl. A MAC broadcast address would be depicted as ffff.ffff.ffff. For the purposes of this book, the authors have truncated the depiction of MAC addresses to simplify discussions. All MAC addresses presented here will be six-digit values (e.g., e5b7cl), appearing without the high order portion of the address (which encodes the manudacturer's designation). The MAC broadcast address will be depicted as ffffff.

MAC address based VLANs—VLANs that are configured based on the MAC address of the endstation.

MAC destination address—MAC address of a network device that receives data. See also **IP destination address, IP source address,** and **MAC source address.**

MAC source address—MAC address of a network device that is sending data. See also **IP destination address, IP source address,** and **MAC destination address.**

Manual username/password—Security mechanism that allows users to establish their own usernames and passwords that do not change unless the users change them.

MBONE—Multicast Backbone. Multicast backbone of the Internet. MBONE is a virtual multicast network composed of multicast LANs and the point-to-point tunnels that interconnect them.

Media—Plural of medium. The various physical environments through which transmission signals pass. Common network media include twisted-pair, coaxial and fiber-optic cable; and the atmosphere (through which microwave, laser, and infrared transmission occur).

Mesh—Network topology in which devices are organized in a manageable, segmented manner with many, often redundant, interconnections strategically placed between network nodes. See also **Full mesh** and **Partial mesh**.

Message digest—Value returned by a hash function. Also referred to as *hash*.

MOSPF—Multicast OSPF. Intradomain multicast routing protocol used in OSPF networks. Extensions are applied to the base OSPF unicast protocol to support IP multicast routing. Defined in RFC 1584.

MPOA—Multiprotocol Over ATM. ATM Forum standardization effort specifying the way that existing and future network-layer protocols such as IP, IPv6, Appletalk, and IPX run over an ATM network with directly attached hosts, routers, and multilayer LAN switches.

Multicast—Single packets copied by the network and sent to a specific subset of network addresses. These addresses are specified in the destination address field. Compare with **Broadcast** and **Unicast**.

Multicast address—Single address that refers to multiple network devices. Also referred to as *group address*. Compare with **Broadcast address** and **Unicast address**. See also **Multicast**.

Multicast Backbone—See **MBONE**.

Multicast group—Dynamically determined group of IP hosts identified by a single IP multicast address.

Multicast Open Shortest Path First—See **MOSPF**.

Multicast registration—Method to filter multicast frames on a switch so that the switch does not send the multicast frames out all of its ports.

Multicast router—Router used to send IGMP Query messages on their attached local networks. Host members of a multicast group respond to a query by sending IGMP Reports noting the multicast groups to which they belong. The multicast router takes responsibility for forwarding multicast datagrams from one multicast group to all other networks that have members in the group. See also **IGMP**.

Multicast routing protocol—Routing protocol used to route multicast packets. See also **DVMRP, MOSPF, PIM dense-mode,** and **PIM sparse-mode**.

Multilayer switch—Switch that filters and forwards packets based on MAC addresses and network addresses. A subset of LAN switch. Also referred to as *Layer 3 switch*.

N

NAK—Negative Acknowledgment. 1. Response sent from a receiving device to a sending device, indicating that the information received contained errors. 2. Response sent to reject a request. Compare to **Acknowledgment**.

Negative Acknowledgment—See **NAK**.

NetBIOS—Network Basic Input/Output System. API used by applications on an IBM LAN to request services from lower-level network processes. These services include session establishment and termination, and information transfer.

Network—Collection of computers, printers, routers, switches, and other devices that can communicate with each other over some transmission medium.

Network address—Network layer address referring to a logical, rather than a physical, network device. Also referred to as a *protocol address*. Compare with **MAC address**.

Network Interface Card—See **NIC**.

Network layer—Layer 3 of the OSI reference model. This layer provides connectivity and path selection between two end systems. The network layer is the layer at which routing occurs. Corresponds roughly with the path control layer of the SNA model. See also **Application layer, Data link layer, Physical layer, Presentation layer, Session layer**, and **Transport layer**.

Network link redundancy—Physical redundant connections between network devices. Also referred to as *backup links*.

Network logon—Security mechanism in which the user must provide a valid username and password in order to gain access to the network.

Next Hop Resolution Protocol—See **NHRP**.

NHRP—Next Hop Resolution Protocol. Protocol used by routers to dynamically discover the MAC address of other routers and hosts connected to an NBMA network. These systems can then directly communicate without requiring traffic to use an intermediate hop, thus increasing performance in ATM, Frame Relay, SMDS, and X.25 environments.

NIC—Network Interface Card. Board that provides network-communication capabilities to and from a computer system.

NNI—Network-to-Network Interface. ATM Forum standard that defines the interface between two ATM switches that are both located in a private network, or are both located in a public network. The interface between a public switch and private one is defined by the UNI standard.

Node—Endpoint of a network connection or a junction that is common to two or more lines in a network. Nodes can be processors, controllers, or workstations. Nodes, which vary in routing and other functional capabilities, can be interconnected by links, and serve as control points in the network. *Node* is sometimes used generically to refer to any entity that can access a network, and is frequently used interchangeably with *device*. See also **host**.

O

OC—Optical Carrier. Series of physical protocols (OC-1, OC-2, OC-3, and so on) defined for SONET optical signal transmissions. OC signal levels put STS frames onto multimode fiber-optic line at a variety of speeds. The base rate is 51.84 Mbps (OC-1); each signal level thereafter operates at a speed divisible by that number (thus, OC-3 runs at 155.52 Mbps).

Open Shortest Path First—See **OSPF**.

OSI reference model—Open System Interconnection reference model. Network architectural model developed by ISO and ITU-T. The model consists of seven layers, each of which specifies particular network functions such as addressing, flow control, error control, encapsulation, and reliable message transfer. The lowest layer (the physical layer) is closest to the media technology. The lower two layers are implemented in hardware and software; the upper five layers are implemented only in software. The highest layer (the application layer) is closest to the user. The OSI reference model is used universally as a method for teaching and understanding network functionality. Similar in some respects to SNA. See **Application layer, Data link layer, Network layer, Physical layer, Presentation layer, Session layer,** and **Transport layer.**

OSPF—Open Shortest Path First. Link-state, hierarchical IGP routing algorithm proposed as a successor to RIP in the Internet community. OSPF features include least-cost routing, multipath routing, and load balancing. OSPF was derived from an early version of the ISIS protocol. Defined in RFC 2178. Compare to **IGRP, EIGRP,** and **RIP.**

P

Packet—Logical grouping of information that includes a header containing control information and (usually) user data. Packets are most often used to refer to network layer units of data.

Parallel routes—Multiple paths from the router to other network devices. All paths can be used to send traffic across the network.

Parallelism—Indicates that multiple paths exist between two points in a network. These paths might be of equal or unequal cost. Parallelism is often a network design goal: If one path fails, there is redundancy in the network to ensure that an alternative path to the same point exists.

Partial mesh—Term describing a network in which devices are organized in a mesh topology; some network nodes are organized in a full mesh; others are only connected to one or two other nodes in the network. A partial mesh does not provide the level of redundancy of a full mesh topology, but is less expensive to implement. Partial mesh topologies are generally used in the peripheral networks that connect to a fully meshed backbone. See also **Full mesh** and **Mesh**.

Peak cell rate—Parameter defined by the ATM Forum for ATM traffic management. In CBR transmissions, PCR determines how often data samples are sent. In ABR transmissions, PCR determines the maximum value of the ACR. See also **ABR, CBR, UBR,** and **VBR**.

Phantom router—In HSRP, two routers share the same virtual IP address and virtual MAC address thus creating a third, non-physical router. Also referred to as *virtual router*. Also see **HSRP, Virtual IP address,** and **Virtual MAC address**.

Physical layer—Layer 1 of the OSI reference model. The physical layer defines the electrical, mechanical, procedural, and functional specifications for activating, maintaining, and deactivating the physical link between end systems. Corresponds with the physical control layer in the SNA model. See also **Application layer, Data link layer, Network layer, Presentation layer, Session layer,** and **Transport layer**.

PIM—Protocol Independent Multicast. Multicast routing architecture that allows the addition of IP multicast routing on existing IP networks. PIM is unicast routing protocol independent, and can be operated in two modes: dense-mode and sparse-mode. See also **PIM dense-mode** and **PIM sparse- mode**.

PIM dense-mode—One of the two PIM operational modes. PIM dense-mode is data-driven and resembles typical multicast routing protocols. Packets are forwarded on all outgoing interfaces until pruning and truncation occur. In dense-mode, receivers are densely populated, and it is assumed that the downstream networks want to receive and will probably use the datagrams that are forwarded to them. The cost of using dense-mode is its default flooding behavior. Sometimes called *dense-mode PIM* or *PIM DM*. Contrast with **PIM sparse-mode**. See also **PIM**.

PIM sparse-mode—One of the two PIM operational modes. PIM sparse-mode tries to constrain data distribution so that a minimal number of routers in the network receive it. Packets are sent only if they are explicitly requested at the RP (rendezvous point). In sparse-mode, receivers are widely distributed, and the assumption is that downstream networks do not necessarily use the datagrams that are sent to them. The cost of using sparse-mode is its reliance on the periodic refreshing of explicit Join messages and its need for RPs. Sometimes called *sparse-mode PIM* or *PIM SM*. Defined in RFC 2117. Contrast with **PIM dense-mode**. See also **PIM** and **Rendezvous point**.

Port—Interface on an internetworking device (such as a router).

Port-based VLANs—VLANs that are configured at the switch port.

Presentation layer—Layer 6 of the OSI reference model. This layer ensures that information sent by the application layer of one system is readable by the application layer of another. The presentation layer is also concerned with the data structures used by programs and therefore negotiates data transfer syntax for the application layer. Corresponds roughly with the presentation services layer of the SNA model. See also **Application layer**, **Data link layer**, **Network layer**, **Physical layer**, **Session layer**, and **Transport layer**.

Prioritization—The process of determining which traffic should go across the network device first.

Priority queuing—Instructing the network device to send any prioritized traffic first and hold the rest of the traffic until there is no more prioritized traffic.

Private key encryption—Digital code used to decrypt/encrypt information and provide digital signatures. This key should be kept secret by the owner of the private key; it has a corresponding public key.

Protocol—Formal description of a set of rules and conventions that govern how devices on a network exchange information.

Protocol address—See **Network address.**

Protocol-based VLANs—VLANs that are configured by the protocol network to which the endstation belongs.

Protocol destination address—Protocol address of a network device that is receiving data.

Protocol Independent Multicast—See **PIM.**

Protocol layer—See **Network layer.**

Protocol source address—Protocol address of a network device that is sending data.

Proxy ARP—Proxy Address Resolution Protocol. Variation of the ARP protocol, in which an intermediate device (for example, a router) sends an ARP response on behalf of an end node to the requesting host. Defined in RFC 1027.

Prune—When the end router detects that there are no group members on one of its interfaces, it stops sending that multicast stream out that interface. Also referred to as *reverse path forwarding* and *Truncated Reverse Path Broadcasting (TRPB)*.

Public key encryption—A digital code used to encrypt/decrypt information and verify digital signatures. This key can be made widely available; it has a corresponding private key.

Q

Quality of Service—See QoS.

QoS—Quality of service. Measure of performance for a transmission system that reflects its transmission quality and service availability.

Queue—1. Generally, an ordered list of elements waiting to be processed. 2. In routing, a backlog of packets waiting to be forwarded over a router interface.

Queuing—A way of lining up network traffic so that it flows according to the prioritization preferences.

R

Redundancy—In internetworking, the duplication of devices, services, or connections so that, in the event of a failure, the redundant devices, services, or connections can perform the work of those that failed. See also **Redundant system**.

Redundant system—Computer, router, switch, or other system that contains two or more of each of the most important subsystems, such as two disk drives, two CPUs, or two power supplies. Also referred to as *component redundancy*.

Reliability—Capability of a network to withstand failures and still maintain network operation.

Rendezvous point—Router specified in PIM sparse-mode implementations to track membership in multicast groups and to forward messages to known multicast group addresses. See also **PIM sparse-mode**.

Resource ReServation Protocol—See **RSVP**.

Reverse path forwarding—See **Prune**.

RFC—Request For Comments. Document series used as the primary means for communicating information about the Internet. Some RFCs are designated by the IAB as Internet standards. Most RFCs, such as Telnet and FTP, document protocol specifications, but some are humorous or historical. RFCs are available online from numerous sources.

RIP—Routing Information Protocol. IGP supplied with UNIX BSD systems. The most common IGP in the Internet. RIP uses hop count as a routing metric. Defined in RFC 1058 and RFC 1723. See also **Enhanced IGRP, IGRP,** and **OSPF**.

Route—Path through an internetwork.

Route authentication—Method in which routers verify valid gateways, and discover invalid gateways and paths in the network.

Router—Network layer device that uses one or more metrics to determine the optimal path along which network traffic should be forwarded. Routers forward packets from one network to another based on network layer information. Routers also perform network layer services on the network.

Routing—Process of finding a path to a destination host. Routing is very complex in large networks because of the many potential intermediate destinations a packet might traverse before reaching its destination host.

Routing Information Protocol—See RIP.

Routing protocol—Protocol that accomplishes routing through the implementation of a specific routing algorithm. Examples of routing protocols include EIGRP, IGRP, OSPF, and RIP.

Routing table—Table stored in a router or some other internetworking device that keeps track of routes to particular network destinations and, in some cases, metrics associated with those routes.

Routing update—Message sent from a router to indicate network reachability and associated cost information. Routing updates are typically sent at regular intervals and after a change in network topology.

RSVP—Resource ReSerVation Protocol. A protocol that supports the reservation of resources across an IP network. Applications running on IP end systems can use RSVP to indicate to other nodes the nature (bandwidth, jitter, maximum burst, and so on) of the packet streams they wish to receive. Defined in RFC 2205.

S

SAP—Service Advertising Protocol. IPX protocol that provides a means of informing network clients about available network resources and services via routers and servers.

Scalability—Capacity of a network to keep pace with changes and growth.

Secret key encryption—Digital code that is shared by two parties; it is used to encrypt and decrypt data.

Server—Node or software program that provides services to clients.

Server block—Network domain that consists of the enterprise servers in the network, and the switching and routing devices required to connect them to the rest of the network.

Session layer—Layer 5 of the OSI reference model. This layer establishes, manages, and terminates sessions between applications and manages data exchange between presentation-layer entities. Corresponds to the data flow control layer of the SNA model. See also **Application layer, Data link layer, Network layer, Physical layer, Presentation layer,** and **Transport layer.**

Shared queuing—Both high-priority and other traffic can be processed by the network device at the same time. Light traffic can be processed at the same time as the high-priority traffic.

Source address—Address of a network device that sends data. See also **Destination address.**

Spanning Tree Protocol—Bridge protocol that utilizes the spanning-tree algorithm, enabling a learning bridge to dynamically work around loops in a network topology by creating a spanning tree. Bridges exchange BPDU messages with other bridges to detect loops, and then remove the loops by shutting down selected bridge interfaces. Refers to both the IEEE 802.1 Spanning-Tree Protocol standard and the earlier Digital Equipment Corporation Spanning-Tree Protocol, on which it is based. The IEEE version supports bridge domains and allows the bridge to construct a loop-free topology across an extended LAN. The IEEE version is generally preferred over the Digital version. Sometimes abbreviated as STP.

Spanning Tree reconvergence—The time that it takes for Spanning Tree to create a new data path through the network.

Spoofing—Action of a packet illegally claiming to be from an address from which it was not actually sent. Spoofing is designed to foil network security mechanisms such as filters and access lists.

Static address—Address that is explicitly configured and entered into the workstation.

Subnet—In IP networks, a network sharing a particular subnet address. Subnetworks are networks that are arbitrarily segmented by a network administrator in order to provide a multilevel, hierarchical routing structure while shielding the subnetwork from the addressing complexity of attached networks. See also **IP address, Subnet address,** and **Subnet mask.**

Subnet address—Portion of an IP address that is specified as the subnetwork by the subnet mask. See also **IP address, Subnet mask,** and **Subnet.**

Subnet mask—32-bit address mask used in IP to indicate the bits of an IP address that are being used for the subnet address. See also **IP address, Subnet,** and **Subnet address.**

Super server—Comprised of several enterprise servers that are consolidated into a single, more powerful machine.

Switch—Network device that filters, forwards, and floods frames based on the destination address of each frame. The switch operates at the data link layer of the OSI model.

Symmetric encryption—Secret key-encryption method that provides data confidentiality. When two endstations use symmetric encryption, they must agree on the algorithm to use and on the secret key that they will share.

T

Throughput—Rate of information arriving at, and possibly passing through, a particular point in a network system.

Token Ring—Token-passing LAN developed and supported by IBM. Token Ring runs at 4 or 16 Mbps over a ring topology.

Traffic prioritization—See **Prioritization**.

Transport layer—Layer 4 of the OSI reference model. This layer is responsible for reliable network communication between end nodes. The transport layer provides mechanisms for the establishment, maintenance, and termination of virtual circuits; transport fault detection and recovery; and information flow control. Corresponds to the transmission control layer of the SNA model. See also **Application layer, Data link layer, Network layer, Physical layer, Presentation layer,** and **Session layer**.

Truncated Reverse Path Broadcasting (TRPB)—See **Prune**.

U

UBR—Unspecified Bit Rate. QoS class defined by the ATM Forum for ATM networks. UBR allows any amount of data up to a specified maximum to be sent across the network, but there are no guarantees in terms of cell loss rate and delay. Compare with **ABR, CBR,** and **VBR.**

UNI—User-Network Interface. ATM Forum specification that defines an interoperability standard for the interface between ATM-based products (a router or an ATM switch) located in a private network and the ATM switches located within the public carrier networks.

Unicast—Message sent to a single network destination. Compare with **Broadcast** and **Multicast.**

Unicast address—Address specifying a single network device. Compare with **Broadcast address and Multicast address.** See also Unicast.

Unspecified Bit Rate—See **UBR.**

User authentication—See **Authentication.**

User authorization—See **Authorization.**

User-level VLANs—Users belong to a specific VLAN, regardless of where they are on the network.

V

Variable Bit Rate—See **VBR.**

VBR—Variable Bit Rate. QoS class defined by the ATM Forum for ATM networks. VBR is subdivided into a Real Time (RT) class and Non-Real Time (NRT) class. VBR (RT) is used for connections in which there is a fixed timing relationship between samples. VBR (NRT) is used for connections in which there is no fixed timing relationship between samples, but that still need a guaranteed QoS. Compare with **ABR, CBR,** and **UBR.**

VINES—Virtual Integrated Network Service. NOS developed and marketed by Banyan Systems.

Virtual IP address—IP address shared by two routers when using HSRP. See also **HSRP, Virtual MAC address, Virtual router,** and **Phantom router.**

Virtual LAN—See **VLAN.**

Virtual MAC address—MAC address shared by two routers when using HSRP. Also see **HSRP, Virtual IP address, Virtual router, and Phantom router.**

Virtual router—In HSRP, two routers share the same virtual IP address and virtual MAC address, thus creating a third nonphysical router. Also referred to as *phantom router.* See also **HSRP, Virtual IP address,** and **Virtual MAC address.**

VLAN—Virtual LAN. Group of devices on one or more LANs that are configured (using management software) so that they can communicate as if they were attached to the same wire, when in fact they are located on a number of different LAN segments. Because VLANs are based on logical instead of physical connections, they are extremely flexible.

VLAN trunking—A single physical link that supports more than one VLAN.

W

WAN—Wide Area Network. Data communications network that serves users across a broad geographic area and often uses transmission devices provided by common carriers. Frame Relay, SMDS, and ATM are examples of WANs.

Web—See **WWW.**

Wide Area Network—See **WAN.**

Wiring closet—Specially designed room used for wiring a data or voice network. Wiring closets serve as a central junction point for the wiring and wiring equipment that is used for interconnecting devices.

Wiring closet switch—Switch used to connect users to the network.

Wiring closet VLAN—VLAN exists on specific wiring closet switches, and do not span the network.

Workgroup server—See **Distributed server.**

World Wide Web—See **WWW.**

WWW—World Wide Web. Large network of Internet servers that provides hypertext and other services to terminals running client applications, such as browsers.

Index

A

ABR (Available Bit Rate), 166, 436
access lists (filters), 180-182, 383, 436
accessing
    applications from servers, 16
    enterprise servers after core switch failure, 307-313
Acknowledge (DHCP), user mobility, 217
acknowledgments, 436
activating hot backup (Spanning Tree), 129–132
address fields (user mobility), 213–214
address resolution, 437
Address Resolution Protocol, *see* ARP
addresses
    barebone network design, 268
    changing user mobility, 210–212
    destination addresses, 28
    IP
        class B, 31
        class D, 57
        complex networks, 387, 390–391
    MAC VLANs (Virtual LANs), 221
    multimedia (complex networks), 376, 383
    source addresses, 28
adds (user mobility), 208

algorithms, 437
    encryption, 185
    TRPB (Truncated Reverse Path Broadcasting) algorithm, 70
analyzing broadcasts-per-second, 42
AppleTalk, 437
Application layer (OSI model), 437
applications
    broadcast processing, 42
    localization, 16
    multimedia, 52–53
        barebone network design, 276
        Internet-to-campus traffic, 106
        LAN design philosophy, 17
        scalable networks, 313–317
    performance, controlling (broadcast frames), 45-47
    sharing, 97-99
architecture
    barebone network design
        building blocks, 264
        core blocks, 265
        server blocks, 265–266
    campus networks
        building blocks, 249–251

      core blocks, 251–253
      server blocks, 253–255
    scalable network design
      broadcast domains, 284, 287, 289, 292
      building blocks, 282, 293–294
      core blocks, 284, 298
      distributed servers, 292
      Internet connectivity, 284
      redundancy, 293
      server blocks, 284, 299–301
      traffic patterns, 285
archives (Internet-Drafts), 433
ARP (Address Resolution Protocol), 437
    requests, 28
    sending broadcast frames, 32–33
asymmetric encryption, 186, 191, 195, 387, 438
ATM (Asynchronous Transfer Mode), 438
    ATM Forum, 433
    LANE (LAN Emulation), 143-145,
      240–241
    prioritizing traffic, 164–166
authentication, 172, 177, 438
    complex networks, 383
      route authentication, 182–183, 322
      scalable networks, 322
authorization, 178–179, 383, 438
automating electronic commerce, 426
autonomous system, 438
Available Bit Rate (ABR), 166, 436

B

backbone (network), 439
    collapsed backbone, 249
    cross-campus traffic, 93-101
    Internet traffic, 102
backing up servers, 127
backup links, 439
backup paths (Spanning Tree), 130-134
backup systems (redundancy), 121-145
    barebone network design, 269–271
    component, 123, 126

    data path, 128-138
    high-level, 124–125
    median, 124
    minimal, 122-123
    network link, 128-138
    parallelism, 134, 136
    scalable network design, 293
    server, 126–128
    wiring closet switch, 329, 335
bandwidth, 439
    allocation, 439
    percentage queueing, 153–154, 439
    priotitizing, 150
    queuing, 155
    super servers, 18
    traffic, 7–8
barebone network design
    building blocks, 264, 271
    core blocks, 265
    cost-efficiency, 266
    distribution switch, 270–271
    Internet connectivity, 266
    mobility, 273–274
    multimedia applications, 276
    nodes, 267–268
    redundancy, 269–271
    security, 275–276
    server blocks, 265–266, 271–272
    services, 276
    simplifying, 276–277
    traffic patterns, 266–269
    wiring closet switch failure, 270
baselines, 9, 115–116, 439
blueprints
    barebone design
      building blocks, 264
      core blocks, 265
      designing redundancy, 269–271
      mobility, 273–274
      nodes, 267–268
      security, 275–276
      server blocks, 265–266
      simplified, 277

building blocks, 249–253
core blocks, 251
customizing, 256–257
scalable network design
broadcast domains, 284, 287, 289, 292
building blocks, 282, 293–294
connectivity, 284
core blocks, 284, 298
server blocks, 284, 299–301
traffic patterns, 285
server blocks, 253–255
BOOTP (Bootstrap Protocol), 439
bottlenecks
baselines, 9
building blocks, 258
troubleshooting, 7–8
breaking up building blocks, 259
broadcast address, 440
Broadcast and Unknown Server, *see* BUS
broadcast domains
barebone network design, 267–268
complex networks
building blocks, 353, 355
core blocks, 350
server blocks, 350
scalable network design, 284, 287, 289, 292
broadcast propagation, 35, 440
broadcast storms, 251, 440
broadcast traffic, 28–29, 45, 47, 54–55
broadcasts, 30–32, 439
DHCP
Discover, 37
Request, 33, 37, 110-111
hexidecimal notation, 28
Layer 2, 28–29
dropping, 40-41
generating, 39-40
IP ARP requests, 110
IPX SAP requests, 33
multimedia (cross-campus traffic), 115
never ending loops, resolving, 133
NIC cards, handling, 44

storing, 38-39
unicasts, 36-38
broadcasts-per-second, 42
broad-spectrum user access failure, 313
browsing
traffic priorities, 150
World Wide Web, 104-105
building blocks, 249–253, 259, 348, 440
barebone network design, 264
bottlenecks, 258
broadcast domains, 353, 355
encryption, 385
nodes
calculating maximum number, 257–258
restrictions, 257
redundancy, 356–358
routers
barebone network design, 271
PIM sparse-mode, 317, 320
scalable network design, 282
broadcast domains, 289-292
redundancy, 293–294
VLANs, 326, 328
VLAN, 391-396
BUS (Broadcast and Unknown Server), 440

C

calculating
building blocks, 257–258
up time (redundancy), 122
campus networks
barebone design
building blocks, 264
core blocks, 265
cost-efficiency, 266
nodes, 267–268
server blocks, 265–266
traffic patterns, 266–269
blueprints
building blocks, 249–253
core blocks, 251

customizing, 256–257
server blocks, 253–255
building blocks, 250
Internet traffic, 101-108
multimedia flooding, 317, 320
resources, user access failure, 313
scalable networks
broadcast domains, 287, 289, 292
building blocks, 282
building VLANs, 326, 328
core blocks, 284
core switch failure, 307, 310, 313
HSRP, 296
Internet connectivity, 284
mobility, 324
multimedia, 313–317
redundancy, 293
router failure, 304
security, 322
server blocks, 284
traffic, 285, 339
transport technologies, 426
voice-over data, 425
campus-to-Internet traffic, 101-104
CBR (Constant Bit Rate), 165, 441
cell delay, 441
centralized servers, 17, 441
changes (user mobility), 208–209
characteristics
barebone network design, 263–264
scalable network design, 281–282
traffic, 313
class B IP address, 31
class D IP addresses, 57
Class of Service, see COS
clients, 441
passing data, 91-92
traffic, 92, 95-97
closet switches (VLANs), 225
collapsed backbone, 249, 441
combining enterprise servers with
distributed servers, 15-16
super servers, 18–19, 21

complex network
complex networks, 345–346
building blocks, 348
broadcast domains, 353-355
redundancy, 356–358
VLANs, 391, 396
core blocks, 348
broadcast domains, 350
redundancy, 359–360
VLANs, 406, 409–410
Internet connections, 349
multimedia addressing, 376, 383
security, 383
encryption, 385, 387
server blocks, 348
broadcast domains, 350
redundancy, 361–362
VLANs, 409, 411
traffic, 349, 418-420
troubleshooting
redundancy, 362, 375
VLANs, 409, 414
user mobility, 387, 390–391
VLANs (user-level), 399, 406
component redundancy, 123, 126, 442
barebone network design, 269
complex networks, 355
computers (endstations)
cross-campus traffic, 93-101
DHCP requests, 110-111
IP ARP requests, 108-110
IPX SAP broadcasts, 109-110
receiving broadcast frames, 41-44
concentrators, 442
configuring
routers with DVMRP, 315
switches, 84
congestion, 442
connections
barebone network design, 268
building block, 292
core blocks, 259

distributed servers, 16
    inter-VLAN, cut-through, 242
connectivity
    bottlenecks, 259
    building blocks, 250
    core switches, 307, 310, 313
    dedicated routers (scalable network
        design), 285
    Internet (barebone network design),
        266, 271
consolidating servers (super servers), 18–19, 21
Constant Bit Rate (CBR), 165, 441
continuous server backups, 127
controlling traffic, 45-47, 292
core blocks, 251, 348, 439, 442
    barebone network design, 265
    broadcast domains, 350
    connections, 259
    encryption, 385
    redundancy, 359–360
    scalable network design, 284
        broadcast domains, 287, 289
        redundancy, 298
        VLANs, 329
    VLAN, 406, 409–410
core switch failure, 307, 310, 313
COS (Class of Service), 441
cost-efficiency (barebone network design), 266
criteria (redundancy)
    high-level, 125
    median, 124
    minimal, 122-123
cross-campus traffic, 93-101
    bare-bone network design, 269
    DHCP requests, 110-111
    distributed servers, 95-97
    distribution switches, 99-100
    file transfers <$endpage>, 95-97
    IGMP queries, 113
    Internet traffic, see Internet traffic
    IP ARP requests, 108-110
    IPX SAP broadcasts, 109-110
    multicast routing, 113

    multimedia broadcasts, 115
    PIM
        dense-mode, 114
        sparse-mode, 114
    VLANs, see user-level VLANs
    see also local traffic
customizing campus networks, 256–257

D

D class IP addresses, 57
data centers (enterprise servers), 14
Data Encryption Standard (DES), 186
Data link layer (OSI model), 443
data load sharing, 289
data path loops, 443
data path redundancy, 128-138
    hot backup, 129–132
    parallelism, 134, 136
data storage backup, 443
data streams, 443
DECnet, 443
decoding, 185
decryption, 185, 444; see also encryption
dedicated bandwidth queuing, 155, 444
dedicated routers, 285
default gateways, 444
delay, 444
DES (Data Encryption Standard), 186
designing
    barebone networks
        building blocks, 264
        core blocks, 265
        mobility, 273–274
        requirements, 263–264
        security, 275–276
        server blocks, 265–266
        simplified, 277
    campus networks
        building blocks, 249–253
        core blocks, 251
        server blocks, 253–255

redundancy, 121-145, 269–271
  high-level, 124-125
  median, 124
  minimal, 122-123
  performance factors, 259
  scalable networks, 314
    mobility, 324
    redundancy, 293
    requirements, 281–282
    security, 322
destination addresses, 28, 35
developing technologies
  electronic commerce, automating, 426
  Gigabit Ethernet, 426
  network management, 427–428
  voice-over data, 425
devices
  building blocks, 250
  component redundancy, 123, 126, 269
  concentrators, 442
  Layer 3 switches, 251
  network link redundancy, 128-138
  routers
    bottlenecks, 258
    broadcast traffic, 36-41
    dedicated routers, 285
    dropping broadcasts, 40-41
    failure, 304
    generating broadcasts, 39-40
    multicast traffic, 113, 313
    PIM dense-mode, 114
    server block failure, 271–272
    sharing applications, 97-99
    storing broadcasts, 38-39
    unicasts, 36-38
  switches, 34-36
DHCP (Dynamic Host Configuration Protocol)
  Acknowledge frame, 444
  Address Lease Time, 444
  complex networks, 387, 390–391
  Discover, 37, 213, 445
  IP scalability, 212–219

NAK (No Acknowledge), 218–219, 445
  Offer frames, 445
  requests, 28, 33, 37, 445
  scalable networks, 326
  servers, 445
digital signatures, 445
Discover (DHCP)
  complex networks, 390
  user mobility, 213–214
distance learning (multimedia), 52
Distance Vector Multicast Routing Protocol, *see* DVMRP
distributed networks (building blocks), 250
distributed servers, 15, 90, 292, 445
  cross-campus traffic, 95-97
  enterprise server comparisons, 15
  Internet traffic
    file servers, 102-103
    sending across backbone, 103
  LAN design, 16–17
  scalable networks, supporting VLANs, 328
distribution centers, 250
distribution switches, 250, 255, 445
  broadcast domains, 353
  complex networks
    redundancy, 356
    user-level VLANs, 399
  failure, 270–271, 304
  scalable network design (redundancy), 282
    configuring VLANs, 335
    providing, 294
  scalable network design, 282
  VLANs (Virtual LANs), 233–236
dividing, 259
DNS (Domain Name System), 210, 218
documents (Internet-Drafts), 432–433
domains
  broadcast
    barebone networks, 267–268
    building blocks (complex networks), 353, 355
    core blocks (complex networks), 350

scalable network design, 287, 289, 292

server blocks (complex networks), 350

distributed servers, 15

enterprise servers, 13–14

downloading files (Internet traffic), 102-103

draft-li-hsrp-00.txt, 143

dropping broadcasts, 40-41

DVMRP (Distance Vector Multicast Routing Protocol), 70–74, 446

complex networks, 376

scalable networks, 315

dynamic filtering switches, 84–85

Dynamic Hosts Configuration Protocol, *see* DHCP

dynamic IP addressing (complex networks), 387, 390–391

dynamic username/password, 176–177

dynamic VLANs (Virtual LANs), 222–223, 446

E

EIGRP (Enhanced Interior Gateway Routing Protocol), 446

ELAN (Emulated LAN), 446

electronic commerce, automating, 426

e-mail

barebone network design (traffic disruption), 272

campus-to-Internet traffic, 101-102

servers, *see* enterprise servers

emerging technologies

electronic commerce (automatic), 426

Gigabit Ethernet, 426

network management, 427–428

VBNS (Very high-speed Backbone Network Service), 427

voice-over data, 425

Emulated LAN, *see* ELAN

encryption, 184–185, 195, 199, 447

asymmetric, 186, 191, 195, 438

complex networks, 385, 387

decryption, 444

hash functions, 191, 194–195

public key, 466

secret key, 469

symmetric, 185–186, 195, 471

end routers, 72–73, 447

endstations

applications, sharing, 97-99

broadcast traffic, 41-44

cross-campus traffic, 93-101

DHCP broadcasts, 110-111

distributed server, 90-93

IP ARP requests, 108-110

IPX SAP broadcasts, 109-110

requests, sending, 91-92

traffic

distributed server path, 90-93

shared distribution switches, 99-100

see also hosts

Enhanced Interior Gateway Routing Protocol, *see* EIGRP

enterprise servers, 13–15, 307, 310, 313

distributed server comparisons, 15

cross-campus traffic, 93-101

email servers, 13, 102

file servers (Internet traffic), 102-103

LAN design, 16–17

server blocks, 253

super servers, 18–19, 21

see also centralized servers

Ethernet, 447

F

failures, 251, 269–270

barebone networks

building block routers, 271

server block routers, 271–272

switches, 272

wiring closet switch, 270

complex networks

redundancy, 362, 375

VLANs, 409, 414

protecting against, 139, 141
scalable networks
    core switch failure, 307, 310, 313
    distribution switch failure, 304
    primary switch, 294
    subnets, 287
Fast Ethernet, 447
fault tolerance (redundancy), 121-145
barebone networks, 269–271
data path, 128-138
high-level, 124-125
median, 124
minimal, 122-123
network link, 128-138
servers, 126–128
FDDI (Fiber Distributed Data Interface), 448
Fiber Distributed Data Interface,
   see FDDI
fields (destination address), 28
FIFO (First In, First Out), 448
file servers (Internet traffic), 102-103
file transfers, 95-97, 448
filters (access lists), 180, 182, 448
complex networks, 383
switches, 84–85
firewalls, 180, 448
flooding, 448
multicast (scalable networks), 314
multimedia, reducing, 317, 320
forwarding
broadcasts (switches), 34-36
traffic (scalable networks), 295
frames, 449
broadcasts, 28–29
    dropping, 40-41
    generating, 39-40
    storing, 38–39
    transmission, 28–29
DHCP
    Acknowledge, 444
    Discover, 37, 445

    Offer frame, 445
    requests, 37, 110-111
IPX SAP broadcasts, 109-110
routing, 36-41
traffic
    cross-campus, 93-101
    Internet, 101-108
    local, 89-93
    paths, 91-93
full mesh, 449

G

gateways
filters (access lists), 180–181
route authentication, 182–183
generating
broadcasts, 39-40
unicasts, 36-38
GI (gateway IP) address field, 213–214
Gigabit Ethernet, 449

H

hardware
component redundancy, 123, 126
prioritizing traffic, 162, 164
routers
    dedicated, 285
    failure, 304
hash functions, 191, 194–195, 449
helper address, 449
hexidecimal notation (broadcast frames), 28
high redundancy (software), 123
high-bandwidth applications, 313–315, 317
high-level redundancy, 124–125
hops, 253, 450
Host Extensions for IP Multicasting
  (RFC 1112), 56
hosts (multicast), 60, 64

hot backups, 129–132, 450
HSRP (Hot Standby Routing Protocol), 141, 143
    router redundancy, 358
    scalable networks, 296
hubs, 451

I-J-K

IDEA (International Data Encryption
    Algorithm), 186
identity, 171–172, 177, 387
IEEE (Institute of Electrical and Electronics
    Engineers)
    802.1q, 243, 451
    specifications, 434
IETF (Internet Engineering Task Force),
    431–433
IGMP (Internet Group Management
    Protocol), 60
    Join messages, 64–65, 451
    queries, 65–67, 451
    real-time imaging (multimedia), 52
    reports, 452
incoming traffic, 104-108
indexes (rfc-index), 431
Info Scout, 430
infrastructure, 322, 30-34
Institute of Electrical and Electronics Engineers,
    see IEEE
integrity, 171–172, 452
    complex networks, 385, 387
    encryption, 184–185, 197
intercepting broadcasts (switches), 34-36
Interior Gateway Routing Protocol, *see* IGRP
intermediate routers, 71, 452
International Data Encryption Algorithm
    (IDEA), 186
Internet, 452
    connectivity
        barebone network design, 266, 271
        complex networks, 349
        scalable network design, 284
    electronic commerce, automating, 426

IEEE specifications, 434
IETF (Internet Engineering Task Force),
    431–433
traffic, 101
    campus-to-Internet traffic, 101-104
    file servers, 102-103
    Internet-to-campus traffic, 104-108
Internet Architecture Board, 431
Internet Engineering Task Force, *see* IETF
Internet Group Management Protocol, *see* IGMP
Internet Protocol, *see* IP
Internet-Drafts, 432–433
Internetwork Packet Exchange, *see* IPX
Internetwork Packet Exchange Service
    Advertisement Protocol, *see* IPX SAP, 454
InterNIC, 431
Inter-VLANs (Virtual LANs), 237–240, 452
    complex networks, 396, 403
    cut-through connections, 242
Intra-VLANs (Virtual LANs), 237–240, 396,
    452
IP (Internet Protocol), 453
    addresses, 453
        barebone network design, 274
        broadcast destination, 29–31
        class B, 31
        class D, 57
        complex networks, 387, 390–391
    DNS (Domain Name System), 210
    multicasts, 57–59, 453
    user mobility, 209–210, 212–219
IP/BootP helper, 390
IPX (Internetwork Packet Exchange), 453
IPX SAP (Internetwork Packet Exchange Service
    Advertisement Protocol), 28, 454
    request scheme, 33
    routing broadcasts, 43

Join messages, 64–65
JoinHostGroup messages, 60

keys (encryption), 185

L

LANs (local area networks), 16–17
    LEC (LAN Emulation Client), 455
    LECS (LAN Emulation Configuration
        Server), 455
    LES (LAN Emulation Server), 455
    LNNI (LAN Emulation Network-to-Net-
        work Interface), 241, 455
    LLUNI (LAN Emulation User-to-Network
        Interface), 241, 456
    see also VLANs
Layer 2
    broadcast frames, 28–29
    switches
        barebone networks, 264
        complex networks, 348
Layer 3 switches, 251
layers
    OSI model
        MAC layer, 28–29
        Network layer, 29–30, 32
    switches, 34, 36
links, establishing new paths, 141
load sharing, 455
local servers, see distributed servers
local traffic, 89-93, 456; see also cross-campus
    traffic
LocalTalk protocol, 456
logons
    authentication, 173–174
    complex networks, 383
    scalable networks, 322
loops, 456

M

MAC (Media Access Control), 457
    addresses
        VLANs (Virtual LANs), 221, 457
        user mobility, 213
        destinations, 457
        sources, 457

    conventions, 28, 465
    layers, 28–29, 35
machines, see endstations
managing networks, 427–428
manual username/password, 176, 457
MBONE (Multicast Backbone), 457
Media Access Control
    see MAC, 28–29, 456
median redundancy, 123-124
mesh, 457
message digest, 457
migration (super servers), 18–19
minimal redundancy, 122-123
mobility, 324
    barebone networks, 273–274
    complex networks, 387, 390–391
    scalable networks, 324
models
    OSI model
        MAC layer, 28–29
        Network layer, 29–30, 32
monitoring networks
    performance (sniffers), 46
    traffic, 115–116
MOSPF (Multicast Open Shortest Path First),
    69–70, 458
MPOA (Multicast Over ATM), 242–243, 458
multicast
    addresses, 458
    complex networks, 376, 383
    groups, 458
    registration, 458
    routing, 113, 458
    traffic, 55–56, 313
    protocols, 68
        DVMRP (Distance Vector Multicast
            Routing Protocol), 70–74
        IP multicast, 57–59
        MOSPF (Multicast Open Shortest Path
            First), 69–70
        MPOA (Multicast Over ATM),
            242–243, 458
        PIM (Protocol Independent Mode),
            74–76, 78–80

requirements, 59
    hosts, 60, 64
    routers, 64, 67
    servers, 60, 64
  switches, 83–85
  traffic (VLANs), 224
Multicast Backbone, *see* MBONE
Multicast OSPF, *see* MOSPF
multilayer switches, 459
multimedia, 314
  applications, 52–53
    Internet-to-campus traffic, 106
    running, 313–317
  barebone network design, 276
  complex networks, 376, 383
  development, 17
  routers, 64, 67
  servers, placing on network, 314
  switches, 81–85
  traffic, 51, 53
    broadcast, 54–55
    multicast, 55–56
    QoS (Quality of Service), 156–157, 162
    unicast, 53
MultiProtocol Over ATM (MPOA), 242–243, 458

N

NAK (No Acknowledge), 218–219, 459
NetBIOS (Network Basic Input/Output System), 459
Network Information Center, *see* NIC
Network layer, 29–30, 32
Network Solutions, Inc, 430
networks, 19, 30–32, 37, 251
  ATM LANE, 143, 145
  barebone, 269–270
    building blocks, 264
    collapsed, 249
    core blocks, 265

    security, 275–276
    server blocks, 265–266
  blueprints
    building blocks, 249–253
    core blocks, 251
    server blocks, 253–255
  broadcasts
    DHCP request scheme, 33
    dropping, 40-41
    generating, 39-40
    IPX SAP request scheme, 33
    storing, 38–39
    traffic, 28–29, 45-47
  complex, *see* complex networks
  connectivity, preventing bottlenecks, 259
  failures, protecting against, 139, 141
  managing, 427–428
  multicast (IP), 57–59
  multimedia flooding, 317, 320
  performance
    distributed servers, 16
    sniffers, 46
  prioritizing, 149–151
  protocols (HSRP), 141
  redundancy, 121-145
    component, 123, 126
    designing, 269–271
    high-level, 124–125
    link, 128-138, 460
    median, 124
    minimal, 122-123
    software, 139
    up time, 122
    VLAN configurations, 329, 335
  resiliency, 123
  routers
    broadcast traffic, 36-41
    dedicated, 285
    failure, 304
    sharing applications, 97-99
    unicasts, 36-38

scalable, 203–206, 220
    redundancy, 293
    requirements, 281–282
servers, 20
    centralized video servers, 17
    distributed, 15, 90
    enterprise servers, 13–14
    super servers, 18–19, 21
    Web-based application servers, 22
services, 276
switches (broadcast traffic), 34-36
topology, updating, 259–260
traffic, 7–8
    baselines, 9
    cross-campus, 93-101
    Internet traffic, 101-108
    local traffic, 89-93
    multimedia, *see* multimedia, traffic
VBNS (Very high-speed Backbone Network
    Service), 427
VLANs, building, 326-328
wiring closet
    scalable network design, 282
    VLANs, 329
see also subnets, 15
Network-to-Network Interface, *see* NNI
never-ending loops, resolving, 133
NHRP (Next Hop Resolution Protocol),
    242–243, 460
NIC (Network Information Center, 44, 358, 430
NNI (Network-to-Network Interface), 460
No Acknowledge (NAK), 218–219
nodes, 461
    barebone networks, 267–268
    building blocks, 257

O

OC (Optical Carrier), 461
open security, 174
OPSF (Open Shortest Path First), 69–70
Optical Carrier, *see* OC

optimal placement, 15
optimizing, 15
OSI model, 461
    Application layer, 437
    Data link layer, 443
    MAC layer, 28–29
    Network layer, 29–30, 32
OSPF (Open Shortest Path First), 462
outgoing traffic
    campus-to-Internet traffic, 101-104
    World Wide Web, 104

P-Q

packets, 462
    multicast flooding, 314
    RSVP (Resource Reservation Protocol),
        157–159
    see also frames
parallel routes, 462
parallelism, 129, 134, 136, 462;
    see also data load sharing
partial mesh, 462
passing data between clients, 91-92
passwords
    barebone networks, 275–276
    manual, 176
paths, 90, 93
    backups (Spanning Tree reconvergence),
        130, 134
    cross-campus traffic, 94-95
    never-ending loops, resolving, 133
    multicast traffic
        PIM-sparse-mode, 317, 320
        scalable networks, 315, 317
    VLANs
        distribution switch redundancy, 335
        wiring closet switch redundancy, 329
patterns (traffic), 7–8
    baselines, 9
    browsing World Wide Web, 104-105
    scalable networks, 285, 301

peak cell rate, 463
percentage queuing (bandwidth), 153–154
performance, 15, 18–22
    bottlenecks, preventing, 259
    distributed servers, 16
    evaluating, 46
    monitoring (sniffers), 46
    traffic baselines, creating, 115–116
phantom routers, 463
Physical layer (OSI model), 463
physical redundancy (Spanning Tree), 129–132
PIM (Protocol Independent Multicast), 74, 463
    dense-mode, 75–76, 114
    sparse-mode, 76, 78–8
        complex networks, 376
        cross-campus traffic, 114
        multimedia flooding, 317, 320
planning networks, 14-15
point-to-multipoint transmissions, 28–29, 34
port-based VLANs, 464
ports, 464
    switches, 84
    VLANs (Virtual LANs), 221
Presentation layer (OSI model), 464
preventing, 259
primary servers, 127
primary switches, 294
priorities (traffic), 149–151, 157-162, 465
    ATM (Asynchronous Transfer Mode)
        networks, 164–166
    hardware, 162, 164
    QoS (Quality of Service), 156
    queuing, 151–155, 341, 465
    scalable networks, 339
    complex networks, 418, 420
private key encryption, 465
processing (broadcast frames), 41-42
Protocol Independent Multicast, see PIM
protocol layer (OSI model), 29–32
protocols, 210
    AppleTalk, 437
    ARP, 28, 32–33

DHCP
    request scheme, 33
    scalable networks, 326
HSRP (Hot Standby Routing Protocol), 141
IP protocol, 29–31
IPX SAP, see IPX SAP
LocalTalk, 456
multicast routing, 68
    DVMRP (Distance Vector Multicast
        Routing Protocol), 70–74
    MOSPF (Multicast Open Shortest Path
        First), 69–70
    PIM (Protocol Independent Mode),
        74–76, 78–80
routing, 136, 138
RSVP (traffic prioritization), 339
software protocols (data path redundancy),
    128-138
Spanning Tree Protocol, 294
user mobility, 209–219
VLANs (Virtual LANs), 222–223
Proxy ARP (Address Resolution Protocol), 465
prune, 72, 466
public key encryption, 186, 191, 466

QoS (Quality of Service), 156–157, 162, 466
queries (IGMP), 65–67, 113
queuing, 151–155, 341, 466

R

real-time imaging (multimedia), 52
receiving broadcast frames, 28–34, 41-44
reconvergence, 130, 134, 470
reducing traffic, 16, 46, 292
redundancy, 121-145, 466
    complex networks, 355
        building blocks, 356–358
        core blocks, 359–360
        server blocks, 361–362
        troubleshooting, 362, 375
    component, 123, 126

data paths, 128-138
    activating hot backup, 129–132
    hot backup, 129
    parallelism, 134, 136
designing, 269–271
distribution switch, 335
high-level, 124-125
median, 124
minimal, 122-123
network link, 128-138
protocols, 141
scalable networks, 293
    building blocks, 293–294
    core blocks, 284, 298
    distribution switch redundancy, 296–297
    server blocks, 284, 299–301
server redundancy, 126–128
software redundancy, 138–145
up time, 122
wiring closet switch, 329
reliability, 467
Rendezvous points, 378, 467
requests
    RSVP (Resource Reservation Protocol), 157–162
    DHCP, 33, 110-111, 217, 390
    endstation paths, 91-93
    IP ARP, 32–33, 108-110
    IPX SAP, 33, 109-110
requirements
    barebone network, 263–264
    multicast, 59
        hosts, 60, 64
        routers, 64, 67
        servers, 60, 64
    scalable network, 281
resiliency, 123
Resource ReServation Protocol, see RSVP
resources
    campus network, 313
    technical information, 430
response times, increasing, 16

RFCs (Requests For Comments)
    1112, 56, 60
    rfc-index, 431–433
RIP (Routing Information Protocol), 467; see also DVMRP
route authentication, 182–183, 467
    complex networks, 383
    scalable networks, 322
router failure, 304
routers
    authorization, 179
    broadcasts
        domains, 353
        dropping, 40-41
        generating, 39-40
        storing, 38-39
        traffic, 36-41
    building blocks
        bottlenecks, 258
        failure, 271
    complex networks
        encryption, 385-387
        multimedia addressing, 376, 383
        user-level VLANs, 399
    component redundancy, 123
    cross-campus traffic, 93-101
    dedicated, 285
    DVMRP, 315
    encryption, 198
    filters (access lists), 180, 182
    hops, see hops
    HSRP redundancy, 358
    IGMP queries, 113
    intermediate routers, 452
    multicast, 64, 67
    optimal paths, 136, 138
    phantom routers, 463
    PIM dense-mode, 114
    queuing, 152–155
    scalable networks
        HSRP, 296
        multicast traffic, 313
    unicasts, 36-38

routing
    broadcast traffic, 36-41
    end routers, 72–73
    intermediate routers, 71
    multicast, 68, 113
        DVMRP (Distance Vector Multicast
            Routing Protocol), 70–74
        MOSPF (Multicast Open Shortest Path
            First), 69–70
    protocols, 317, 320, 468
    pruning back, 72
    redundancy, 141
    tables, 468
    unicasts, 36-38
    update broadcasts, 28
Routing Information Protocol, *see* RIP
RSVP (Resource Reservation Protocol),
    156–162, 339, 467
running multimedia applications
    Internet-to-campus traffic, 106
    scalable networks, 313–317

S

SAP (Service Advertisement Protocol), 468
scalable networks, 203–206, 282, 292, 313–317,
    469
    building blocks, 282
        broadcast domains, 289, 292
        redundancy, 293–294
    complex networks, 376, 383
    core blocks, 284
        broadcast domains, 287, 289
        redundancy, 284, 298
    distributed servers, 292
    distribution switches
        failure, 304
        redundancy, 296–297
    failures, 304
    HSRP, 296
    Internet connectivity, 284
    mobility, 324

    prioritization, 339
    requirements, 281-282
    route authentication, 322
    security, 322
    server blocks, 284
        broadcast domains, 284, 287
        redundancy, 299–301
    traffic
        dividing, 295
        multicast traffic, 315, 317
        patterns, 285, 301
        prioritization, 339
    user mobility, 206
        adds, 208
        changes, 208–209
        IP protocol, 212–219
        moves, 207
        protocols, 209, 211–212
    VLANs (Virtual LANs), 220
        ATM LANE (ATM with LAN
            Emulation), 240–241
        building, 326, 328
        distribution switch, 233–236
        dynamic, 222–223
        IEEE 802.1q, 243
        Inter-VLANs, 237–240
        Intra-VLANs, 237–240
        MAC address, 221
        MPOA (MultiProtocol Over ATM),
            242–243
        ports, 221
        protocols, 222–223
        traffic, 224
        user-level, 225–228
        wiring closet, 229–233
schemes, 19
    DHCP request schemes, 33
    IP ARP request schemes, 32–33
    redundancy
        core switch failure, 310, 313
        scalable network design, 293–294,
            298–301

secret key encryption, 469
security, 171–172
    authentication, 172, 177, 182–183
    authorization, 178–179
    barebone networks, 275–276
    complex networks, 383-387
    digital signatures, 445
    encryption, 184–185, 195, 199
        asymmetric, 186, 191, 195
        hash functions, 191, 194–195
        symmetric, 185–186, 195
    filters (access lists), 180-182
    firewalls, 448
    redundancy, 121-145
        barebone networks, 269–271
        component, 123
        high-level, 124-125
        median, 124
        minimal, 122-123
        up time, 122
    scalable networks, 322
    servers, backing up, 127
segments, 30–32
sending
    broadcast frames, 28–34
    files (Internet traffic), 102-103
    endstation requests, 91-92
server blocks, 253–255, 348
    barebone networks, 265–266, 271–272
    broadcast domains, 350
    distribution switches, 255
    encryption, 385
    redundancy, 361–362
    RSVP (traffic prioritization), 339, 341
    scalable networks, 284
        broadcast domains, 287
        redundancy, 284, 299–301
        router failure, 335
        VLANs, 329, 409-411
servers, 20
    authentication, 174–175
    authorization, 179

    backing up, 127
    barebone network design, 268
    broadcast domains, 355
    centralized video servers, 17
    client/server traffic, 92
    DHCP, 37
    distributed, 15, 90
        cross-campus traffic, 95-97
        scalable network design, 292
    DNS (Domain Name System), 210, 218
    e-mail servers, 101-102
    enterprise servers, 13–14
    failures, 272
    file servers, 102-103
    filters (access lists), 180, 182
    IPX, routing broadcasts, 43
    multicast, 60, 64
    multimedia servers, 314
    redundancy, 126–128
    super servers, 18–19, 21
    traffic, 93-101
    Web servers, 22, 104
Service Advertisement Protocol, *see* SAP
services
    barebone network design, 276
    InterNIC (Network Information
        Center), 430
Session layer (OSI model), 469
shared queuing, 154–155, 469
sharing
    applications, 97-99
    data load sharing, 289
    distribution switches, 99-100
    whiteboard applications. 92-93
shifts in LAN design philosophy, 16–17
sites (Web)
    ATM Forum, 433
    IEEE, 434
    Internet-Drafts, 433
    InterNIC, 431
sniffers, 46

software, 128, 138
  multimedia, 313–315, 317
  prioritizing traffic
    QOS (Quality of Service), 156-162
    queuing, 151-155
  redundancy, 138–145
    data path, 129
    network, 123
source addresses, 28
Spanning Tree, 129–132, 469
  reconvergence, 130, 134
  redundancy, 294
spoofing, 470
static addressing, 210, 470
storing broadcasts, 38-39
streaming video (unicast traffic), 53
subnets, 30–32, 470
  addresses, 470
  barebone networks, 274
  cross-campus traffic, 101
  end routers, 72
  enterprise servers, 14–15
  masks, 470
  scalable networks, 287;
    see also broadcast domains
super servers, 18–19, 21, 470
switches, 35, 471
  barebone networks
    failure, 270–272
    wiring closet, 264
  broadcast domains, 353
  broadcast traffic, 34-36
  complex networks, 348
    redundancy, 356
    user-level VLANs, 399
  core switch failures, 307, 310, 313
  distribution switches, 250
    cross-campus traffic, 99-100
    failure, 304
    redundancy, 296–297, 335
    scalable network design, 282
    VLANs (Virtual LANs), 233–236

  Layer 3 switches, 251
  multilayer, 459
  multimedia, 81–85
  RSVP (Resource Reservation Protocol), 157–162
  VLANs (Virtual LANs), 225
  wiring closet switches, 329
symmetric encryption, 185-186, 195, 387, 471

T

technologies
  emerging
    automated electronic commerce, 426
    Gigabit Ethernet, 426
    voice-over data, 425
  publications, 435
  VBNS (Very high-speed Backbone Network Service), 427
telephone system broadcasts, 30-34
throughput, 471
titles of RFCs, 432–433
Token Ring, 471
topologies, updating, 259–260
traffic, 15, 90, 93, 339
  barebone networks, 266–269
  baselines, 9, 115–116
  broadcast traffic, 28–29
    controlling, 45-47
    receiving, 41-44
    transmission, 28–29
  building blocks, 258
  client/server traffic, 92
  complex networks, 349, 358
  core blocks, 252
  cross-campus, 93-101
    DHCP requests, 110-111
    distributed servers, 95-97
    distribution switches, 99-100
    IGMP queries, 113
    IP ARP requests, 108-110

IPX SAP broadcasts, 109-110
multicast routing <$startpage>, 113
e-mail, 272
Internet traffic, 101
  campus-to-Internet traffic, 101-104
  Internet-to-campus traffic, 104-108
  see also Internet traffic
local traffic, 89-93, 101
monitoring, 115–116
multicast
  configuring routers, 313
  PIM sparse-mode, 317, 320
  scalable networks, 315, 317
multimedia, 51, 53, 115
  broadcast, 54–55
  multicast, 55–56
  unicast, 53
paths, 90-93
patterns (scalable networks), 285, 301
priorities, 149–151
  ATM (Asynchronous Transfer Mode)
    networks, 164–166
  complex networks, 418, 420
  hardware, 162, 164
  QoS (Quality of Service), 156–157, 162
  queuing, 151–155
reducing, 16
scalable networks
  distributed servers, 292
  dividing, 295
  multimedia sources, 313–317
troubleshooting, 7–8
VLANs (Virtual LANs), 224
voice-over data, 425
transmissions (point-to-multipoint), 28–34
Transport layer (OSI model), 471
transport technologies, 426
triple (3DES), 186
troubleshooting
  broadcast traffic, 45-47
  complex networks, 409, 414
  network traffic, 7–8
  redundancy, 362, 375

scalable networks
  core switch failure, 307, 310, 313
  distribution switch failure, 304
  router failures, 304
TRPB (Truncated Reverse Path Broadcasting)
  algorithm, 70
trunking (VLANs), 243

U

UBR (Unspecified Bit Rate), 166, 472
unicasts, 472
  complex networks, 376, 383, 403
  routing, 36-38
  traffic, 53, 314
unplugging computers from network, 46
up time requirements, 122
updating network topology, 259–260
user authentication, 172, 177-179, 322
user mobility
  complex networks, 387, 390–391
  VLANs (Virtual LANs), 228
user-level VLANs, 399, 406, 472
usernames
  dynamic, 176–177
  manual, 176
  passwords, 176–177
  scalable networks, 322
users
  distributed servers, 16
  mobility, 206
    adds, 208
    barebone network design, 274
    changes, 208–209
    IP protocol, 212–219
    moves, 207
    protocols, 209, 211–212
  passing data, 91–92
  passwords, 276
  scalable networks, 324
  VLANs (Virtual LANs), 225–228
utilities (sniffers), 46

V

VBNS (Very high-speed Backbone Network Service), 427
VBR (Variable Bit Rate), 165–166, 472
video
    multicast requirements, 61–62, 64
    unicast traffic, 53
videoconferencing, 52, 150
VINES (Virtual Integrated Network Service), 473
virtual IP address, 473
virtual MAC address, 473
virtual routers, 473
VLANs (Virtual LANs), 220
    ATM LANE (ATM with LAN Emulation), 240–241
    complex networks
        building blocks, 391, 396
        core blocks, 406, 409–410
        server blocks, 409, 411
        troubleshooting, 409, 414
        user-level, 399, 406
    distribution switch, 233–236
    dynamic, 222–223
    IEEE 802.1q, 243
    Inter-VLANs, 237–240
    Intra-VLANs, 237–240
    MAC address, 221
    MPOA (MultiProtocol Over ATM), 242–243
    ports, 221
    protocols, 222–223
    scalable networks, 326, 328
    traffic, 224
    trunking, 243
    user-level, 225–228
    wiring closet, 229–233
    see also LANs
voice-over data, 425

W-Z

WANs (Wide Area Networks)
    Internet traffic, 101-108
        campus-to-Internet traffic, 101-104
        Internet-to-campus traffic, 104-108
        see also Internet traffic
    prioritizing, 149–151
    scalable networks, 285
Web sites
    ATM Forum, 433
    IEEE, 434
    Internet-Drafts, 433
    InterNIC, 431
Web-based application servers, 22
whiteboard applications, sharing, 92-93
wiring closet switches, 282, 474
    barebone network design, 264
    broadcast domains, 353
    complex networks, 356
    failures, 270, 301
    VLANs (Virtual LANs), 225, 229–233, 329
workgroup servers, 15, 474

Your IP (YI) address field, 216